SECONDARY EDUCATION IN A CHANGING WORLD

Series editors: Barry M. Franklin and Gary McCulloch

Published by Palgrave Macmillan:

Girls' Secondary Education in the Western World:
From the 18th to the 20th Century
Edited by James C. Albisetti, Joyce Goodman, and Rebecca Rogers
(2010)

Race-Class Relations and Integration in Secondary Education:
The Case of Miller High
By Caroline Eick
(2010)

Teaching Harry Potter: The Power of Imagination in Multicultural
Classrooms
By Catherine L. Belcher and Becky Herr Stephenson
(2011)

The Invention of the Secondary Curriculum
By John White
(2011)

Secondary STEM Educational Reform
Edited by Carla C. Johnson
(2011)

New Labour and Secondary Education, 1994–2010
By Clyde Chitty
(2013)

Secondary Education and the Raising of the School-Leaving Age:
Coming of Age?
Tom Woodin, Gary McCulloch, and Steven Cowan
(2013)

SECONDARY EDUCATION AND THE RAISING OF THE SCHOOL-LEAVING AGE

COMING OF AGE?

TOM WOODIN, GARY MCCULLOCH, AND
STEVEN COWAN

palgrave
macmillan

SECONDARY EDUCATION AND THE RAISING OF THE SCHOOL-LEAVING AGE
Copyright © Tom Woodin, Gary McCulloch, and Steven Cowan, 2013.

First published in 2013 by
PALGRAVE MACMILLAN®
in the United States—a division of St. Martin's Press LLC,
175 Fifth Avenue, New York, NY 10010.

Where this book is distributed in the UK, Europe and the rest of the world,
this is by Palgrave Macmillan, a division of Macmillan Publishers Limited,
registered in England, company number 785998, of Houndmills,
Basingstoke, Hampshire RG21 6XS.

Palgrave Macmillan is the global academic imprint of the above companies
and has companies and representatives throughout the world.

Palgrave® and Macmillan® are registered trademarks in the United States,
the United Kingdom, Europe and other countries.

ISBN: 978–0–230–34039–8

Library of Congress Cataloging-in-Publication Data

Woodin, Tom.
    Secondary education and the raising of the school-leaving age :
coming of age? / Tom Woodin, Gary McCulloch and Steven Cowan.
        pages cm. — (Secondary education in a changing world)
    Includes bibliographical references.
    ISBN 978–0–230–34039–8 (hardcover : alk. paper)
    1. Education, Compulsory—Great Britain. I. McCulloch, Gary.
II. Cowan, Steven. III. Title.

LC135.G7W66 2013
379.2'30941—dc23   2013014589

A catalogue record of the book is available from the British Library.

Design by Newgen Knowledge Works (P) Ltd., Chennai, India.

First edition: October 2013

10 9 8 7 6 5 4 3 2 1

For
Susan, Ella, and Eva
Sarah
Shaoling and Yanhua

Contents

Series Editor's Foreword

Among the educational issues affecting policy makers, public officials, and citizens in modern, democratic, and industrial societies, none has been more contentious than the role of secondary schooling. As we develop the Secondary Education in a Changing World series with Palgrave Macmillan, our continuing intent is to provide a venue for scholars in different national settings to explore critical and controversial issues surrounding secondary education. We envision our series as a place for the airing and resolution of these controversial issues.

More than a century has elapsed since Emile Durkheim argued the importance of studying secondary education as a unity, rather than in relation to the wide range of subjects and the division of pedagogical labor of which it was composed. Only thus, he insisted, would it be possible to have the ends and aims of secondary education constantly in view. The failure to do so accounted for a great deal of difficulty with which secondary education was faced. First it meant that secondary education was "intellectually disoriented," between "a past which is dying and a future which is still undecided," and as a result "lacks the vigor and vitality which it once possessed."* Second, the institutions of secondary education were not understood adequately in relation to their past, which was "the soil which nourished them and gave them their present meaning, and apart from which they cannot be examined without a great deal of impoverishment and distortion." (10). And third, it was difficult for secondary school teachers, who were responsible for putting policy reforms into practice, to understand the nature and the problems and issues that prompted them.

In the early decades of the twenty-first century, Durkheim's strictures still have resonance. The intellectual disorientation of secondary education is more evident than ever as it is caught up in successive waves of policy

---

* E. Durkheim (1938/1977), *The Evolution of Educational Thought: Lectures on the Formation and Development of Secondary Education in France* (London: Routledge and Kegan Paul), 8.

changes. The connections between the present and the past have become increasingly hard to trace and untangle. Moreover, the distance between policy makers on the one hand and the practitioners on the other has rarely seemed as immense as it is today. The key mission of the current series of books is, in the spirit of Durkheim, to address these underlying dilemmas of secondary education and to play a part in resolving them.

The raising of the school-leaving age (ROSLA) can be viewed as a technical matter, part of the gradual expansion of secondary education and of schooling in general around the world over more than a century. Yet this is to ignore the real significance of the school-leaving age for compulsory education systems and in regulating the transition between school and society. The achievement of the current volume, *Secondary Education and the Raising of the School-Leaving Age: Coming of Age?*, by Tom Woodin, Gary McCulloch, and Steven Cowan, is that it demonstrates that the school-leaving age has been consistently at the heart of vigorous debates about the character and aims of secondary education. Families, employers, and the state have been actively involved in contesting when children and youth should be obliged to attend school rather than be allowed to go to work and make a living. Teachers and other educators have also engaged in this argument, not always in support of a longer school life for pupils who preferred to be elsewhere. This is a lively debate in our own time, when in many countries the compulsory school age is continuing to rise, and when the rewards and challenges of this upward growth remain under close scrutiny.

Woodin, McCulloch, and Cowan locate their study in the broad context of international and global discussion of the school-leaving age. Their particular focus is on how this debate has played itself out in Britain. Here, they range widely from the disputes over compulsory schooling, apprenticeship, and half-time education in the nineteenth century, to the current initiative to increase the participation age to 17 and then to 18. It is the efforts to raise the age from 14 to 15, which bore fruit in 1947, and then to 16 as occurred in 1972 that are explored in particular detail, as the authors make use of extensive archival records to understand the hopes and aspirations, as well as the doubts and reservations, that underlay these changes. They document the reforms that took place at a national level and also highlight the contributions made by individual reformers, schools, and localities in this long-term process. The work argues convincingly that the success of the campaign to raise the school-leaving age signified in an important sense the "coming of age" of secondary education in the modern era, but also that it came close to being derailed. Overall, this book makes an important contribution to the international literature as the first work to investigate the historical development of the raising of the school-leaving age critically and in depth.

As the fifteenth volume in our series, *Secondary Education and the Raising of the School-Leaving Age* develops further many of the arguments raised in earlier volumes about the expansion and globalization of secondary education. It offers the foundation for additional volumes that might explore a number of these emerging trends in educational provision for secondary school-aged youth as well as suggesting new areas of inquiry for the series as we extend our focus more deliberately beyond the United States and United Kingdom.

BARRY M. FRANKLIN
Series Coeditor

Acknowledgments

We acknowledge the generous financial support of the Economic and Social Research Council for funding the project Raising the School-Leaving Age: Policy and Practice in Historical Perspective RES-062–23–1494 on which this work is based.

We would like to thank various archives including the Institute of Education Archives, National Archives, National Archives of Scotland, Modern Records Office, Churchill College Cambridge, Bodleian Library, East Sussex Record Office, Essex County Record Office, Gloucestershire Record Office, Centre for Kentish Studies, Lancashire County Record Office, West Yorkshire Archive Service, London Metropolitan Archives, Manchester Archives and Local Studies, Manchester University, Tameside Local Studies, and Leeds University Special Collections. We are also grateful for the advice and feedback of colleagues at a number of conferences including the History of Education Society, the Social History Society, the British Educational Research Association, and the International Standing Conference for the History of Education, as well as a large number of invited seminars in the United Kingdom and around the world. Our students at the Institute of Education London have also been a constant supply of advice and discussion around this project.

The chapters in this book also draw upon articles published in the *Journal of Education Policy*, *History of Education*, and *British Educational Research Journal*.

Timeline: Extension of the School-Leaving Age in Britain

1870   Elementary Education Act: Establishment of School Boards. Byelaws compelling attendance from age 5 to 13

1876   Elementary Schools Act. Establishment of Attendance Committees

1880   Elementary Education Act: Compelling attendance between ages of 5 and 10

1893   Elementary Education (School Attendance) Act: Compulsory attendance to age 11

1899   Leaving age extended to 12

1901   The Education (Scotland) Act of 1901 extended the age of compulsory education in Scotland to 14

1902   Creation of local education authorities with powers to provide schooling other than elementary

1917   Lewis Report proposed school-leaving age of 14 with no exemptions, followed by attendance for less than 8 hours a week or 320 hours a year at day-continuation classes up to the age of 18

1918   Education Act: Leaving age raised to 14. Proposes day-continuation classes to 18

1921   Education Consolidation Act confirms raising of school age to 15/16

1922   *Secondary Education for All* published, R. H. Tawney

1926   Hadow Report: *The Education of the Adolescent*, Board of Education Consultative Committee

1929   Trevelyan Education Bill to raise leaving age to 15 defeated

1936   National Government legislates for ROSLA to 15 with exemptions

1939   Emergency legislation delays implementation of ROSLA arising from 1936 Act

1938   Spens Report, Board of Education Consultative Committee
        Recommends ROSLA to 16
1944   War-time Coalition government legislates for ROSLA to 15 and
        to 16 when practical. County Colleges envisaged
1947   Labour government implements ROSLA to 15
1959   Crowther Report: *15 to 18* produced by the CACE. Recommends
        ROSLA to 16
1963   Newsom Report: *Half Our Future*. Recommends ROSLA to 16
1964   Conservative government agrees upon a date of 1970–1971 for
        ROSLA to 16
1968   Labour government delays ROSLA for two years
1972   Conservative government implements ROSLA to 16
2008   Labour government: Education and Skills Act: RPA to 18
2013   RPA to 17 comes into force
2015   RPA to 18 comes into force

Acronyms

A&B	Architects and Building Branch of the Ministry of Education
AEC	Association of Education Committees
AMA	Assistant Mistresses Association
AST	Australian States & Territories
BBC	British Broadcasting Corporation
BERA	British Educational Research Association
BRICs	Brazil, Russia, India, China
CAB	Cabinet
CACE	Central Advisory Council for Education (England)
CBI	Confederation of British Industry
CERI	Centre for Educational Research and Innovation
CP	Cabinet Papers
CSE	Certificate of Secondary Education
CYEE	Central Youth Employment Executive
DCSF	Department for Children, Schools, and Families
DES	Department of Education and Science
DfE	Department for Education
DfES	Department for Education and Skills
EFA	Education for All
EMA	Education Maintenance Allowances
FBI	Federation of British Industries
FE	Further Education
GCE	General Certificate of Education
GCSE	General Certificate of Secondary Education
GNP	Gross National Product
HMI	His/Her Majesty's Inspectorate
HMSO	His/Her Majesty's Stationery Office
HORSA	Hutting Operation for Raising the School-Leaving Age
IBE	International Bureau of Education
ILEA	Inner London Education Authority
ILO	International Labour Office
IMF	International Monetary Fund

ITBs	Industrial Training Boards
IQ	Intelligence Quotient
LEA	Local Education Authority
LMS	Local Management of Schools
MP	Member of Parliament
MSC	Manpower Services Commission
NA	National Archives
NAHT	National Association of Headteachers
NAS	National Association of Schoolmasters
NEET	Not in education, employment, or training
NEL	National Education League
NSW	New South Wales (Australia)
NUT	National Union of Teachers
OECD	Organisation of Economic Cooperation and Development
OFSTED	Office for Standards in Education
ROSLA	Raising of the School-Leaving Age
RPA	Raising the Participation Age
RSLA	Raising the School Leaving Age
SAC	School Age Council
SED	Scottish Education Department
TES	*Times Educational Supplement*
TUC	Trades Union Congress
TVEI	Technical and Vocational Education Initiative
UNESCO	United Nations Educational, Scientific and Cultural Organisation
WEA	Workers' Educational Association
WTO	World Trade Organisation
YOP	Youth Opportunity Programme

Chapter 1

Introduction

The expansion of compulsory education represents a fundamental social transformation of the modern world. Raising of the school-leaving age (ROSLA) has been at the heart of this process. Schooling is commonly seen as a turning point in the lives of young people after which they are considered fit to participate more fully in society, literally coming of age. Debates over the length and content of this process have been both perennial and intense. ROSLA has not been a technical change but rather an historical shift, which has affected the ways in which we understand not only education but also youth, welfare, employment, and inequality. Yet, comparatively little has been written on the topic.

There are few aspects of social life that have been immune to the extension of compulsory education. The fortunes of economic competitiveness, modernization, democracy, citizenship, social justice, and human flourishing have all been tied to increasing the years of mandatory schooling. Expanding education within a "knowledge economy" has become a key target for those seeking to explain failures in the past and to herald progress in the future. Even revisionist perspectives that, from the 1960s and the 1970s, viewed schooling in terms of social control and the reproduction of inequalities, nevertheless agreed that compulsory education was growing in importance. Moreover, the centrality of education and learning in contemporary societies can be identified across the world. Compulsory schooling is a deeply embedded feature at the heart of national identities. In the West, fears about the "emerging" economies of China, India, Brazil, Russia, and others, where the expansion of education is much commented upon, have fuelled this agenda. Indeed, the demise of natural resources, the relocation of manufacturing industry to developing countries, the rise of service industries, and the intensification of technological innovation have all led to a renewed focus upon learning and skills. Countries such as the Netherlands, Belgium, Hungary, and some American states now have a school-leaving age of 18 and voluntary staying on has increased elsewhere. A related set of assumptions permeates the Millennium Development Goals to which universal access to primary education is central.

Our contemporary context provides an important departure point for an historical exploration of the school-leaving age not only in England but also Scotland and the United Kingdom more generally. In England, the 2008 Education and Skills Act legislated to make participation in education and training compulsory up to 17 from 2013 and 18 from 2015, a policy decision informed to some extent by historical analysis. From 1997 to 2010, Labour governments generally tended to play down the relevance of historical explanations, but such comparisons became prominent in this case. The then–secretary of state for education, Ed Balls, made direct comparisons with the 1918 Education Act that raised the hope of education to 18. He invoked the post-1945 need to rebuild a democratic society as presaging the concerns of the early twenty-first century. Despite the clear differences between the raising of the school-leaving age and the more diffuse notion of "participation," which could include various forms of certified education and training, extending compulsion in education clearly lent itself to historical inquiry.[1]

The related notions of "policy memory" and "policy amnesia" are useful to develop an understanding of both past and present. It is possible to develop "policy learning" from the past if we are sensitive to the fact that apparently similar measures may acquire very different meanings across historical contexts. Long-term policy oscillations in key debates over the school-leaving age resurface in complex ways in different historical settings. By examining broad historical transformations, continuing dilemmas and repeated practices can be identified in secondary education. Historical "lessons" rarely come in the form of detailed and precise prescriptions but rather depend upon an awareness of long-term structural factors that constrain the freedom for action in the present. Despite the lack of a sustained study in this area, judging by a recent spate of publications, there is clearly an appetite for linking historical analysis to contemporary policy development.[2]

The progressive raising of the school-leaving age has not been a neutral reform or an isolated case of educational history but has been rooted in particular historical contexts. In Britain, areas of welfare, such as health, experienced a sudden and visible increase in state direction, control, and ownership after 1948 with the creation of the National Health Service, whereas state educational provision developed more incrementally but nonetheless significantly. At the heart of ROSLA lies this interconnection between prosaic detail and its broader social significance. The title of G. A. N. Lowndes's book *A Silent Social Revolution* well captured the sense that profound changes were resulting from accumulating reforms, even if it underestimated the controversy that underlay them.[3]

In view of these educational and social implications, it is surprising that there has been no major historical treatment of ROSLA, either in the United Kingdom or internationally. But it is possible to identify important commentaries and debates at moments when ROSLA became more prominent in public discourse. The successive raising of the school-leaving age reveals that change took place at moments of heightened social crisis and deeply felt social changes. The key dates when the age was raised represent historical turning points for a collective negotiation of the purpose of education within a divided society. In Britain, compulsory education developed in the nineteenth century and was extended in stages up to the present day. A number of education acts from 1870 introduced compulsory universal education and served to harness and regulate the use of literacy within a society coming to terms with industrialization and imperial expansion.[4] This legislation came in the wake of the extension of the franchise in 1867 to a wider section of the population, which had stimulated widespread debate and moral panic among the upper and middle classes. It also responded to a gradual decline in the need for child labor and would encourage nascent economic demands for a labor force educated to a basic level. After 1880, as compulsion came to be accepted by influential sections of public opinion, the school-leaving age was extended from 10 to 11 in 1893 and to 12 in 1899, although some areas raised it beyond that (such as Scotland where the leaving age became 14 before it did in England).[5]

The key stages of ROSLA in the twentieth century followed soon after the two world wars and helped to crystallize an impulse for educational progress. The 1918 Education Act raised the age to 14 with no exceptions, a measure that was implemented in 1921. In the early twentieth century, ROSLA became central to a progressive educational alliance spearheaded by reforming institutions such as the International Labour Office (ILO) and social democratic parties. The British economic historian and doyen of educational progressives, R. H. Tawney, placed ROSLA at the heart of social change in arguing that education made a vital economic, social, cultural, and moral contribution to national life. He conceived of schools as quasi-religious, spiritual retreats, away from the dangerous and demeaning workplace, which allowed young people to mature in an enlightened environment.[6] Tawney was a key influence on the Hadow Committee, which recommended raising the school-leaving age to 15 and the introduction of secondary education.[7] In extending education, ROSLA also hastened its reorganization. Similarly, professional groups such as teachers were keen to express their support for the measure in the interwar years. This viewpoint was reflected in publications such as *The Extra Year* (1938), which was sponsored by a number of teacher unions.[8] This progressive energy had helped to build the momentum behind the 1936 Education Act that raised the leaving age to 15 with what were described as "beneficial" exemptions, but was cancelled due to war. Finally, the 1944 Education Act paved the way to raise the leaving age to 15 in 1947 and to 16 when feasible. ROSLA established a crucial framework in which divided forms of secondary education developed in the United Kingdom.

This national experience helped to inform I. L. Kandel's international study of the school-leaving age, as part of a UNESCO (United Nations Educational, Scientific, Cultural Organisation) project reviewing compulsory education across the world, which appeared in 1951. Kandel summarized a number of national research projects on the topic. In its early years, UNESCO developed the idea of "fundamental" education, as one basis for nurturing intellectual and moral solidarity following wartime loss and destruction. It should not be surprising that the themes identified by Kandel reappear throughout the history of the school-leaving age and included equality of opportunity, education as an investment, and education and child labor laws. Each of these reflected continuing dilemmas of educational policy and practice.[9]

At times ROSLA has appeared to be an almost inevitable reform but, on closer analysis, tenacious strands of opposition can be identified. Following the 1944 Education Act, ROSLA to 16 remained on the statute book for 28 years before being implemented on the final crest of the postwar consensus that had seen the construction of the "welfare state." But the power of a changing progressive alliance was still discernible in 1972 and ROSLA served as a catalyst for the reform of curriculum, pedagogy, and personal relationships in schools, which in turn stimulated further resistance. Edited collections by J. W. Tibble[10] and Barry Turner[11] were published to reflect academic, practitioner, and political debates over the issue. Experimental projects tested out new ideas and more informal relationships between teachers and pupils whose self-expression was fostered.[12]

As a more critical and sustained response to some of the changes wrought by ROSLA, Dan Finn charted the changing connection between schooling and employment.[13] The rise of vocationalism in the 1980s led Finn to explore youth employment initiatives and he noted that education was coming to replace work for many young people. His subtitle of "training without jobs" testified to the disaffection felt by many pupils. For those more sympathetic to the changes wrought in the 1980s, higher levels of compulsory schooling came to be seen as a positive development. The Organisation for Economic Co-operation and Development (OECD) publication, *Compulsory Education in a Changing World* (1983) had been more neutral about the topic although it addressed the school-leaving age only tangentially. This was a study that appeared at a moment of transition to a new educational phase pervaded by neoliberal ideas relating to the economy.[14]

In recent decades, raising the school-leaving age has served as a measuring stick for economists who analyze the effects of compulsory education. The historical experiences of particular countries such as Greece, Canada, and the United Kingdom have been mined to show that increasing the years of compulsory education have had a positive outcome in terms of individual earnings—a correlation made in a mountain of research reports.[15] The association between income and education reflects wider trends about the role of knowledge in the economy but necessarily hides more complex issues such as the quality and range of schooling, in addition to the effect on families, inequalities, and institutional factors, which can be more difficult to chart.[16]

These stages of growth took place over prolonged periods of time, involving intricate debate and the formation of coalitions that shaped and reshaped educational policy. In the process, the purpose, content, and nature of secondary education has remained entwined in a set of thorny and enduring conflicts. From its beginnings, different stakeholders advocated multiple visions for secondary education: who it is for, should it be a common or differentiated experience, where should it take place and, crucially, for how long it should last. The role of ROSLA in these wider educational debates has been underplayed, being viewed as a technical mechanism, a discrete legislative act that enabled children to remain in school for longer periods of time. Historians of education have tended to focus upon issues such as selection and the comprehensive movement, a debate that lent itself more directly to a particular form of class analysis which became prevalent from the 1960s.[17] Brian Simon recognized the raising of the age in the 1940s as one significant element in educational advance that responded to a progressive social movement. It was seen as "a rapid and major thrust forward" and underlay the development of secondary education for all. Simon's account of raising the age to 16 is more muted and crowded out by the issue of comprehensive schooling.[18] But the broad issue of "secondary education for all" cannot in fact be fully understood without reference to the school-leaving age. In addition, ROSLA connects to another major postwar educational development, that of the expansion of higher education that was often pitted against ROSLA. Extending the leaving age was also presented in tandem with further education (FE), as a broader type of tertiary education, if not as an alternative.

Our approach aims to uncover complex patterns of educational change in relation to wider social, economic, political, and cultural issues, thus placing the history of ROSLA within a much wider set of structures. A decisive dilemma has been the issue of whether education was considered to be a cost or an investment that boosts human capital. Raising the leaving age has been viewed as a way of improving opportunity and social justice, whether in a limited sense of helping more pupils to climb an educational ladder or in terms of more fundamental social change. However, critics of ROSLA have underlined the escalating costs of welfare, the existing needs of the labor market and the fact that the tax burden could be ill-afforded and better-utilized elsewhere. Families have feared a loss of income consequent upon ROSLA. Educators and teachers have pointed to competing priorities in debates on ROSLA, as well as a predicted cost in terms of educational standards. As a result, on each occasion when the school-leaving age was raised, resources and arguments have had to be deployed, against significant opposition, to show that such a change was both desirable and achievable. Differing evaluations of the economic "return" from education, over variable timescales, proved to be the cause of considerable disagreement.[19]

Overall shifts in the relation between education and employment can be identified to the extent that early twentieth-century reformers, reacting against the effects of industrialism, had campaigned to keep children away from the demeaning experience of work and industry. By contrast, contemporary impulses have aimed to reconnect education with the experience of work. This relationship remains unresolved to the present day. ROSLA stimulated a widely felt need to adopt new forms of curriculum and pedagogy that served to reignite long-simmering tensions over the academic-vocational or education-training divide. Disagreements over the points at which common and differentiated curricula began and ended intensified as secondary education for all became a reality. ROSLA was itself in constant competition with the demand for part-time post-compulsory education, for example, in the form of day-continuation schools in the interwar period as well as later proposals for county colleges. Within both camps of "education" and "training," contrasting opinions found a home. Even among those who favored equality for all, a differentiated approach could unexpectedly result. Most negatively, inadequate forms of "training" came to be presented as one solution to problems of antisocial behavior and "delinquency" among the "nonacademic."[20] Writing in the late 1950s, Raymond Williams had noted that extending culture might also lead to its transformation.[21] This has been visible in the arena of education where a number of stakeholders have battled over competing visions.

ROSLA has highlighted the transition points or boundaries between school, work and citizenship during an historical phase in which new ideas about youth and young people were becoming prevalent. Put simply, more schooling served to prolong childhood. Indeed, a hierarchy of educational "stages" of personal development has come to suffuse educational thinking, a development nurtured by ROSLA. Schools have recognized the maturity of older pupils while simultaneously infantilizing them. Jane Pilcher for example has related the changing school-leaving age to conceptions of children and childhood, which have denoted "an increasing division between the world of the child and the world of the adult, and a lengthening of the chronological markers assigned to childhood."[22] Between the phases of childhood and adulthood, that of "adolescence" emerged from the late nineteenth century. According to John Springhall, the school-leaving age operated to postpone wage earning by the adolescent for a few short years, and hence postponed the responsibilities of adulthood.[23] School was a formative experience for middle-class and upper-class adolescents, but for the average state-educated adolescent, leaving school and making the transition to earning wages was a "rite of passage" although not always a straightforward one. Springhall argues, indeed, that the concept of adolescence "came of age" in Britain in the 1950s, leading to the first distinctive youth subcultures.[24] Jon Savage's recent work, looking especially at the United States, also claims that the concept of what became known as the "teenager" as a distinctive phase of life was triumphant in postwar society, and again links this to the rise of consumerism.[25] While ROSLA has been widely cited as a root cause of the growth and expansion of childhood, education has less commonly provided the locus for a wider discussion of the topic.[26] Indeed, ROSLA can be read as an attempt to regulate adolescence and enlist it to support competing versions of the national interest.

Despite the apparent uniformity of ROSLA, in reality it has impacted unequally across the social spectrum, inscribing a deeply felt sense of failure, which was heavily determined by wider inequalities. It was motivated, in part, by a desire to channel wider social formations in relation to class, gender, disability, and race. The vast majority of people affected by ROSLA were working class. "Successful" pupils have tended to accept a subordinate status while concerns have been repeatedly expressed over others who contested the expected forms of subjectivity consequent upon retaining successively older age groups in schools. The specter of unschooled and unregulated youth has continually haunted public debate and policy discussions. Multiple "problems" have resulted, whether in terms of "failure" at school, subsequent unemployment, delinquency, or antisocial behavior. During the postwar years, in the process of bringing a new group of young people into schools, deficit views proliferated. Those affected by ROSLA were often viewed as locked within their own limited mental and geographical horizons and incapable of engaging with the wider public world. As a result, preparations for ROSLA emphasized private lives and personal development and therefore contributed to a growing privatization of life in the postwar years, a development that would be effectively harnessed by the new right in the 1970s and the 1980s. Such concerns have been felt in recent debates over the more marginal category of "NEETs," those not in education, employment, or training, a residual grouping that has generated fear among policy makers.[27]

Regional disparities became marked as a result of ROSLA. Throughout the twentieth century, many parts of southeast England were cushioned from the effects of ROSLA where higher voluntary staying-on rates prevailed in comparison with other areas in the north of the country, particularly the northeast. These differences made for variable approaches to the school-leaving age, which developed in the United Kingdom within a devolved system. The resulting relations between the local and national provides a continuing theme for analysis. ROSLA was not simply imposed from the center but was interpreted by local education authorities, schools, and individual teachers. In each case, wider forms of inequality encroached upon these relationships.

Although in recent years, social class has become an absent presence in political and social discussion, its relevance to education can be easily identified. Alongside class, ROSLA was deeply implicated in other divides that have muddied the waters of class analysis. Changes in the school-leaving age have had drastically different implications for girls and boys. While policy makers have tended to take the male student as the norm, the reality on the ground could be starkly divided along gender lines. For much of the twentieth century, girls often shouldered the burden of unequal schooling, for instance, in fulfilling domestic duties rather than attending school.[28] In the postwar world, issues of race also became prominent so that, by the 1970s, the schooling experiences of black and minority ethnic communities could be a world apart from other groups at a time when Bernard Coard wrote about how education could "make the West Indian child educationally sub-normal."[29] Despite the silence of many archival sources on this topic, race was simmering beneath the surface of debates on ROSLA in the 1960s and the 1970s. In addition, disabled children—often categorized as "defective," frequently faced a different form of compulsory schooling from that of their peers.

But ROSLA did not simply equate with growing inequality. Supporters asserted that a universal leaving age of 16, when public exams took place, was essential to the construction of a common secondary curriculum that would help to enhance equality of opportunity. Paradoxically, it was the very success of growing numbers of individuals from all marginalized groups that fed into arguments for extending mandatory schooling. The presence in schools of increasing numbers of working class, black, female, and disabled students made it clear that most, if not all, were potentially capable of success and that vast resources of untapped potential existed in hitherto unexpected places—a powerful argument that overlapped with those who asserted the economic need for a more skilled labor force.[30]

The school-leaving age has traversed the shifting notions of compulsion and freedom. While enforcement has been a vital lever in guaranteeing secondary education for all, it has also generated contrary tendencies. It is no coincidence that debates on increasing compulsory education developed alongside ideas of "deschooling" and "social control," which focused on the harmful effects of schools.[31] Libertarian ideals emanating from both the left and right have highlighted the potential for individuals, families, and communities to exert greater control over the education of children.[32] Indeed, the popular acceptance of compulsory schooling surely represents a major form of mass socialization from the mid-nineteenth century. The debate over whether young people went to school "willingly" or "unwillingly" hides the fact that, over time, the importance of schooling has steadily saturated the collective consciousness.[33]

However, we should resist simplistic accounts of progress in relation to ROSLA. As a reform it has been bitterly resisted. The history of ROSLA was closely tied into political battles and much debated at cabinet meetings while political parties competed tenaciously to gain political ascendancy in the world of education. In the 1940s, the Labour minister Ellen Wilkinson had to put up a considerable fight to secure the agreement that the school-leaving age should be raised in 1947. Similar battles were fought in the 1950s and the 1960s within the Conservative Party when the decision was made to raise the age to 16 in 1970, although it was subsequently delayed for two years to 1972. It helped the party to come to terms with an expanding welfare state, to fend off Labour criticisms, gain kudos with the voting public, and to respond to the long-term demands of the economy for higher skill levels.

ROSLA to 16 came about in the face of intransigent opposition among those who were extremely doubtful about the educability of all young people and feared moral decline and a breakdown of the social order. It was achieved contrary to the considerable criticism and claims that the material structures were not "ready" for such a change. ROSLA was not a solitary or isolated event but involved protracted debate and complex negotiations throughout an education system in which schools and local education authorities enjoyed a great deal of autonomy. Between 1964 and 1972, critical voices became increasingly vociferous during the prolonged period of preparation. Those who were attracted by "tradition" and "standards," coalesced around the Black Papers on Education, the first of which appeared in 1969. Yet, ROSLA represented an expanding sense of possibility and opportunity. For example, as a direct result of raising the leaving age in 1972, examination entry significantly increased and, for the first time, the age of school leaving corresponded with the age at which public examinations were held. Somewhat unexpectedly, this led to the reduction of experimentation with integrated studies and other courses. It took time to fill out the new educational framework and, in subsequent years, there were many initiatives in technical and vocational education that, it was believed, would appeal to this age group.

This study is largely based upon original archival and documentary research.[34] A range of primary historical sources is examined, many of them for the first time. These include not only the key published sources such as *15 to 18* (Crowther Report, 1959) and *Half Our Future* (Newsom Report, 1963) but also policy documents, minutes, memos, correspondence, curriculum materials, and inspection reports produced by politicians, government departments, and the Schools Council. In addition, we have uncovered a range of local material that illuminates the role played by local politicians, civil servants, teachers, and others. Educational policies are not simply implemented but have to be reinterpreted at every stage so that meanings and practices of similar policies can vary quite widely. Comparing documents arising from other pressure groups, political parties, and public bodies including trade unions such as the National Union of Teachers (NUT), the Confederation of British Industry (CBI), and the BBC (British Broadcasting Corporation) helps to elucidate these issues. The wider international context is examined through a mixture of documentary analysis and a critical assessment of historical writing on the topic; the work of the UNESCO and the OECD has been crucial here. While this project has not engaged directly with the experience of pupils, student voices do occasionally emerge through surveys, enquiries, and local material. The principal focus of this study is on ROSLA to 16 in 1972, which represented a central shift in the history of compulsory schooling, but it extends back in history as well as forward to current debates. Chapter 2 offers an overview of the ways in which the extension of compulsory education has spread across the globe. Chapters 3 and 4 provide the historical background by charting the emergence of compulsion as well as its gradual extension up to 1947, ROSLA to 15 and the development of secondary education. Chapter 5 examines how and why ROSLA to 16 regained attention and support in the 1950s up to the formal commitment to go forward with it. In chapter 6, initial preparations are reviewed, and also the continual hesitations that led to a delay in its adoption. Chapter 7 analyzes the final stages in preparing for ROSLA to 16, while chapter 8 charts how it was put into practice nationally and locally. The two final chapters seek to connect these historical developments with the contemporary scene in the twenty-first century, and then to appraise the lasting significance of these changes.

Chapter 2

The School-Leaving Age in International Perspective

The raising of the school-leaving age (ROSLA)[1] has been a historical process common to many countries. The school-leaving age lends itself to international comparisons and often serves as a marker of progress and educational development. In recent decades, the extent of compulsory education has become tied into key discourses in international arenas and reflects the increased worldwide interest in education, not least by bodies including the United Nations Education, Scientific and Cultural Organisation (UNESCO), the Organisation of Economic Cooperation and Development (OECD), and the World Bank. Within nations, comparative performance tables can stimulate both the fear of being left behind as well as offer the reassurance that the seemingly intrepid step toward raising the leaving age is in fact tried and tested. Although it appears relatively straightforward to make international comparisons on school-leaving ages, the reality may be more complex. This is because, for example, differential enforcement rates may exist, the duration of schooling does not necessarily translate into quality of experience, and countries with a low official leaving age may in fact record high levels of participation and achievement.

The experience of ROSLA in Britain can be usefully placed within a set of wider historical contexts. The oscillation between viewing ROSLA as a specific technical measure, and as a more profound and contested social reform, has permeated international debates on the topic. Those countries that first went through a process of industrialization and modernization have provided a dominant model of compulsory education. In particular, this was shared by many European countries, Australia and New Zealand and the United States, although the latter came early to support compulsory education. A common framework for understanding the historical development of ROSLA can be developed by charting successive broad stages in the development and extension of compulsory education. In doing so, it remains hard to escape a progressive narrative when discussing the gradual raising of the school-leaving age.[2] Indeed, only a few examples of reducing the age can be identified and these exist within an overall picture of extending compulsory education. The contemporary appetite for education also supports a theme of incremental and inexorable expansion.[3]

The Rise of Compulsory Education

It was from the mid-nineteenth century that compulsory schooling came to be introduced, enforced, and normalized against other forms of education and learning, which became increasingly marginal by comparison. Schooling would gradually become an institutionalized and naturalized part of the life course leading to widespread acceptance. The intense arguments that took place around the formation of compulsory education provided a crucial framework in which debates over ROSLA would take place in the coming decades and centuries. A number of overlapping motivations can be identified in the creation of national systems of compulsory education. The European model of education developed in relation to other broad historical transformations: the Reformation and Counter-Reformation, the Enlightenment, the development of the state in society, and the dominance of a market economy characterized by urbanization and industrialization. The individual was conceived as capable of being formed and transformed through an educational process, a shift that gave rise to complex processes of socialization and self-development. Schooling would become central to the process of state formation and the forging of a national identity.[4]

Compulsory education has become closely associated with the rise of democracy as twin elements in a story of growth. The interconnection between education, democracy, and modernization should not be seen as inevitable, however, a point illustrated by the ways in which compulsory schooling developed in very different contexts.[5] There is considerable evidence that schooling could be associated with less democratic forces. Early examples of compulsory education can indeed be identified such as a compulsory attendance law in Weimar, in 1617. By the late eighteenth century, both Prussia and Austria had introduced a significant element of compulsory schooling. These laws arose out of the attempts of the growing absolutist state to contain social tensions that emerged between feudalism and a nascent capitalism in which limited personal autonomy and the expansion of literacy developed.[6] Nineteenth-century educational arguments over compulsion had been partly prefigured in earlier debates over schooling and, to some extent, apprenticeship. The affinities between education and social control would later be rediscovered in contests over the nature of ROSLA.

Compulsory educational systems emerged across much of Europe, North America, and Australasia in the late nineteenth century. In Britain, mandatory education directly challenged the ideology of laissez-faire, a doctrine that had become pervasive. The use of the state to achieve universal compulsory schooling was a challenge to dominant ways of thinking that revolved around the freedom and autonomy of the individual. In fact, state action was needed to police and regulate a shifting market economy. Democracy was still at a nascent level in nineteenth-century Europe where education was not simply conceived as a form of individual mobility but also as a confirmation of hierarchy and class structures.[7]

Universal education was a reform associated with a particular model of nation building in Western Europe.[8] The concern to build and restore national pride in the wake of war and colonial adventures was often prominent in the passing of compulsory education laws. For example, the French politicians of the Third Republic, who were still licking their wounds from defeat in the Franco-Prussian War (1870–1871), embarked on an active program of schooling that would result in a state controlled, universal, and free education system. In doing so, they built upon a range of educational ideas, initiatives, and laws that had been stimulated since the French Revolution.[9]

In many countries, the rise of democracy, through extending the franchise, created pressures to both respond to popular demands as well as to regulate the forms of learning and literacy, and thus, the subjectivity of future generations.[10] The rise of a visible working class that had developed independent and autonomous forms of literacy and learning struck a note of discord among the bourgeoisie. Reforms in education helped to assuage middle-class stereotypes about a potentially rebellious and recalcitrant working class who appeared to threaten social norms. Equally, evidence of apparent working-class respectability served to calm these fears and justify an extension of both the franchise and education.[11]

In turn, changes in the labor market lent a force and influence to these arguments for compulsion with evidence that the need for, and value of, child labor was declining in the late nineteenth century, although this would be a slow process.[12] The demand for skilled labor, and a more educated and literate workforce, was beginning to be felt in diverse areas such as the railways and post office. By the early twentieth century, the growth of clerical and administrative work had become marked. The resulting worries about children roaming the streets and gaining premature independence helped to justify state compulsion to provide a greater regulation of young people and a growing social interest in protecting children.[13]

Compulsory education emerged as one significant arena in which wider social divisions could be handled and regulated. This was not always a conscious realization but arose from attempting to balance the tensions between control and freedom that were widely felt, in differing ways, across the social spectrum. There was widespread ambivalence about state control, not just by laissez-faire economists but by families losing the right to send their children to work as well as working-class leaders who became anxious about state "mis-education."[14] However, the labor movement would come to argue the need for free universal education and actively campaign for it and, certainly in Britain, it was a pioneer in calling for raising the leaving age to 16 as early as the 1890s.[15] Similarly, a significant body of bourgeois opinion remained firmly opposed to educating the working class, alarmed that it might foment insubordination and even revolution. The middle classes active in educational reform became keen to remodel the working class along lines sympathetic to their own vision of society. At the same time, they identified education as a source of knowledge and social standing and actively defended superior educational routes for their own children.[16] Gender issues were also prominent in establishing universal education. Girls and boys were to be socialized into accepting differing social assumptions about appropriate life paths for men and women.[17]

The battle to convince public opinion of the necessity for state education was not won overnight, nor did legislative enactments lead to a sudden shift in opinion. Positive reasons for embracing compulsory schooling took time to embed themselves in the minds of those in positions of influence. Universal compulsory education was established gradually and, in many countries, required a series of legislative changes. Even then, legal frameworks and structures did not always reflect the reality on the ground and school attendance often fell far short of the legislative intention. Legal stipulations were initially quite low in terms of the duration and hours of schooling.

Compulsory education legislation was not always accompanied by effective enforcement regimes. Countries varied in terms of ensuring attendance and those, such as Italy, that had only recently been unified, struggled to achieve uniform levels of school attendance across the whole country. Nevertheless, schooling was gradually becoming a part of national expectations, and it was no coincidence that the Italian children's character, Pinocchio, was locked up after not going to school.[18] For many decades after the passage of such laws, young people could be found working in industry, domestic labor, and agricultural work rather than attending school. In many cases, exemptions were allowed for a variety of reasons, not only employment related. For example, in New Zealand, following the 1877 Education Act, children could be absent from school if they were adequately educated elsewhere, if they lived more than two miles from a school, if there were impassable roads, due to sickness, or if they had already achieved an adequate level of education.[19] Unsurprisingly, attendance remained a major issue with enforcement continuing to be lax in many areas and it would not be until 1914 that "the battle of compulsory attendance had been won."[20] As late as the 1950s, in many parts of the world, it was estimated that over 50 percent of pupils were still not attending school regularly.[21]

The processes of mass socialization by which many people came to accept and, in some cases, embrace schooling in terms of opportunity and individual expression drew upon varied resources. Enforcement and punishment regimes were gradually developed and, in one sense, a particular version of education was imposed upon a reluctant working class.[22] The fine line between the harsh attendance officer and the more "caring" teacher and social worker was often traversed in enforcing school-leaving ages. Indeed, in developing attendance at school, caring and control became overlapping practices rather than polar opposites.[23] In part, inducements to parents played a role in this battle including child benefits, traveling expenses, school materials, and medical services. But these tended to be placed alongside fines and penalties, which were more feasible as the number of recalcitrant children reduced in number. Those who did not fit with this model were gradually categorized as truants and, later, as "deprived" or "deviant," and "special" forms of provision were developed to meet their needs.[24] In this way, schools became central agencies for the creation of citizens, designed to inculcate a shared national character in future generations.[25]

The US historical experience lends some credence to these perspectives even though much has been written about its exceptionalism. Education played a central role in socializing waves of immigrants from other cultures who went through an educational melting pot of Americanization. The rapid urbanization of the United States also fostered educational growth as one means of handling the ensuing social tensions and potential for social breakdown.[26] Moreover, the early extension of the franchise in the United States, along with the development of common schooling, encouraged a notion of the United States as a land of opportunity. The dates of enactment of compulsory schooling laws among American states reveal that, following the early examples of Massachusetts in 1852 and the District of

Columbia in 1864, most others followed suit in the 50 years after 1870, for instance, Michigan in 1871, California and New York in 1874, Ohio in 1877, and Idaho in 1884. Unsurprisingly, the southern states generally lagged behind and did not pass such laws until into the twentieth century, with the exception of Kentucky (1896) and West Virginia (1897). This apparent tardiness is related to the fact that it allowed time to pass segregation laws in the wake of the Civil War (1860–1865) and Reconstruction, thus excluding ex-slaves from the benefits of education, although a number of black schools and colleges were established. Initially laws only required attendance for a number of weeks in a year. The gradual enforcement was related to the growing availability of school places. Alabama's compulsory attendance law, introduced in 1915, required attendance for 80 days a year but allowed for a number of exemptions according to distance, health, level of education, and domestic responsibilities. Enforcement was weak and almost nonexistent among black communities.[27] It was against this background that the landmark Supreme Court case, Brown v. Board of Education of Topeka in 1954, in rejecting the claim of "separate but equal" schooling, gave rise to an explosive controversy in the ensuing decades.

It has been commonly argued that compulsory attendance laws responded to the rising popularity of schooling. In this sense, they represented the formalization and institutionalization of existing social changes.[28] While laws responded to rising levels of voluntary enrollment, they also gradually facilitated an acceptance of universal and compulsory schooling. David Tyack has noted the "symbolic" phase of legal compulsion that eased the way for future bouts of legislative action on compulsory schooling accompanied by stricter enforcement.[29] The claim that laws did not increase attendance may have been true over the initial decades after a law was passed, but in subsequent decades they became part of the common sense of schooling, particularly when the social, economic, and political context became conducive to full enforcement of the law.

Secondary Education and the School-Leaving Age

As state education expanded, a range of new interest groups made the case for further extensions in the school-leaving age. During the early twentieth century, professional groups proliferated across many societies, not least in education even though teachers commonly operated on the boundary between professionalism and trade unionism. Teachers and their trade unions would often find themselves in the contradictory situation of supporting ROSLA while reacting negatively to the thought of having to teach actual students who did not necessarily accept the necessity to remain in school.[30]

The creation of compulsory education and its extension through ROSLA was widely perceived to be a fundamental social change. The very first International Conference on Public Education, held in Geneva in 1934 and organized by the International Bureau of Education (IBE) with the support of the International Labour Office (ILO), was on the topic of "compulsory education and the raising of the school leaving age." This subject was chosen to garner maximum international interest. The event generated a series of recommendations that could be adapted to the needs of different countries, a format that continued for many years. Indeed, national, regional, and local conditions all tempered the universal nature of this reform. It was argued that teaching and education were expected to develop

> the potentialities of each culture in accordance with its historical traditions, and to encourage between the various cultures the harmony which will generate peace and concord; and...be kept in line with social and economic developments, by means of international co-operation on the widest possible scale.[31]

This friction between the universalism of ROSLA and its specific national and cultural location suffused debates on the issue. The conference contributed to a growing body of opinion in favor of the creation and extension of secondary education up to the age of 14 at least.[32] The ILO itself published a report that argued for a dual approach to restricting child labor laws while extending educational opportunity.[33] In the twentieth century, as the school-leaving age was gradually raised in many countries, the need and demand for more specialized forms of education was recognized. As compulsory schooling was lengthened, separate forms of education—elementary and secondary—came to be seen as complementary to one another.[34]

The extension of "universal" compulsory education had not meant that everyone followed identical educational pathways. While basic and elementary schooling became available to all, in reality wealthier groups benefited from secondary education and private schools, which provided access to higher education and to more prestigious and remunerative employment. From the mid-twentieth century, the notion that secondary education should be a common educational experience available to all gained widespread acceptance across developed nations. There had been many calls to introduce secondary education in earlier decades as well as practical examples that supported this trend. Secondary education for all also implied a higher school-leaving age and a common curriculum for all. However, secondary education would often be further divided in ways that confirmed wider class and gender divisions.

Educational expansion appeared possible during the extraordinary postwar years of economic growth when developed countries witnessed sustained increases in their standard of living. Each generation was enjoying greater prosperity than the previous one, and education became tied into these improved life chances. A mutually reinforcing process developed between the needs of the workplace and the demands of individuals for improved economic well-being. On an international level, ideas of modernization and economic competitiveness began to saturate policy discussions and educational policies were seen to help countries avoid being left behind.

As education came to be conceived as increasingly central to the economy, society, and culture, efforts were made to embed sympathies for compulsory education. Although ROSLA promoted the professional autonomy of schools and teachers, it released contrary pressures that tied schools into the fortunes of their communities. It was argued within UNESCO that parents needed to

> appreciate school work and welcome compulsory education for their children, schools should be integrated as closely as possible with the community; schools should play their part in raising living standards in the community, and in its social, economic, civic, artistic and cultural advance.[35]

During the twentieth century, educationists focused upon their role in protecting children from the dangers of the workplace and the wider social environment, allowing time for them to mature in a supportive and enlightening setting. The sphere of education was one in which schools and teachers enjoyed considerable professional autonomy. In some cases, this involved applying a scientific rationality to the learning of young people; in others, progressive educational traditions were adapted to new cohorts of pupils remaining in school. Yet, signs of the breakdown of this professional vision were also perceptible in the face of such calls for integration with the community.

Compulsory and universal schooling was central to postwar social reconstruction. The new educational systems in West Germany and Japan were specifically devised to foster democratic values. In response to Article 26 of the Universal Declaration of Human Rights, UNESCO embarked on a project to encourage "the universalisation and prolongation of free compulsory education." Accordingly it commissioned a number of national studies of compulsory education in countries including Australia, France, United Kingdom, Ecuador, Iraq, and Thailand with an overall summary by Isaac Kandel. A number of international conferences were held including regional groupings in such areas as South East Asia.[36]

The three decades following the Second World War witnessed a bout of legislation, which raised the school-leaving age. In Britain, the 1944 Education Act raised the age to 15, achieved in 1947, and to 16 in 1972. In 1943, following the Youth and Welfare Act of 1940, the Australian state of New South Wales raised the age to 15 with New Zealand following suit in 1944. By achieving a higher threshold of voluntary participation, more people became willing to countenance increased educational compulsion.[37] That Britain was about to raise the age certainly impacted across the Commonwealth countries.[38] In West Germany, the federal states extended the duration of compulsory schooling from eight to nine years between 1949 and 1969. The quality of German education has been attested by many commentators. Although it has been widely argued that increasing the years of schooling makes a substantial economic difference to both individuals and societies, one research study on West Germany found no economic returns resulting from this extension of compulsion and suggested it may have been because, for those on a vocational track, essential employment-related skills were not learned in the final year of schooling but had already been achieved much earlier than might be the case in the United States or United Kingdom.[39]

It is commonly argued that decreasing economic returns tend to result from each successive increase in ROSLA. According to this reasoning, it has proven to be relatively more valuable for countries with lower educational levels to catch up with "advanced" countries, which has resulted in a process of "convergence" across developed nations.[40] During the postwar period, under the pressure of industrial competition, the school-leaving age was even raised by multiples of two and three years in certain cases. For instance, Portugal raised the age by 2 years and France increased it from 14 to 16 in 1967 although later legislation enabled more vocational routes to be pursued from the age of 14. In 1980, compulsory school attendance in Greece was increased by three years.

From the establishment of education systems, international comparisons have not only been expressed in economic terms. The Boshevik Revolution of 1917 and the expanding influence of the Soviet Union brought a political and ideological element to the fore of these comparisons. The 1919 Soviet Communist Party Congress approved a new system of universal education, which was initiated with intensive literacy campaigns. There was an early aspiration to create a national system of schooling with a leaving age of 18 although this would not be achieved for several decades. Central control was established over the education system in order to support a planned economy, but Soviet education drew upon older enlightenment traditions. Following considerable expansion in the 1930s, a 7-year course was introduced in 1949, from ages 7 to 14, and this was further extended by the Khruschev reforms after 1958. By the 1970s, general education had become the norm for many 17- to 18-year-olds. The expansion of the formal education system was seen as a principal means of forging the new workers who would contribute to the achievement of socialism. Developments in engineering and science proceeded rapidly. The launch of the Sputnik satellite in 1957 had a huge impact in focusing attention on education and helped to justify raising the school-leaving age across the "free" world.[41] Other socialist countries would carry out literacy campaigns in the coming years, as a way of helping to achieve desired social changes, for example in Cuba in the 1960s and Nicaragua in the 1980s.[42]

During the postwar years, ROSLA was central to the reorganization of education systems in many nations. In Scandinavian countries and in Britain, where common forms of schooling developed, these dual reforms were difficult to disentangle.[43] In 1970, the Spanish General Education Act raised the age to 14, enabling access to secondary education, a move that coincided with a significant reshaping of the whole education system, the most significant change since the Moyano Act of 1857, which had established a system of elementary education.[44] Regional disparities were prominent in areas such as Malaga, which only had 67 percent of the school places it required. In such cases, the capacity to provide universal schooling continued to be undercut by material shortages. Extending universal education depended not only on political support and a regime of enforcement but also on spaces in schools being available.[45] It was a challenge familiar in many poorer countries.

Compulsory Education in Developing and Emerging Economies

The creation and extension of compulsory education has provided a powerful set of models for so-called developing and emerging countries, many of which are attempting to concertina similar levels of educational growth into a comparatively short time span compared to the long maturation period that took place in Europe and, to a lesser extent, North America, Australia, and New Zealand. Historically, the aspiration for full-time universal schooling had proved problematic for countries without the ability to provide the resources for it. Compulsory education was viewed by some as "expensive and elitist," and part-time schooling was considered as an alternative.[46] However, the Millennium Development Goal of ensuring universal access to primary education for all children as well as gender equality in education resulted from growing international pressures and a number of agreements on education. Specifically, it built upon the Education for All movement coordinated by UNESCO and developed through the Global Declaration on Basic Education in Jomtien in 1990 and the Dakar framework on Education for All, in 2000.

These developments coexisted with strategies to counter the use of child labor, which has proved to be a continuing issue. In 1973, the ILO adopted a Minimum Age Convention that raised the recommended standard for employment in developing countries from 14 to 15 years or the age at which compulsory education ended, whichever was the higher. Such declarations on their own had limited impact but contributed to a growing set of concerns about young people.[47] Similarly, calls from UNICEF (United Nations Children's Fund) and other bodies to respect the rights of children supported a growing recognition of the need for education for all young people. One example has been Lesotho, where the 2010 Education Act made primary education free and compulsory as a contribution toward achieving the Millennium Development Goals. Despite this, in 2012, 18 percent of children were still not in primary school with costs, such as uniforms and learning materials, preventing many from attending.[48] The World Bank has also supported a major strategy for increasing secondary education in sub-Saharan Africa. Enrollment remains a major objective in Ghana where progression rates from primary to secondary school were 90 percent in 2012 but enrollment rates can fall below 50 percent as many pupils drop out.[49] It proved difficult to implement free and compulsory basic education, introduced in 1995, in the face of ongoing economic difficulties that left families facing significant sacrifices in order to send their children to school.[50] Issues of equity and efficiency are therefore considered essential in the development of secondary schooling for all. Although raising the school-leaving age can be less of a priority in sub-Saharan Africa, it is nevertheless connected to creating a basic infrastructure of schooling.

However, we must question the assumption that education necessarily leads to development. The correlation between longer compulsory schooling and the wealth of a nation, the relationship is not a straightforward one. For example, some Caribbean islands have 12–13 years of compulsory schooling, similar to Belgium, the Netherlands, and Germany with leaving ages of 18. Countries as diverse as Mexico, Namibia, and Peru enjoy more than ten years of compulsory schooling, not far off the rates for many

Western countries. In virtually every nation, children enter school between 4 and 8 and remain there for a period of between 4 and 13 years, averaging around 8 to 9 years of schooling. This clearly hides a wide range of national differences, not just in terms of duration but also content and quality.[51]

The tension between competing priorities of elite higher education and mass basic education has been at the crux of developing national systems of education. The division can be particularly marked where there is an absolute scarcity of resources. A common response to problems of economic development has been to train leaders in "elite" institutions. This dilemma is actively felt in Western countries where common and elite forms of education have often coexisted in a strained relationship. Emerging economies have recently joined this race through the development of elite technical institutions. But this can create difficulties in terms of exacerbating inequalities and perpetuating differences between rich and poor and between ethnic groups. For example, India, which has embraced a technical educational revolution in producing high volumes of well-qualified graduates, nevertheless has a literacy rate of 60 percent and only a 40 percent gross enrollment in secondary education, compared to an average of 70 percent in East Asian countries and 82 percent in Latin America.[52]

Since independence in 1947, gradually rising literacy levels in India have provided a basis for educational expansion. Higher educational institutions have been tied to economic growth, but the chasm between social groups and classes has been widened by this very inequality of educational provision. As a result, inequalities can be juxtaposed in quite a stark manner whereby new IT and call centers staffed by graduates coexist with communities that remain rooted in rural and traditional livelihoods. Moreover, it is somewhat ironic that World Bank and OECD reports have noted how unequal educational opportunities can generate lower levels of stability, economic investment, and growth, whereas equality can underpin higher levels of health, education, and general well-being.[53] While some states in India enacted compulsory education laws, this was not found to correlate with levels of enrollment, which varied considerably across the country.[54]

The accentuation of diverse educational experiences in many developing countries has also led to a counterreaction in favor of education for all. In this context, a number of significant attempts to develop compulsory education have been made. The introduction of the commitment to provide free compulsory education in India has become a key mechanism to extend education in a country with a billion people. In 1968 and 1986, the National Policy on Education made attempts to establish a uniform 12-year pattern of schooling with the final two years comprising an upper secondary stage. The Indian constitution was amended in 2002 to incorporate the responsibility of the state to provide "free and compulsory education to all children of the age of six to fourteen years."[55] It took a number of years for this aspiration to be translated into law. In theory the state had already been responsible for ten years of compulsory education but the number of children not in school, and those in poor quality provision, remained high. The 2009 Right of Children to Free and Compulsory Education Act has been widely seen as a turning point in Indian educational history. Yet critics complained that there was no commitment to quality, no clear understanding of where the resources would come from to fund this development, limited means of enforcement, and ambiguity over the responsibility for ensuring attendance. Powers to implement legislation have been devolved to state- and district-level authorities and civil society and private organizations that continue to play a strong role in sponsoring and providing schooling.[56] The persistence of administrative difficulties, funding shortfalls, and the demand for child labor all hamper the shift to a "national" system of compulsory education. In recognizing the need to challenge inequality, the law is again playing a symbolic role in attempting to clear a path for the gradual implementation of compulsory schooling, to

> create a humane and equitable society that incorporates the secular values and the ethnic, religious and cultural diversities of India...the objectives of democracy, social justice, and equality can be achieved only through the provision of elementary education of equitable quality to all.[57]

In the nation that by 2025 will have the largest population of children, this aspiration will not easily deal with deeply ingrained forms of inequality. Given the rapidity of change in India, one might expect the emerging education system to become a locus for conflicts between these countervailing forces of modernity, opportunity, tradition, and hierarchy.[58]

By contrast, South East Asia provides a different set of issues relating to compulsory school-leaving ages. Many of these countries have been categorized as "emerging," although Japan has been a leading economic power since the 1960s, a position that is now rapidly also being assumed by China, South Korea, and, to a degree, Vietnam. Compulsion has not always been central to educational thinking in these countries but a significant expansion of schooling has been made in its absence. Japan achieved very high rates of participation with only limited compulsion. In South Korea, a 1948 law introduced a partially compulsory education system that was implemented in 1953. Even though only primary education was both compulsory and free, enrollment rates for secondary education were equivalent to those in industrialized countries. After the Japanese occupation in 1945, adult literacy rates in South Korea stood at 22 percent but then rose dramatically to nearly 90 percent by 1970 and almost 95 percent by 1990.[59] Despite these achievements, the national preoccupation with the educational success of children has given rise to serious social concerns including the disturbing numbers of student suicides annually. While some areas have experienced significant increases in educational participation, provision remains limited in some areas.

South East Asian countries have experienced rapid educational change. The Asian "tigers" are often held up as examples of neoliberalism in action, illustrating the ways in which education is closely tied into the skill formation of knowledge-based economies.[60] In Singapore, the development of an independent educational system was closely tied into a nation-building project following its break away from the Malaysian Federation in 1965. In line with other countries across the region, high enrollment rates were achieved through voluntary action and, by the early twenty-first century, only 3 percent of each age cohort was not enrolled in primary schools. Compulsory education was introduced as a means of responding not only to external economic forces but also to fears of potential ethnic separation and conflict within.[61] It was not until 2003 that compulsory education was implemented for the age group 6–15 to provide a "common core of knowledge...for a knowledge-based economy" that would help to "build national identity and cohesion." Education was seen as "the most effective long-term solution to achieve growth and stability for the nation, in addition to preparing young Singaporeans to participate in a modern economy."[62]

The association between education and democracy is a contingent historical outcome clearly illustrated in South East Asia, where the expansion of schooling has not necessarily been linked to an equivalent extension of democratic processes as was the case in Britain. In Indonesia, during the rule of the Western-backed President Suharto (1967–1988), who installed a military-led government, the country witnessed a significant growth in basic education when the numbers of primary schools increased from 65,000 in 1973 to 130,000 in 1984 catering for 26 million pupils. However, educational expansion may have laid the groundwork for a change of regime and has certainly continued apace since that time. In 1984, a six-year mandatory education was introduced and increased to nine years only one decade later in 1994. In 2010, it was announced that 12 years of compulsory schooling would be introduced by 2014 despite the fact that the country was struggling to meet the material needs of the earlier increases. The way in which contemporary economic discourses continue to pervade political thinking on the nation was clearly indicated by Vice President Boediono's argument that it would increase the country's "academic standing" and improve economic performance. Indeed, The *Jakarta Post* quoted Boediono as claiming, "We will use this program to increase the quality of the nation."[63]

It does not necessarily follow that each increase in the school-leaving age will result in a positive democratic outcome. One study found no causal effect between increasing the duration of compulsory schooling and increased political participation.[64] This contrasts with many popularly held assumptions, as well as a range of empirical and theoretical studies, that connect the level of education and, in some cases, years of schooling, to rising political participation, and other personal and social benefits.[65] However, whether antidemocratic forces can coexist for long with increasing levels of education is more contestable. Although compulsory education can respond to a range of motivational factors, the long-term implications of a well-educated population is an uncontrollable and unpredictable force. The growing sense of subjectivity and self-awareness in China, within a restrictive civil society, may be a case in point.

Both Brazil and China have taken significant steps to increasing compulsory education, yet they have done so in ways that contradict many dominant ideas, for example, through concerted state action. In contrast to many other South East Asian countries, China has used legal measures to extend compulsory education alongside a process of devolution.[66] Both China and India have resorted to a range of private providers to help expand educational capacity. This reflects the characteristic way that China, in supporting nine years of compulsory schooling since the mid-1980s, has sought to retain central state control while embracing a more diverse marketplace.[67] In such a large country, the financing and administration of this measure has been devolved on a regional basis.[68]

The School-Leaving Age in a Changing World

Historical issues have remained pertinent to contemporary settings in Western nations. From the 1980s, the new framework of compulsory primary and secondary education became an increasingly contested territory. ROSLA as a topic tended to die down in international debates in comparison with the pressing concerns of selective and common schooling, curriculum and pedagogy and raising standards. One OECD study in 1983 found that compulsory schooling had become a common experience and "a primary social institution."[69] It was suggested that education received relatively limited public attention, and that "its goals, processes and practices have tended to be taken as given."[70] But the extension of educational systems resulting from ROSLA also led to reorganization. It was not always possible simply to extend what was already in existence; incorporating the full cohort of older pupils created problems that could not be met from within existing frameworks.

The relative isolation of schooling was not to last. With more and more resources being devoted to compulsory education, wider interests demanded a voice in their deployment. While ROSLA enhanced professional interests by emphasizing the importance of education, it paradoxically served to break down the barriers between schools and interest groups who felt that education might serve their interests. New alliances across business, politics, and civil society all began to encroach upon secondary education and led to closer scrutiny of schools and a gradual breaking down of the autonomy enjoyed by education systems. Expansion has gone hand in hand with a closer relationship to work and society. The consequent reconfiguration of compulsory schooling has undermined many assumptions and traditions.[71] Teachers and schools have had to meet targets, accountability measures, and inspection regimes that tie the teacher to a particular set of practices connected to the assumed needs of the economy.

It is from within this shifting context that compulsory education is being extended. The educational scene has become dominated by neoliberal discourses in which education has played an important, but secondary, role to economic interests. Drawing on the philosophy of thinkers such as Friedrich Hayek and Milton Friedman, it has been argued that "free markets," limiting the restrictions on capital and supporting transnational corporations are essential to the prosperity of nations. As a modern incarnation of human capital theory, a highly skilled workforce is viewed as a necessary prerequisite for wealthy nations to attract inward investment. Business leaders and a range of intermediate agencies have all actively pursued these policies and pushed governments to liberalize their economies. For example, the World Bank, International Monetary Fund (IMF), World Trade Organisation (WTO), and OECD have been instrumental in promoting discourses of privatization and marketization.

In the early years of the twenty-first century, lifelong learning in a "knowledge economy" has become a popular idea. Economic globalization has encouraged higher expenditure on education, which is increasingly expected to serve wider economic needs.[72] The new climate has proved conducive to international comparisons in which proxy measures, such as the duration of compulsory schooling, have become one important way to judge contemporary educational systems and evaluate their success. Education for all and a state-imposed period of compulsory schooling is seen as a support for human capital, for democracy and, symbolically at least, creates a level playing field. As more students now remain in education and attend university, a range of pathways have opened up with the blurring of a training/education divide. Attention has focused upon policy borrowing across countries in which apparently similar policies can mask ideological intent and imposed changes.[73] Just as exams do not necessarily provide the skills required by economies, the existence of certain education policies and structures do not always indicate the quality and range of education available in any given country.[74]

Transition has become a key word related to the duration and extent of compulsory education. It has also generated tensions as new pathways and options have been encouraged, so that the sharp break between schooling and other forms of learning and training has begun to break down. Young people may now need to negotiate different assumptions about their identity in relation to a range of learning, training, and part-time employment routes.[75]

It has become a contradictory but common observation that extending compulsory education contributes to economic development as well as social cohesion, civil society, and social well-being.[76] In addition, education is widely associated with improved health, gender equality, lower fertility, and birthrates as well as lower child mortality. These benefits have been accompanied by new forms of governance that have called into play a diffuse range of networks to support increases in compulsory education by tackling those now considered to be "at risk" or described as "NEET"—not in education, employment, or training.[77] The effects of bringing recalcitrant pupils into learning situations can be felt by teachers in the classroom where the quality of learning experiences may be adversely affected. For instance, Spanish free and compulsory education was increased from the age of 14 to 16 in 1990. It was found that teacher absenteeism increased by approximately 15 percent as a result of this reform and the figure rose to 50 percent in regions with traditionally lower staying-on rates. In other words, ROSLA can be a partial measure in the drive to improve the quality of education. These moments of transition may be particularly acute in cases where the age is raised by more than one year at a time. The adjustments in attitudes among both teachers, pupils and parents to the new situation may indeed take some time to settle down.[78] Educators thus continue to face contradictory processes of teaching more mature pupils who are nevertheless to remain as pupils. In this way, ROSLA has intensified the educational affinities between support and control in requiring tough and stringent enforcement mechanisms, including penalties and fines, in addition to a range of welfare, pastoral, and support mechanisms that nurture the potential for learning in pupils.

A number of examples illustrate these changes. All Australian states have recently raised the school-leaving age, a widely recognized national priority; indeed, the orchestration of education policy across the states has been pursued under a "collaborative federalism."[79] The 2009 *Compact with Young Australians* emphasized the right of and need for all young people to complete Year 10 and then to remain in education, training, and employment until the age of 17. These policy documents have been heavily influenced by globalized discourses of competitiveness, placing Australia "ahead," "behind," and "equal to" other nations according to a range of criteria. Despite Australia being placed highly in league tables, the Compact introduced a sense of urgency to the national situation in claiming that "too many young Australians achieve only minimum standards. At 74 percent, Australia's secondary school completion rate is among the lowest in the OECD."[80] This anxiety was to be addressed through increased opportunities for all 15- to 24-year-olds.

Responding to the global context has become the most significant incentive to raise compulsory education. For instance, in New South Wales, the age of compulsion was increased from 15 to 17 in 2009.[81] In 2008, the state premier, Morris Lemma, had argued that the education system was becoming dated; compulsion had to be extended to meet new challenges "including climate change, globalization and the growing strength of the Chinese and Indian economies."[82] With raising the age to 18, many countries are more relaxed about encouraging a range of vocational options, not simply enforcing a common curriculum. In 2006, in Western Australia, the compulsory school-leaving age was raised to 16 and then 17 in 2008, and young people must now be in full-time school, work, approved training, or a mixture of these until they are 17. This created problems of tracking young people as such flexible schemes can be difficult to administer. Ironically, extending compulsion appears to be the means of dealing with attendance issues among younger cohorts. It has even been claimed that attendance is in decline with 30 percent of students in Western Australia judged to be at risk.[83]

The United States illustrates a different model of federalism in which most states start education at ages 6 or 7 and complete between 16 and 18. There has been a growing tendency for states to raise the age to 18. By June 2010, 19 states had a leaving age of 16; 11 an age of 17; and 20 states had raised the age to 18 as had the District of Columbia, American Samoa, and Puerto Rico.[84] Maryland has also followed suit more recently. Undoubtedly, this trend reveals that education is being conceived as an economic benefit in the face of challenges from China and other emerging economic powers. That compulsory education has become a live public issue was reflected in President Barack Obama's 2012 State of the Union address when he moved into a territory traditionally occupied by the states in calling for new laws:

> When students don't walk away from their education, more of them walk the stage to get their diploma. When students are not allowed to drop out, they do better...I am proposing that every state—every state—requires that all students stay in high school until they graduate or turn 18.[85]

Extending compulsion is also viewed as a convenient way of addressing a range of social problems. A coordinated approach to the welfare and education of young people to 18 is being highlighted. Research for the Bill Gates Foundation declared that the United States was suffering from a "dropout epidemic," which had a particularly harsh impact upon ethnic minorities since approximately half of African Americans, Hispanics, and Native Americans did not graduate from high school.[86] Bodies such as the National Association of Secondary School Principals have actively supported raising the level of compulsory education on these grounds.[87] The "dropout crisis," which sees up to an estimated 1 million school children leave school early, is commonly linked to a range of social problems; such young people are "more likely to commit crimes, abuse drugs and alcohol, become teenage parents, live in poverty and commit suicide."[88] States such as Indiana and New Hampshire have experimented with a range of measures including parental involvement, alternative and supplementary support, connecting anti-truancy action to reengagement policies, exit interviews, early warning systems, and preventative counseling.[89] However, these policies challenge deeply embedded ideas about freedom and fears of state action. Raising compulsory education to 18 will not easily overcome strongly felt opposition to compulsory education.[90] Attempts to raise the age in Massachusetts, Minnesota, and New Jersey have all recently proved unsuccessful, with state politicians recoiling from the prospect of increased spending on education and related welfare measures.[91] Moreover, research has claimed that increased compulsion will not necessarily improve high school completion rates,[92] a claim that is attractive to these skeptics, particularly in a time of economic recession.

Despite the strong contemporary tendencies in favor of extending compulsory education, we should guard against the view that raising the school-leaving age is in any way inevitable or part of a consensus. It is possible to identify very real obstacles and opposition to compulsory education and ROSLA especially at a time of global economic downturn. For developing countries, reducing child labor remains central to educational strategies on education for all.[93] Notions of the "knowledge economy" and global convergence often underestimate the fact that many sectors of manufacturing and agriculture still make considerable use of child labor. In these areas of the world, the notion of a separate stage of the life course associated with childhood remains muted. In the nineteenth century, it was common to view child labor as important for both the national and family economy, and there have continued to be strong echoes of this idea over the past century, adapting to changes in the social and cultural context.

Overall, ROSLA has impinged upon a wide variety of educational forces and concepts that varied in divergent national settings. It often resulted from disjointed and contested policy processes within these particular cultural contexts. The actual meanings of ROSLA within each country thus need to be placed within their specific historical location. Achieving legislation was one thing; implementing changes in the years following reform quite another. The ways in which these changes worked through in the English and, to some extent, the British experience, provides a fascinating insight into the growth of compulsory education.

Chapter 3

Framework for ROSLA: Establishing Compulsion

In the late nineteenth and early twentieth centuries, a system that developed to meet the social class interests of Victorian elites continued to shape educational discourses and practices.[1] During this period, legislation was introduced to compel parents to send their children to school. This was continually subject to challenge and opposition over extending the age of compulsion, which was entangled with other key social issues. Schooling came to be seen by many as the preferred institutional setting in which to place working-class children deemed too young to work. The expansion of a national schooling system underpinned by legislative requirements upon parents to send their children to school entailed an historic rebalancing of social relations between individual independence and the rights of parents and families on the one hand, and agencies of the state, both locally and nationally, on the other. With the advent of elected school boards to coordinate educational provision locally, following the 1870 Education Act, issues of schooling and childcare became linked inexorably with political processes. The establishment of compulsion in this broader social and political context provided the framework for the raising of the school leaving age (ROSLA).

Tentative Beginnings

The politics of extending compulsion in schooling was, from the beginning, closely intertwined with the issue of the role and place of children and juveniles within the national and regional labor force. Resistance to extension of compulsory schooling tended to come from those with vested interests in maintaining the supply of the relatively cheaper labor of children, as well as from many parents who felt that a delay in realizing the earning potential of their offspring served little purpose. Their child would secure work in the same shop, warehouse, large house, factory, trade, or utility company regardless of whether they left school at 12, 13, or 14. By contrast, supporters of extending schooling came from a range of moral, social, political, and educational positions and thus never formed a coherent social movement. This partly explains why employers, conservatives, and the Anglican and Catholic hierarchies were able to limit the rate of progress toward the compulsory provision of schooling for all children up to an agreed leaving age.

A key development arising from the introduction of a national educational system was the emergence of a large and powerful professional interest group, which in turn was to play a major role in shaping future public debate about education.[2] This included teachers, school boards officials, officers and inspectors from within the government Board of Education, and professionals working within teacher training colleges. Britain expanded during this period into the preeminent global industrial and imperial power, creating a need for ever-increasing numbers of clerically and administratively capable employees, far beyond the ability of traditional apprenticeship-based mechanisms for reproducing such human capital within the population. In particular, the demand from commerce for female clerical employees at the beginning of the twentieth century would help to bring about changes in attitudes toward the need for secondary schooling for girls. Calls for the extension of schooling during the nineteenth century and into the twentieth century should be understood in relation to these broader socioeconomic trends. Sometimes calls for the extension of schooling did not arise from "educational" interests at all. It is notable how social Darwinism and eugenics, both powerful intellectual and social currents from the last two decades of the nineteenth century, gave rise to contradictory arguments on education.[3]

In introducing the 1870 Education Act, William Forster emphasized that the concept of state intervention to regulate children's lives was not new. Under the Poor Law, attendance at school could be a condition of receiving relief, and the 1857 Industrial Schools Act enabled magistrates to sentence children found begging to spend time at an industrial school.[4] Direct state involvement in the provision of schooling began during the 1830s with the establishment of a formal committee to operate a scheme to offer grants for school building to religiously controlled educational organizations. Schemes of inspection followed, having the effect of extending the supervisory link between schools and the state.[5] Over the following two decades, five separate pieces of legislation were passed relating to compulsory purchase of land for the purpose of building schools. This led to the 1855 School Grants Act, which stipulated that where monies from the Treasury had been made to acquire land for schools, to develop the buildings, or for their repair, they could not be sold without express permission from the government. The state was developing a stake in the development of a national system of elementary schooling designed to accommodate working-class children. These incremental changes would reach a threshold after which state intervention would become the norm.

Initially the teachers struggled to secure regular attendance of pupils at the school because many were half-timers engaged in paid labor, and some would not have been able to afford the full-time fees. The problems faced by the schools are reflected in the diary of a Mr. Gardner who was a teacher at Shepherd Street School in Preston in 1871.

> Very few children present in time for opening. Great difficulty in getting punctual attendance. Half-timers almost as bad as the full-day scholars. One reason may be that the mothers of many of the children are employed in the mills and are thus, to some extent, prevented from pushing their children off to school. The breakfast time allowed in the mills is from 8 to 8.30 in some instances but most commonly from 8.30 to 9 o'clock.[6]

Gardner's diary describes a social setting in which parents left their homes early in the morning in order to arrive at the mill for the morning shift. Their children were left to their own devices if they were too young to work. The immediate area described by Gardner suffered from extensive poverty and a lack of employment.

School provision and attendance were bound up in such local circumstances. The successive industrial acts and legislative changes that instituted schooling were uneven in their reach. Despite barriers to school attendance, participation grew steadily during the period from 1820 to 1870 but, for many, especially those living in the poor rural areas, and those from the expanding mining and manufacturing districts, school life amounted to little more than two or three years in total.[7] Although the picture of school attendance and participation remained a mixed one, the number of pupils and schools of all kinds grew steadily in line with population growth, making the presence of education in the country increasingly visible. W. B. Stephens's extensive study of the geography of literacy in Britain during the first half of the nineteenth century describes a picture of widely varying standards of provision and opportunities.[8] Parochial variations also existed so that one parish might have strong local schooling traditions whereas a neighboring parish offered little to nothing for the children of the poor. This is not to deny the presence and tradition of literate practices and forms of learning located within working-class movements and communities.[9] However, in a changing society in which clerical and administrative competence opened up opportunities for nonmanual forms of employment, schooling would gradually come to be perceived as an essential stage in the lives of a majority of children.

State intervention was also developing in schooling for the middle and upper classes who were catered for through a separate system of schools, funded through scholarships arising from accumulated bequests or through fees paid by parents. It was within this class-based sphere that forms of post-elementary or secondary schooling were to develop as preparation either for university or as early induction into a profession such as surveying or estates management. For many girls, secondary schooling was to focus upon preparation for a middle-class household, management of domestic servants, supervising a growing family and certain cultural attributes considered suitable for women. Given that the social prestige of such schools derived from the social status of their clientele, the philosophy and curriculum arising from them came to exert a considerable influence upon subsequent debates about the form that secondary education should take. At the top of this movement were the great "public" schools such as Rugby, Harrow, Shrewsbury, Charterhouse, and Eton where boys from gentry and aristocratic families were groomed for future political and social leadership prior to their time at Oxford or Cambridge University.[10] Alongside such schools there existed a spread of endowed grammar schools, some dating back several centuries, most of which remained focused around a classical studies curriculum. Some schoolmasters offered "modern" subjects on a fee basis, which meant that sons of prosperous traders and farmers might be attracted to public schools as day boys alongside the resident boarders.[11]

As the prosperous middle class expanded in the early Victorian period, demand for new boarding schools grew. These were often modeled on the pattern of established public schools and not only retained elements of the classics but also included modern subjects such as geography, science, modern European languages, and history. By the 1860s, a new sector had arisen almost everywhere across Britain, of private schools designed for the prosperous middle classes with a curriculum to some extent tailored to the future needs of this social class, although there were many small schools that struggled to survive.[12] The state intervened in 1840 with the passing of the Grammar Schools Act, which permitted the Court of Chancery to rule on changes within endowed grammar schools toward including branches of science and literature other than Greek or Latin. The law also provided for Chancery to decide upon amalgamations of grammar schools located in the same towns, but made special exemption of a list of named great schools that were to lie outside of the terms of the legislation, thus consolidating their independence from the gradually extending reach of legislation in relation to issues of schooling. This independence was to be further consolidated in 1868 following the Clarendon Report, when the Public Schools Act detailed the responsibilities of governing boards of these few schools in order to strengthen their role in preparing the next generation of the social elite.[13]

For the history of compulsory education such early beginnings, however partial and class biased, nevertheless laid the ground for the idea that Parliament and politics in general had legitimate concerns within the sphere of education and could legislate where necessary. While the Clarendon Report was being prepared, a parallel enquiry into the efficiency and effectiveness of the grammar schools was also underway led by Lord Taunton. The purpose of this enquiry was to address the palpable deficit in secondary schooling, which led to shortages of sufficiently trained young people needed to staff expanding agencies such as the post office, banks, railway and shipping companies, ports, or indeed state departments. The Taunton enquiry recommended that a national framework be established and proposed a solution reflecting the social-class interests of the authors. There was to be a group of schools where the leaving age was 18, whose purpose was to prepare pupils for university entrance and the professions. The next type of school would be intended to train boys to the age of 16 or 17 for occupations in the military services or government departments, both nationally and at a local level. The final type of secondary school envisaged by the Taunton enquiry commissioners was for boys up to the age of 15 where modern subjects would be taught to sons of farmers, businessmen, and skilled workers. These schools were to be included under secondary school regulations because state-supported elementary schooling extended only to the age of 12. Following this, in 1869, the government passed the Endowed Schools Act that regulated the purpose and scope of such schools. The title of the Act reveals an interesting coda—"and otherwise to provide for the advancement of education." For the first time in British legislation, the idea of extending secondary schooling was linked explicitly to a wider conception of educational advance.[14]

Running in tandem with the acts outlined above was another set of legislation that directly regulated the working lives of children, thus interposing the state between employer and child and parent and employer. These were collectively known as the Factory Acts, and their cumulative effect was to enable children to undertake schooling in the working week. The 1802 Factory Act had been passed in the face of growing concern about the moral and social behavior of young people whose brief lives had been dominated by working in the cotton industry. It stipulated that employers of apprentices were required to provide time for the study of arithmetic, writing, and reading for the first four years of a seven-year apprenticeship. This was to be included within the normal 12-hour working day, rather than in addition to it. The idea of an apprenticeship was to prepare a young person for a lifetime working within an occupational field, including eventually training the next generation of apprentices. Like other early attempts at social legislation, the 1802 Act failed to address the main issues and problems that gave rise to it in the first place. An example of this tendency was that apprenticeships were for boys rather than girls, yet the moral concern expressed in relation to the proposed legislation related largely to the conduct of young women who had been exposed to influences at their workplaces, considered by many to be immoral. Apprenticeship continued to be a widespread experience for working-class boys.[15]

The 1833 and 1844 Factory Acts applied to labor in the textile industries and regulated hours of work for children and women. A key feature of these pieces of legislation was their use of ages to define "childhood." Under the 1833 Act, no child under 9 years of age was to work in industry, and a "child" under 18 was not to work nights. Children aged 9 to 13 were to receive 2 hours of education per day. From 1844, children aged from 9 to 13 had a maximum of 9 hours of work per day. Those aged 13 to 18 had a maximum of 12 hours per day with further restrictions on hours for Sundays. Meal breaks became a statutory requirement. This legislation established what was known as the "half-time" system of school and work, widely criticized by the end of the century but still common until the end of the First World War.[16] In 1847, maximum working hours in the textile industry for children under 18 were fixed at 10 hours per day. This was followed in 1850 by state-regulated working hours of 6:00 a.m. to 6:00 p.m. or 7:00 a.m. to 7:00 p.m., depending upon whether it was summer or winter. A time limit on Saturday working of 2:00 p.m. was also instituted for all children between the ages of 13 to 18.

Subsequent Factory Acts further regulated the free exchange between employer, parents, and children in relation to permissible employment. The Factory and Workshop Act of 1878 applied previous Acts to all trades rather than just textiles or mines. The age limit on child employment was raised to ten and linked to compulsory schooling up to that age. Children who were 10 to 14 years old were limited to half-day working. The 1891 Factory Act further extended the age limit for employment from 10 to 11. This series of legislative steps took longer to embrace the needs of women and children in textile and other industries than was the case with the Mines and Collieries Act of 1842, which prohibited all women, as well as girls and boys under ten years old, from working underground in coal mines.[17]

These reforms established a clear connection between industrial reform and the idea of extending school provision for the poorer classes. Through such steps, a space was created within public discourse concerning what ought to happen with children being subjected to the effects of paid work. In subsequent decades, as calls for the extension of compulsory schooling developed, the link between the provision of schooling and concerns about the relation of young people to industry remained in the forefront of public and political debates.

The Advent of Compulsion

With separate government enquiries and Acts focused upon elite schools and those for the middle class, there remained an equivalent interest in the educational condition of the poorer classes. In 1858, under the chairmanship of the Duke of Newcastle, a Royal Commission was established to report on the state of "popular" education in England. An explicit concern was to act in the face of the visible numbers of children present at all times in public spaces. Another concern was to propose a system that would help to equalize provision of elementary schooling across all districts, an implicit call for expansion. Added to this was a concern to find some way of managing and regulating such a nationwide system without overburdening the state department. Ensuring that all children acquired degrees of "useful knowledge" was an urgent matter.[18] The report published in 1861 was to inform public discussion for nearly a decade, before the Liberal government of William Gladstone backed a bill drafted by William Forster that reflected most of the issues outlined by the Newcastle Commission Report.[19]

The 1870 Act required district authorities to make provision of sufficient school places for all children aged 5–13 who lived in the district. Where this was not achievable under current local arrangements, the Act provided for the establishment of elected school boards charged with ensuring that such places were provided. A key shift was related to the powers granted to the Education Department to issue regulations about the way publicly funded elementary schools would operate. School boards were given powers to remit fees for families assessed to be too poor to pay, previously one of the main barriers to many continuing their schooling. However, the reform applied only to areas where there were "gaps" in provision, which was unsatisfactory to many Liberals. Feeling was especially high among nonconformists who opposed the continuing dominance of Anglican interests in publicly funded elementary schooling. The Act permitted a six-month period for districts to increase provision before facing compulsion to establish an elected school board, and this allowed Anglicans to increase the number of schools they controlled by 30 percent.[20] Nonconformists were also angered by the way that payments to defray school fees for necessitous children would be paid to diocesan authorities.

The creation of a unified national system was further ensured by the provision that from 1871 only elementary schools falling within the jurisdiction of the school boards would receive building and maintenance grants, effectively forcing all schools to be included within the new structures. In time this would adversely affect many schools in working-class districts.[21] The most significant power granted to these boards was the ability to pass byelaws requiring parents to send their children to school if they were between the ages of 5 and 13. Although the decision was delegated and decentralized, it created powers to compel parents and young people to attend school, even though these provisions fell far short of the educational ambitions of those who had campaigned for legislation.

The provision barely concealed the entrenched hostility to compulsion coming from influential sectors of society. Harold Silver has described the scale of opposition as "mountainous," arguing that in the decade following the 1870 Act, something of significance changed the balance of wider public opinion toward favoring the principle of compulsion.[22] He adds that there was no inevitability of an eventual movement in that direction. One answer to the problem posed by Silver is that the actions and example of the school boards themselves contributed substantially to changed opinion, especially in working-class districts where school board elections galvanized cooperative and labor movement interests either around Liberal candidates or sometimes around independents. Another explanation was the social and moral impact of the continuing and expanding presence in the public domain of child destitution, which was coming to be seen by many as presenting a threat to social stability. Earlier arguments about securing rising educational involvement by strengthening factory legislation to require an educational test before employment of a child was permissible, no longer seemed credible in the face of concentrations of deprivation apparent in many parts of the country. While one section of the working class appeared to be growing in respectability in ways that appeared positive to middle-class onlookers,[23] another section struck a note of fear and discord. In 1857, at an educational conference called to remedy the "evil" of the "insufficient attendance of the working classes" in schools, Albert, the Prince Consort, had noted that boys were part of a family's "productive power" while girls should be the "hand maiden of the house." But this picture was clearly challenged by the fact that 600,000 children aged 3–15 years were absent from school but employed, over 2.2 million were absent with their whereabouts unknown. The urge to control this potentially chaotic situation that resulted from a changing labor market brought an element of urgency to the argument for compulsory schooling.[24]

A number of school boards had passed byelaws requiring some periods of compulsory attendance, but the usual tendency was for these to be hedged with various exemptions. This blunted the edge of criticism against the principle of compulsion reducing it to practical instances and cases. The school boards were able to access funding from the Education Department as well as from locally levied education rates, a provision that made expanding educational funding into a focus of intense political division with representatives of local business interests often resisting expansion. Newly enfranchised parents who could vote tended to support such expansion along with the rising trade union and labor movement.

The idea of an "education system," based upon compulsory schooling would, over the coming decades, become embedded in political and social debates. One of the weaknesses of the 1870 Act was the lack of any local structures to monitor and enforce attendance. The Elementary Schools Act of 1876 required local authorities to establish school attendance committees where no effective school board had been established. The Act also placed a duty upon parents to secure adequate provision for their children. The financial disincentives arising from payment of fees for schooling were further alleviated by the Act granting powers to local poor law guardians to offer assistance in proven cases. Forster left office in 1874 and was able to respond to nonconformist critics by pointing to an increase of nearly 5,000 additional schools on top of the nearly 5,300 that existed when he took office. Although he recognized that the campaign to extend schooling had been only partially successful, his claim was that the 1870 Act triggered a momentum that would not be stopped.[25] The evident weaknesses of the 1870 Act, which merely permitted the framing of byelaws, were reduced through the Elementary Education Act of 1880, when local boards were enabled to pass byelaws compelling children between five and ten years of age to attend school.

The personal drive and political character of key individuals constituted a key factor in the movement toward compulsion. The Liberal MP for Sheffield and supporter of the trade union and cooperative movements A. J. Mundella, for example, played a significant role in the passing of the 1876 and 1880 Acts. He introduced three bills in Parliament to increase the school-leaving age. Such pressure led to a bill requiring school attendance committees to be established where no board had been created, under Section 7 of the Elementary Education Act of 1876. Of equal political significance was the campaign of the National Education League (NEL) centered round Birmingham and led by George Dixon and Joseph Chamberlain. Their concern was to create an elementary school system free of sectarian bias and control. The link with Mundella was William Dronfield from Sheffield who became secretary of the NEL in 1869. It was Dixon who co-sponsored the three private Member's Bills with Mundella.[26] This kept the pressure upon Conservatives and Anglicans who felt it necessary to organize a countermovement called the National Education Union.[27]

From this point onwards, the campaigns to extend and resist extending compulsory school attendance helped not only to shape political allegiances at the highest levels, but also to define the political stances of the main party groupings. Many of the major political figures of their times became directly involved in this issue. A growing influence from the 1870s was the National Union of Elementary Teachers. One consequence of the establishment of school boards was the creation of a powerful teacher trade union that was to become one of the leading voices in subsequent decades for the continued extension of compulsory schooling. Within a decade of its formation, it was part of the campaigning group supporting initiatives from cooperative societies, nonconformists, and Liberals, drawing a majority of their members from the board schools rather than those working in voluntary schools.[28]

Despite the 1876 Bill being proposed from the House of Lords by Viscount Sandon, a Conservative Cabinet member, many Conservatives fought to prevent the bill from passing. In this they had strong support of the Anglican and Roman Catholic hierarchies, but Sandon's measure eventually passed with the backing of Liberals after many on his own benches voted against what was a government measure. This development illustrates how problematic is the view that raising the school-leaving age was a process of steady extension and expansion of the schooling system, as in part, Sandon's bill was an attempt to divert and preempt future initiatives in the event of the Liberals returning to office.[29]

When Gladstone returned to office in 1880, he appointed Mundella as vice president of the Committee of Education. Mundella was permitted to act as though he held the formal office of president because the politicians occupying that post lacked an active interest in educational matters and concentrated instead on other aspects of their political role. Gladstone's support for Mundella partly arose from his need to secure the support of rising Liberal/Labour representatives in the growing northern cities and Mundella fitted the profile perfectly. However, without the formal title of president and without membership of the cabinet, his radicalizing potential could be held in check. Mundella's role within the history of raising the school-leaving age can therefore be viewed as part of a wider strategy to create clear political divides in the minds of urban electorates between Conservative and Liberal Parties, a strategy that in part led to a split in Conservative Party ranks between social traditionalists and democratic conservatives. From the inception of compulsory education, the school-leaving age was heavily involved within the conflicts of party politics.

When Lord Salisbury regained office in the summer of 1886 for his second administration, it became clear that any future Gladstone-led administration could act to limit funding of nonboard, "voluntary" elementary schools, thus posing a fundamental threat to the Anglican and Catholic schools. His response was to establish a commission of enquiry chaired by Lord Cross whose design was to lay the ground for a restructuring of the elementary school system.[30] One way of doing this was to define more precisely the bounds of what elementary education was and to propose a clearer distinction between that and secondary education provision. Arising from the report of the Cross Commission, schools began to provide for activities such as woodwork and laundering. Additionally, following fashions of the time, certain styles of physical exercise and activity began to be introduced. Elementary schools became interested in hygiene, gardening, and home management, leading to a wider range of values and thinking about the purpose of schools moving considerably beyond the limitations of the prescribed code that for so long had restricted what could or could not be included within the curriculum.[31]

A significant development that was to have important consequences for future discussions occured with the 1889 Welsh Intermediate Education Act, which required county councils in Wales to provide for intermediate and technical education committees. The proposals would first have to be submitted to the Charity Commission and would permit half of the cost of classes to come from the Treasury. "Intermediate education" within the terms of the Act was education other than elementary, which could include subjects such as classical languages, the Welsh language and modern European languages, science, and mathematics. "Technical education" was to incorporate activities recognized by the Department of Science and Art, which required the use of a range of materials and tools, training leading to commercial and administrative skills and knowledge, and studies relating to particular occupations and industries such as agriculture.[32]

Once the local frameworks arising from this Act were in place, some forms of continuing schooling or training beyond elementary levels were present across Wales, and this led to higher levels of participation than were found in the English counties. The Liberal politician Arthur Acland, appointed as vice president of the Committee on Education and a member of the cabinet in Gladstone's final administration in 1892, was one of the main promoters of the Act. The evident success of the measure in stimulating attendance at secondary level informed his book of 1892, which became a key reference for educational reformers campaigning for the extension of the school-leaving age and expansion of secondary education.[33]

The 1891 Elementary Education Act instituted free schooling for the mass of children from the working class and made further inroads into the residual communities of non-attenders. The ages mentioned within this piece of legislation implicitly recognized the role of "higher" elementary study by specifying 15 as the upper limit rather than 14. In terms of the public debate concerning when schooling should begin, specifying the age of three is also of interest and reflected a rising awareness of the value of "infant" education. Each child registered at a public elementary school was to be worth 10 shillings (one-half of a pound sterling), and schools in receipt of such grants were not allowed to charge additional fees. The "school pence" had been a barrier for many from the poorest sections of working-class communities, and removal of fees meant that children could attend without their parents' ability to pay acting as an obstacle.[34]

Each legislative step led to gradual increases in rates of attendance and in the duration of schooling. It helped to normalize the idea that children passed through certain stages of development and that, between certain ages, they should attend school before going out to work. As this grant based on per capita payments was to be calculated on "average" attendance, the 1891 Act created a funding framework that provided a positive incentive for head teachers and school governors to register and retain pupils. Their work was strengthened by the local board attendance officers who worked to enforce regulations.

This was extended after the 1889 Royal Commission on the Blind and the Deaf recommended that blind children receive compulsory education in board schools. A two-stage education was envisaged, elementary and technical. Legislation followed with the Education of Blind and Deaf Mute Children (Scotland) Act of 1890 and the Elementary Education (Blind and Deaf Children) Act of 1893 in England. School authorities now had responsibility to educate blind children between the ages of 6 and 16 as well as deaf children between the ages of 7 and 16. In some senses, this outstripped what was commonly available for other children and represented a considerably stronger provision than was available for most children for decades to come.[35]

At the same time, secondary education was being expanded and redefined. A significant focus for this arose in 1894–1895 through the enquiries and report of the Bryce Commission on secondary education. The enquiry stage of the commission revealed that provision of secondary schooling across the country was woefully inadequate and virtually excluded working-class children. The fact that there were places where ex-elementary school pupils who had completed the higher grade had progressed into grammar schools suggested that there was both unmet potential and need. Bryce discovered in a survey of 7 county authorities that in 4 of these only 4 percent of girls and boys remained at school after the age of 14. An even starker figure was the discovery that just 1 percent aged 16 remained in schooling elsewhere. The recommendation from Bryce was for the administration and funding of all schooling to be unified.[36]

Bryce was responsive to wider public discussion about the critical lack of educational opportunities relating especially to technical and scientifically based industries. An 1893 report from the Department of Art and Science revealed declining provision in economically critical areas.[37] Later in the same year, the vice chancellor of Oxford University convened a conference of educationalists to discuss the state into which secondary education had fallen and to consider measures to effect an improvement.[38] In 1895, Henry Craik, who was to play a prominent role for almost 20 years in the direction of Scottish education, published a key work raising fundamental issues concerning the expansion of the education system under state control.[39] For thinkers such as Craik, the creation of effective, modern schooling systems was an essential aspect of creating modern and stable states, capable of addressing the social concerns of the majority.

Such state-led interventions functioned throughout this period as points in which government attempted to wrest some degree of control and influence in a social and political debate. The Bryce proposals were to fall far short of the political ambitions of many across the political spectrum. They advocated that secondary schooling should be made available for 10 percent of children over 14 and that this be structured into 3 tiers or grades, effectively reflecting social-class divisions and interests. However, the dominant sentiment behind the official report set the tone for future debates and action in relation to the extension of secondary schooling and consequently in relation to extending the age of compulsory attendance.[40] Before the development of a national framework in which secondary education could develop, central rationalization was deemed to be necessary. The Board of Education Act of 1899 brought together the functions of the Education Department, the Science and Art Department, and those powers of the Charity Commissioners relating to educational charities, to create a new Board of Education. In the same year, the age of compulsory attendance at school for all children was raised to 12 years of age.[41]

Conservative politicians came under pressure from church representatives who were becoming increasingly concerned about the drift of congregations away from the established church and the success of board schools in relation to the "voluntary" elementary schools provided through the diocesan authorities. John Gorst, the vice president of the Committee of Council on Education, managed to engineer a test case in which the official auditor found that the highly influential London School Board had breached its statutory limitations by providing education paid for through local rates and state funding that was beyond the legal definition of elementary schooling. Thus its work in areas such as sciences and arts for higher-grade classes was deemed illegal. The judgment of the auditor, Cockerton, was upheld twice on appeal, producing a situation where the tendency of many school boards to provide for older age groups was rendered illegal. The resistance to this creeping extension of activity beyond the statutory age of compulsion primarily arose from private colleges, endowed grammar schools that were struggling financially, and church interests, who wanted to hamper the further expansion of the school boards.[42]

The political aim of Gorst and the Conservative leader Arthur Balfour was to achieve a mechanism through which grants for salaries and upkeep of both board schools and denominational schools could be equalized, thus appeasing church interests and reassuring the lobby representing endowed and private schools. Such concerns were sufficiently strong during a period of Conservative government to restrict the growth of post-elementary education. This would necessitate creating a different political settlement to that initiated by Forster's 1870 Act.

Extending the Leaving Age

The 1902 Education Act marks one of the key points in the developing narrative of raising the school-leaving age because it permitted new local and county education authorities to make provision for post-elementary education. It reduced by two-thirds the number of responsible bodies for the provision of schooling, including the abolition of elected school boards, and rationalized things such as paying teachers, funding school building, and providing learning materials and facilities. Denominational groups secured formal representation on local education authorities (LEAs), while continuing to have a majority position on school governing bodies. The denominational bodies would also exercise control over religious education in their schools, a provision that outraged nonconformists who objected very strongly to the idea that ratepayers should be paying for sectarian schooling. The Act overcame the block on "higher-tops" or post-elementary schooling arising from the Cockerton Judgement, and in the decade following 1902, nearly a thousand new secondary schools were to open with more than one-third of these being for girls. However, such schools remained fee-paying although a part of an elected and accountable local structure of administration and management.

The growth of secondary schools came to an abrupt halt in 1914 due to the outbreak of war, but the first decade of the twentieth century was a period in which secondary education became available to a degree in virtually every district across the country. It became integrated into the politics of local government, setting the scene for many more people to become involved in issues around post-elementary schooling. The distinction between elementary and secondary education became clarified. The 1902 Act also established a Board of Education consultative committee whose purpose was to undertake detailed investigations into specific topics. In 1908 and 1909, there were two enquiries into questions of school attendance.[43]

The production, publication, and subsequent reception of reports such as these both responded to wider public and professional discussion around the issue of providing secondary schooling, and helped to provoke further debate. The Regulations for Secondary Schools of 1904 produced by the board framed secondary education around a four-year course running from the age of 11 to 15. In 1907, the powers of LEAs were extended to include provision of education other than elementary and to offer scholarships (payments of fees) for children between the ages of 12 and 16.[44] As the need for more teachers grew, it became necessary to seek recruits from elementary schools to become pupil teachers, and in the same year there was an extension of free places paid for by the LEAs to fee-paying secondary schools. Thus, although there was no major legislation between 1902 and 1918, the period was highly significant in laying the basis for the extension of secondary education.

In Scotland, meanwhile, separate legislation had, since the 1870s, provided for its own process of increasing the school-leaving age.[45] The minimum school-leaving age in Scotland was only 10, although local authorities could forbid full-time work up to the age of 14. The Education (Scotland) Act of 1901 extended the age of compulsory education in Scotland to 14, leading also to the spread of supplementary courses of a practical kind for working-class children, alongside the academic leaving certificate, which had been established in 1888.[46] Moreover, the Education of Defective Children (Scotland) Act of 1906 enabled for the provision of special schools while, in 1913, similar acts in England and Scotland required authorities to ascertain which children between 5 and 16 were indeed "defective"; only the uneducable child was to pass to the care of mental deficiency committees.[47] Judgments about types of children would become widespread in the coming years and the 1921 Education Act required authorities to determine which children were "imbeciles" and thus uneducable.[48]

Debates on the value of raising the school-leaving age continued during these years. An article in the *Westminster Review* in March 1907 called for a reduction in the schooling age. The author felt that schools were doing little to fit boys for industry or girls for domestic duties: "It throws boys upon the labour market ignorant, vulgar, and frivolous; and it turns out girls with but a shadow of knowledge of real matter-of-fact household economies... mere giggling ninnies with a capacity for little beyond frivolity and trashy literature."[49] Yet this was also a time of increasing concern for the problem of what was described as "boy labour." In 1904, a published study by E. J. Urwick explored the "species of man-child" who "from early youth has to make his living solely by physical strength and the exercise of mother-wit stiffened by a little elementary education, without any technical training either at the hands of organised educational authority or through the rougher methods of apprenticeship."[50] Urwick concluded that either day-school education should be made compulsory beyond the age of 14, or evening school should be made compulsory, and that since public opinion was not ready for the former, the latter should be provided as soon as possible.[51] Evidence provided for the Poor Law Commission and the consultative committee of the Board of Education in the first decade of the twentieth century, in addition to an enquiry conducted in Glasgow by William Kennedy and a young economic historian, R. H. Tawney, highlighted this issue further. Tawney's study showed that in Glasgow, although most working-class boys left school at 14, apprentices were not taken on until they were 16. According to Tawney, during this gap of two years, they took on temporary work that gave no preparation to their future vocations and accustomed them to purely casual labor. Boy laborers such as messengers, milk boys, and van boys had no educational content in their work, and were likely to be dismissed when they began to ask for adult wages.[52]

These concerns about school leavers were shared by Charles Trevelyan, a Liberal politician and undersecretary of the Board of Education in the Liberal government from 1908 until 1914. At the opening of a new secondary school for girls in 1910, Trevelyan argued that the board should require children to stay in school long enough to profit by their education: "One or two short years were not for a boy or girl to profit by any kind of secondary education."[53] Moreover, according to Trevelyan, it was the mass of children from 14 to 18 years of age that formed the most neglected part of the population. He went so far as to suggest that LEAs should be given compulsory powers to require a child to continue education after 14 where that child was not employed or was engaged in degrading and useless employment, or employment that would lead him or her nowhere.[54] In 1911, the president of the Board of Education, Walter Runciman, introduced a School and Continuation Class Attendance Bill that proposed the complete abolition of half-time education and the establishment of a school-leaving age of 14, which was, however, to be subject to variation on the basis of local opinion on whether it should be higher or lower than this. As was already the case in Scotland, children would not be allowed to leave school one by one as they reached the relevant birthday, but would be retained until a fixed date, and this principle was maintained in subsequent legislation. However, the Liberal government, under pressure in a range of areas, did not proceed with the 1911 Bill.[55]

By the outbreak of war in 1914 there were 200,000 pupils attending various forms of post-elementary schools. This represented about one in six of the age cohort. The vast majority worked for low wages in unrewarding and insecure jobs supplementing meager family incomes. The war produced a contradictory situation in relation to schooling and child welfare. During the fighting, many children in schools were better off than they had been previously because of the rise in wages and availability of work for parents and older siblings. There was rising prosperity despite a wartime cutback in school-based services from 1916. Following the Military Services Act of 1916, which conscripted most men between the ages of 18 and 41, local employers advertised for replacement employees and offered attractive wages resulting in a reduction of school attendance. LEAs were inundated with claims for exemption certificates on the basis that the proposed employment was useful to the war effort. Those over 12 years who were already half-timers often ceased attending school altogether, while many other children between 12 and 14 sought proficiency certificates enabling them to leave officially before they reached 14.[56]

Adding to pressure on LEAs, local employers' organizations lobbied for a relaxation of local byelaws. As the main breadwinner was often away on military service, the income from older siblings became a necessity for many families. The president of the Board of Education, H. A. L. Fisher, conceded that this trend had become widespread reporting to Parliament that on official data supplied via LEAs, 600,000 children had been put to work during the preceding three years. Under questioning, he conceded also that the likelihood was that just as many more would have been working unofficially.[57]

The nature of some of the work was a cause for widespread concern. Both girls and boys of 14 were employed in munitions factories and earned as much and sometimes more than their fathers would have done before the outbreak of war. Older girls in semiskilled manufacturing at higher wages and in skilled administrative work were openly employed during this period.[58] It is against this backdrop of a rising concern about the place of "juveniles" in a new postwar social order that debates on raising the school-leaving age need to be seen. Added to these social concerns were those arising from medical officers' reports concerning the general size and ill-health of much of the British urban population and these were confirmed by military officers having to refuse admission to so many thousands of boys of military age who were sick and weak and unfit for service since they fell below the minimum standards for recruitment.[59]

The Government had established a commission to report on youth employment after the war, and its report was published in 1917, under the title *Juvenile Education in Relationship to Employment after the War*, but has usually been known as the Lewis Report.[60] Its concerns and recommendations reveal much about what had happened within the education system since the start of the war. Lewis recommended that juvenile employment bureaus be strengthened and that local employment committees should in future play a more active role in planning for what happened to children after leaving school. The report firmly recommended ROSLA to 14 with no exceptions, followed by attendance for at least 8 hours a week or 320 hours per annum at day-continuation classes up to the age of 18 years. This reform, it affirmed, would require a complete "change of temper and outlook,"[61] but it acknowledged that general opinion was not ready for an increase in the school-leaving age to 15.[62] It also suggested that with an extended leaving age it would be necessary to have a less "bookish" form of education for the pupils affected: "Education is a mental process, but the truth that for many children, especially those who will live by their hands, the best avenue to the mind is through the hands has not yet worked its complete revolution in the pedagogic methods of the 19th century."[63]

It was the Lewis Report that was to lay the ground for several of the main features of the Education Act of 1918 taken through Parliament by the president of the Board of Education, H. A. L. Fisher. When he introduced his bill in Parliament, Fisher made it clear that, although it was an Education Bill, it was designed to address a range of social issues:

> Prompted by the deficiencies which have been revealed by the War; [the Education Bill]...is framed to repair the intellectual wastage which has been caused by the War; and should it pass into law before peace is struck it will put a prompt end to an evil which has grown to alarming proportions during the last three years—I allude to the industrial pressure upon the child life of this country—and it will greatly facilitate the solution of many problems of juvenile employment, which will certainly be affected by the transition of the country from a basis of war to a basis of peace.[64]

The relationship between employment and education was strongly emphasized in a way that expressed the moral positioning of the proposed legislation.

Fisher's Act has been seen as a landmark in the history of British education, but many of its provisions were not implemented due to severe cutbacks in government finance for public services after the Great War. Even before becoming law, compromises were necessary in order to secure a majority in Parliament. On the issue of post-14 continuation schools, one of the key features of the proposed legislation, Fisher later admitted to the problems he faced:

> I was compelled in order to overcome the resistance of the Lancashire members to compulsory part-time continuation schools, to introduce an amendment postponing for seven years the application of the scheme to young people between sixteen and eighteen, a concession seemingly great but in reality of little practical importance, since several years would be needed before an adequate supply of efficient teachers would be forthcoming, yet without which the Bill would not have passed.[65]

Those who were opposing his proposals were formed from an alliance of factory owners and landowners, the Catholic and Anglican Church hierarchy, and members of Parliament from all three political parties seeking to appease voter resistance to child labor in factories and in farming. Fisher betrayed an insouciance regarding implementation dates especially when one recalls the loss of half a million young men to the labor force and the consequent urgency of establishing an effective system to replace them.

The Education Bill was one of the major gestures toward social reform from the Lloyd George government, proposing to raise the school-leaving age from 12 to 14, make access to day-release training, a right for young workers, and establish day-continuation schools under LEA control in all areas. It received active support from the Trades Union Congress, which had campaigned vigorously for ROSLA and for continuation schools since the 1890s.[66] The Act eventually required LEAs to plan to cater for children who were likely to continue their education "in schools other than elementary."[67] The somewhat tortuous wording reveals the extent to which vested interests in grammar and private schools resisted the idea of LEAs encroaching onto their territory. In Section 3 of the Act, the proposals for day-continuation schools were outlined but then qualified with "if practicable" at the end of the clause. Responsibility for preparing such schemes lay with the LEAs rather than central government and any plans were to include proposals for how pupils who qualified should be able to pursue to secondary level without the encumbrance of fees. LEAs were to have powers over enforcing school attendance, and from thence forward only schools recognized by the LEA would count in terms of attendance regulations. Children would begin and end attendance when school terms started and finished rather than when they reached or were approaching a certain age.

Employing children under the age of 12 was to be illegal. Children were not permitted to work in mines, factories, workshops, or quarries. Entertainments in which children appeared required a license issued by the LEA. Before any employment certificate was issued, inspectors had to be assured that the work would not be prejudicial to health or physical development. Breach of these regulations would incur specified penalties. LEAs were to be able to offer scholarships to pay fees to secondary schools and to provide maintenance allowances to support such scholarships. Such powers however were permissive rather than directive and subject to local byelaws and discretion thus enabling little action to be taken. The only fees allowable in elementary schools were to be for school meals.[68]

In 1921, the Education (Consolidation) Act was passed, finally raising the compulsory age of schooling to 14 without exemptions. The social and economic interests that had sought to reverse the pattern of extending the school age and thereby extending the reach of the state into family life were defeated. The experience of regression during the War came as a warning to campaigners for educational extension that gains made in previous decades could be reversed in certain circumstances. From then on, the debate concerning raising the compulsory school age was to focus upon what happened after the age of 14 and on the extent to which new, purpose-built secondary schools, now distinct from elementary schools, would cater for all young people between the ages of 14 and 18. LEAs were required to submit schemes covering their areas including provision for secondary education in the form of continuation schools,[69] thus establishing the defining relationship between a strengthened central Board of Education and the still relatively new LEAs. Section 20 of the Act required LEAs to provide "courses of advanced instruction for the older or more intelligent children" including those who stayed on beyond the age of 14.[70]

LEAs were also empowered to extend their involvement at the other end of the age spectrum by providing nursery schools for children from two to five years of age.[71] This extension arose directly from the realization that many British children, especially those from the urban working classes were ill-nourished and unhealthy. LEAs acquired a specific duty to attend to the "health, nourishment, and physical welfare" of children as well as to specifically educational concerns. In relation to school attendance, Part IV of the Act specified the following:

> It shall be the duty of the parent of every child between the ages of five and fourteen, or, if a byelaw under this Act so provides, between the ages of six

and fourteen, to cause that child to receive efficient elementary instruction in reading, writing and arithmetic.[72]

The law therefore established unequivocally a balance of duties and responsibilities between the LEA and parent in relation to the child who was defined as both belonging to the family and to the civil community in which she or he lived. Additionally, in Part VIII of the Act, LEAs acquired extensive powers of inspection of workplaces and of public spaces to restrict the employment of children of school age.

Moreover, the extension of compulsory education led directly to the claim that new forms of schooling would be necessary for the majority of those affected—this assumption would become commonplace for much of the twentieth century. The Federation of British Industries (FBI), at the same time as requesting a delay in raising the school-leaving age, also called for differing forms of education for "the more promising children" who should attend secondary schools and the "less promising children" who should continue in elementary schools to improve their character, general intelligence, and powers of observation.[73] These assumptions about differentiation paradoxically tied in with opposing progressive views on the emerging education system shared by Tawney and others. An article in the *Athenaeum* in April 1917 claimed:

> Schools are not merely intellectual training grounds; they are also communities for developing social and moral qualities rightly expected from all, whether they be lady factory inspectors or tailoresses, doctors or street sweepers.[74]

The patchwork of legislation that was the legacy of the previous hundred or more years, deriving from industrial, public health, welfare, employment, and education acts was also consolidated into one unified piece of legislation by the 1921 Act. Thus 1921 provided a new framework from which calls for secondary education for all would be increasingly heard in the coming years.

Chapter 4

ROSLA and the Emergence of Secondary Education

After the First World War, and over the following 30 years, the issue of raising the school-leaving age was to be at the center of a strong educational campaign. Its advocates were often fervent in their support for such a measure and in many cases saw it as the key to further educational progress for the majority of children and for social progress more generally. Debate over the school-leaving age accompanied the emergence of a new kind of secondary education, designed to permit all children of the age range to take part rather than to exclude all but an academic elite. Foremost among the proponents of raising of the school-leaving age (ROSLA) at this time was the socialist intellectual R. H. Tawney. Yet issues around the school-leaving age continued to be controversial, and the measure was vigorously opposed on social and economic grounds especially in times of financial hardship. In the event, despite several false dawns, the school-leaving age was not raised even to 15 until after the Second World War, and ROSLA to 16 was destined to take even longer to achieve.

Secondary Education for All?

The Liberal pledge of forging a "land fit for heroes" was, by 1922, turning sour, as many of the key provisions in the 1918 Education Act remained to be implemented. The Geddes Committee, established in response to the postwar financial crisis, recommended severe spending cuts. Fisher himself lost the argument in cabinet and had to admit in 1922 that plans were being considered to raise the school attendance age from five to six years. Fisher tried to argue that the proposed cutbacks were temporary and that when economic and financial recovery arrived, the future for education would once more be bright. Brian Simon has pointed out that such a view ignored the fact that the cutbacks in expenditure would have long-lasting effects such as the reverse in numbers of teachers, cessation of building or repairing new schools, and reductions in training, all of which would require several years of planning before the negative impact could be reversed.[1] The Federation of British Industries (FBI) however, took the opposite view to that held across the labor movement and instead supported calls for a freeze on teacher salaries, increases in fees for secondary schooling, and raising entry into school to six years of age.[2] Although Fisher presented a Bill to the House of Commons to raise the age of entry to six years, nothing came of it, possibly because it was understood to be so politically dangerous for all parties involved in the coalition government. Had the proposal proceeded, using Fisher's own estimates, almost 740,000 children below the age of six would have ceased to attend school and this would have entailed a saving of the salaries of at least 12,000 teachers.[3]

It was within this turbulent and sometimes-embittered atmosphere that in 1922 R. H. Tawney produced a key report, *Secondary Education for All*, published by the labor Party.[4] The publication symbolized the break being made by the Labour movement from the Liberals and it was to set the terms for future debate within the educational world. Tawney was a major figure within the national educational system. By 1922, he had been a leading member of the Workers' Educational Association for nearly 20 years; he was a member of the Board of Education Consultative Committee whose remit was to produce official reports on issues of educational importance; he was convenor of the Labour Party subcommittee on education charged with producing policy in advance of a general election; and he had been a major contributor to academic and policy debate about the link between youth employment and nationwide underachievement in education. His personal influence was strengthened by his position as a leader writer for the influential liberal newspaper, the *Manchester Guardian*.[5]

As an expert in the detail of the 1918 and 1921 Acts, Tawney was able to exploit the sense of failure and inertia brought about by the government raising expectations legislatively while cutting back on spending and thus rendering the legislative provisions inoperable. The arguments within *Secondary Education for All* mirrored the theoretical ambitions behind the 1921 Act of accepting diversity in provision and moving in stages toward raising the leaving age. Tawney agreed with the drift of the 1921 Act in seeing local education authorities (LEAs) as the instruments for educational progress. He diverged sharply from the Liberal line by plainly, and in simple language, opposing exemptions for the purposes of employment and part-time provision. The appearance of commonsense in his writing arose from the way that he appeared to argue for the realization of much that was already agreed in previous legislation but had lain fallow by ineffective Liberal and Conservative governments. The three core issues were separation of primary and secondary stages at the age of 11 within a continuous system, incorporation of existing forms of full-time secondary provision into LEAs with equal grant support, and extension of secondary education to 16 years of age without exemptions.[6]

This took head-on the Fisher compromise of day-continuation schools, which had been envisaged as places where young employees would secure day release from employment in order to pursue vocationally related courses. For Tawney, continuation schools should only be considered in relation to adolescents who had left school at 16; they "cannot be accepted as a substitute for the development of a system of secondary education" he thundered; continuation schools should continue secondary, not elementary education.[7] He argued in detail that indirect benefits arising from extending education for all children to 16 far outweighed any immediate, direct costs, and showed how increased spending on secondary education could reduce spending elsewhere such as unemployment benefits.

Financial constraints following the "Geddes Axe" rendered Liberal and Labour councilors at district and county council level powerless to take action to expand secondary school provision. This served to highlight the impotence of Section 46 of the 1921 Act, which theoretically empowered LEAs to pass byelaws requiring school attendance up to the end of the school term when a pupil was 15 as long as some occupations were exempted. However hamstrung such councilors were, supporters of raising the leaving age could nevertheless point to the fact that the principle had been conceded in legislation. Financial cuts to education in the 1922/23 budget led to a reduction of funded secondary places across the whole country to just 70,000; 15,000 fewer than in 1919. While Tawney and Labour offered a beacon of hope for the future, the reality on the ground was that the cause of extending secondary schooling and with it, the gradual raising of the leaving age, was set in reverse.

As the Conservative/Liberal coalition broke down in 1924, Labour became the largest party in Parliament for the first time. Although the government led by Ramsay MacDonald lasted only nine months, they nevertheless left the door open for an electoral victory for the Conservatives. Labour's first education minister was Charles Trevelyan, who had defected from the Liberals to Labour in 1919 and who was to be a key ally for Tawney.[8]

The Board of Education Consultative Committee chaired by William Hadow and including Tawney began working at this time to examine the education of the adolescent. The eventual report, published in 1926, stated that the case in favor was proven as "young persons" who left school "prematurely" would suffer from social and intellectual deterioration, which rendered much of the expenditure on schooling before the age of 14 a waste. Thus for reasons of cost-effectiveness alone, schooling should be extended to the point where pupils could benefit most from it. This is why Hadow described the then age of compulsory attendance to 14, effectively 13 for many, as a paradox.[9]

The central argument within the Hadow Report was that if the future strength of the national economy lay in "the intelligence and character" of the young, it made sense to ensure that they were educated. Reflecting a growing awareness of the separate stage of adolescence, it argued that schooling to 15 was a necessity to achieve full physical and intellectual development of young people:

> It is unreasonable to attempt to harvest crops in spring, or to divert into supplying the economic necessities of the immediate present the still undeveloped capacities of those on whose intelligence and character the very life of the nation must depend in the future. There is no capital more productive than the energies of human beings. There is no investment more remunerative than expenditure devoted to developing them.[10]

Beyond these metaphors of natural growth, further arguments were needed to address the concerns of employers, parents, costs to the exchequer, the negative costs arising from premature leaving, and the impact upon the labor market. It was an argument of applied economics rather than the financial auditing mentality that dominated thinking within the Treasury.

The figure for attendance in public elementary schooling after the age of 14 was, according to Hadow, 170,893 pupils in 1922/23, or 26.1 percent of the cohort size when aged 10/11.[11] It was recognized that of these a majority left full-time schooling before they reached the age of 15. Therefore the first step in making progress toward raising the age to 15 should be to seek abolition of all forms of exemption below the age of 14. Despite these figures, the Hadow committee identified steady rises in the proportion of those staying on to 15 and beyond and attributed much of it to the effects of the 1918 legislation. They also identified significant regional disparities and suggested that continuing attendance reflected the extent to which LEAs had implemented fully provisions in the 1918 Act to keep pupils at school until the school term in which their fourteenth birthday fell.[12]

The obstacles facing reformers were formidable and included opposition from parents who were reliant upon the early earnings of their 14-year-old children. There was the issue of a lack of sufficient numbers of suitable buildings to accommodate an entire extra cohort. Additionally, the perennial problem of teacher supply was outlined. Of these, the problems of parental opposition in poorer areas appeared the most formidable: "Under existing economic conditions, the pressure to curtail the education of children who ought to remain at school is too often almost irresistible."[13]

Against this difficulty, the report argued that as a uniform raising of the age of attendance would be applied, there would be a general benefit arising from greater employment being available arising from taking a cohort out of the labor market. It was claimed that raising the school age should be accompanied by an extension of the system of maintenance allowances for poorer families and that as the reform would uniformly affect everyone, the traditional costs associated with staying on at an existing type of secondary school would not exist.

Hadow recommended a date of September 1932 for raising the age to 15. The chief gain, it was argued, would be that "education shall have larger opportunities of moulding the lives of boys and girls during the critical years of early adolescence."[14] No doubt as a concession within the committee in order to secure an agreement, the report stated that any further extension would involve making the fullest possible use of existing provisions within the 1918 Act for part-time continuing education.

The report triggered widespread debate culminating in a national conference held in October 1927 on the education of the adolescent, presided over by Hadow himself and sponsored by the National Union of Teachers (NUT) and Workers' Educational Association (WEA), among others.[15] Percy Jackson, the chairman of the progressive West Riding LEA, reported that the Association of Education Committees (AEC) had approved a policy for the school age to be raised within six years. He argued, following Tawney's line, that the cost effects of such a proposal would be neutral. For Tawney extending the school age was an investment that would yield rewards in the future.[16]

The Conservative government elected to office in 1924 made no further progress on this issue, and Tawney and his associates were confined mainly to local initiatives. For example, Tawney suggested that Durham, as a leading LEA controlled by Labour, might be able to submit byelaws raising the school age to the Board of Education.[17] Moreover, he proposed privately, that the government should tell LEAs in mining areas, where employment prospects were especially limited, that they should make arrangements for keeping boys at school to 15, and offer to pay the cost of maintenance itself. "It is clearly the reasonable policy," he argued, "and it would be the thin end of the wedge."[18] He encouraged Trevelyan to maintain pressure on educational policy both within the Labour Party and more broadly:

> Education now is good politics, as shown by the fact that at the last election both Tories and Liberals felt obliged, in imitation of us, to produce an educational programme. But our people are apt to be extremely conventional and timid, and to gib at anything educational as unpractical and unpopular (which it isn't).[19]

This was an early recognition that such educational issues as ROSLA might become electorally significant for political parties concerned with public opinion. Meanwhile, these developments were met with disbelief and criticism not only among some employers but within society at large. E. T. Good, writing in the *English Review* in 1926, warned that the "industrial efficiency of our race" was being undermined by "too much schooling," which had "converted a brave, enterprising, and intensely industrious nation into jellyfish, fops and loafers."[20] The momentum for raising the school-leaving age was being considered "regardless of cost or consequences" and a "sifting out" process was favored whereby most "boys should get into industry, and girls into the kitchen, at a very early age, after a very few years at school."[21] Political strategists were weighing up the relative importance of such contrasting views.

In 1929, the Labour Party returned to office with another minority government led by Ramsay MacDonald. Before the election, Labour had promised to raise the school-leaving age to 15 with immediate effect, with a further extension to 16 as soon as this was possible. Its educational policy now included part-time compulsory continuation schooling or training until 18. To appease parts of its own electoral base, Labour promised to offer extended maintenance grants to families along with the building of specialist secondary schools. Its president of the Board of Education was again Charles Trevelyan, who remained fully committed to ROSLA even in a growing financial crisis in the aftermath of the stock market crash in the United States. Echoing contemporary economic thinking, Ramsay MacDonald argued that by taking 400,000 young people out of the labor market there would be a corresponding increase in jobs for those presently unemployed or underemployed.[22] Even if the financial climate was unpromising, the political situation appeared to favor a speedy resolution to the struggle to raise the school-leaving age.

Despite such commitments, the proposed program of legislation for the next session of Parliament failed to include reference to a forthcoming Education Act. This omission was picked up by the *Manchester Guardian*, and a lengthy editorial of July 9 entitled "The School Leaving Age" commented on the lack of any proposals and how the plans being made by LEAs on the basis of known government policy would be unclear.[23] All of the important bodies representing LEAs had declared themselves in favor of the age of school attendance being raised to 15. It was pointed out that the president of the Board of Education wanted the reform along with the minister for Labour J. H. Thomas and that the Liberal Party would back such legislation. The Hadow Report wanted to raise the leaving age to 15 immediately and the same view had been confirmed by other respected sources.[24] Ranged against the policy were "certain industrial interests" objecting to "a diminution in the supply of juvenile labour" and the Treasury, which was opposed to the expenditure involved on principle. Sensing the seriousness of the omission of the policy from the government's program, the *Manchester Guardian* editorial urged that "strong and vocal public opinion is needed to support this policy and to overcome difficulties."[25]

The *Manchester Guardian* returned to the fray with an editorial on "The Educational Programme" at the end of October 1929. It again stressed the cross-party Liberal-Labour support for the proposed measures especially for raising the leaving age. It noted that LEAs had been warned to make immediate preparations to retain children at school for an additional year within 18 months from the present date, but expressed anxiety that "a lethargic minority" might postpone action waiting for a change in the political situation.[26]

The Labour chancellor, Philip Snowden, opposed the proposals on the grounds of the onset of severe economic difficulties. Despite this formidable opposition to central government spending on social and welfare services, Trevelyan presented his proposals once more to cabinet.[27] He pointed to the dip in student numbers in the years 1932 and 1933, which would be followed by a sudden rise of over 100,000 in 1934 due to the postwar jump in the birthrate. Trevelyan concluded that the cost of raising the leaving age should be offset against "the saving in unemployment benefit and poor relief which is bound to result."[28] Trevelyan then made a statement in the House of Commons stating that a bill would be introduced to raise the leaving age to 15 by September 1931.[29] This statement was followed up in September with announcements to LEAs outlining plans for assistance with expanding school buildings and facilities at a 50 percent rate, rather than the previous 20 percent ratio between local and Treasury funding.[30] Trevelyan appeared to have reversed the hesitation that had characterized government inaction on the issue since the end of the War.

A date of April 1, 1931, was announced, which would give LEAs a year and a half to prepare.[31] Trevelyan felt that by declaring a definite date "anxieties" within Labour Party ranks would be placated. He was also concerned to work closely with directors of education who were preparing local secondary reorganization plans following the recommendations of the Hadow Report of 1926. This proposal linked ROSLA with wider proposals for structural reorganization of the system, which was already a familiar theme and was to continue to be a prominent aspect of the reform in later years. The issue related to English and Welsh schools only, as no legislation was required for Scotland where the change could be brought about by an administrative order made by the secretary of state for Scotland. Trevelyan reported to cabinet that the "traditional" opposition to raising the leaving age from Yorkshire and Lancashire textile districts had been more muted due to the well-defined and publicly known stance of the Labour Party on the issue. He had come under pressure from Labour MPs from the north to legislate quickly rather than nearer to the next general election.[32] Eustace Percy, the former president of the Board of Education, argued that secondary reorganization and a raised school-leaving age was to be supported in principle and implemented at the "proper moment" but resistance from the labor market, parental resistance, and the need to improve educational conditions all meant that the time was not yet ripe for such a course of action.[33]

However, there was also evidence of support from different quarters of the country. In 1930, the *Countryman* magazine carried out a survey of elementary school subscribers and found that, despite the difficulties that teachers and pupils faced in terms of travel and resources, a "strong faith in a great ideal" was evident based "not on the labour market but the child's welfare."[34] In part, this was a gendered vision based upon the professional experience of the "woman teacher" who argued for the care of children over the exigencies of the labor market or the structure of the education system.[35] In 1929, a long-standing director of education argued that Trevelyan had ignored the fact that raising the leaving age was at heart "a moral question" that, if not acted upon, would hasten moral degeneracy among the young.[36]

In discussions with LEAs the purely educational concerns supporting reform, which had been prominent in the Hadow Report, took second place to the question of raising maintenance allowances for 14-year-olds.[37] Trevelyan preferred LEAs to adopt what he called a "liberal scale" for such allowances because it was something that would significantly appease parental opinion in textile and other manufacturing districts.[38] In his presentation to cabinet, Trevelyan pointed out the cost savings in unemployment benefit that would not have to be paid out if just one-third of the vacancies that would in normal circumstances have gone to 14-year-olds were taken up by registered unemployed. His estimate of savings was £4.5 million per annum. Once again the economic arguments were to take precedence over educational ones.[39] Trevelyan's political instincts can be seen through his proposal that 75 percent of the costs of the proposed reform should fall on the Treasury, with just 25 percent coming under local authority rates so as to minimize rises in locally levied rates. This was a double-edged sword as such a move strengthened the hand of Snowden and the Treasury.

Trevelyan had decided upon a strategy of pushing the forward momentum of political support for his proposals, and announced in early January 1930 at the North of England Education Conference that he would be introducing a bill that included proposals to raise the leaving age to 15 and later at a suitable date to 16.[40] He published the Education (School Attendance) Bill proposing implementation of leaving at 15 by the end of Easter 1931. This met with strong opposition by the Catholic hierarchy who feared a loss of influence should secondary schools be brought firmly under LEA direction. They became active with Labour Party MPs representing constituencies where working-class Catholics were a large part of the Labour base.[41]

The biggest hurdle that Trevelyan faced arose, however, from the estimates of costs for maintenance allowances to parents for children aged over 14, who would otherwise be earning a wage. Snowden at the Treasury insisted on a clause requiring families to submit to a means test before receiving such payments. This crossed a bridge that most Labour MPs would not accept, as means testing had become hated as a way of humiliating the poor. The Catholic hierarchy's opposition materialized in the form of an amendment tabled by a Labour MP to delay legislation until agreement had been reached on how to fund voluntary provided schools. This amendment also proposed delay until 1932. The bill even as amended, was defeated in the House of Lords, leaving the government with the option of forcing its passage through the House of Commons. Snowden's demands for cuts in expenditure by all departments were supported by virtually all of the cabinet and as Trevelyan's bill ran into the sand, he resigned as president of the Board of Education, leaving office for the final time.[42] The following month he explained his decision to his constituents in Newcastle. The failure of his bill, he insisted, was a lost opportunity to improve equality of opportunity for the children of the workers as compared with the well-to-do:

> Better schools were being everywhere prepared and in that extra year there would have been an opportunity not now afforded in a large number of schools for the beginning of science, for practice in manual instruction and for broader interests which disappear for the boy and girl when industry begins.[43]

It was an opportunity that was not to return for another decade.

The Education Act of 1936

Within six months of these events, the Labour prime minister, MacDonald, announced he was forming a government of national unity. He took with him only two of his cabinet colleagues, and they were promptly expelled from the Labour Party. A new government of an entirely different political character was formed and the subsequent general election confirmed this change. The Conservatives were back in effective control of the political agenda, and the cause of raising the leaving age once more, as in 1919, seemed set for a reverse. Nevertheless, the campaign in favor of extending the school-leaving age continued unabated.

Tawney continued arguing the view that he had elaborated upon since 1922. In an important two part feature in the *Manchester Guardian*, he deplored the real terms cut of up to 13 percent on expenditure from when the National Government took office. He stressed that education spending was investment and that the lack of funding was leading to a "general paralysis of educational development and in some areas a decline in educational standards." He pointed to the contradictory situation of there being many unemployed teachers claiming benefits while schools were short-staffed. There was a danger that the higher numbers of adolescents leaving school at 14 arising from the postwar bulge in the birthrate would suddenly raise youth unemployment to record levels. Raising the school-leaving age to 15 was, he argued, an urgent necessity. By retaining up to 400,000 boys and girls in school not only would it save money on unemployment payments but would also give older juveniles a greater chance of securing employment as well as some adults.[44]

This general perspective toward raising the leaving age was reflected in a key publication emanating from the Department of Economics at Manchester University, an in-depth study of employment conditions and prospects for juveniles in Lancashire.[45] The authors painted a grim picture of the social malaise brought about by prevailing conditions. This amounted economically to "squandering real national capital in the form of skill and energy of the rising generation."[46] The findings from their research revealed that in Lancashire, 22 percent of 14-year-olds who had left school in the Easter or July of 1932 were still unemployed in the autumn (September) of that year. The total number of unemployed leavers from secondary schools and junior technical colleges was even higher because at the age of 16 it was more difficult for them to find jobs.[47] Their conclusion could not have been more emphatic: "On social and educational grounds, the case for the lengthening of school life for all children, and not merely for those who are unemployed on leaving, is overwhelming."[48] The authors noted that in districts where authorities had acted upon the provisions to offer distinct secondary schooling, particularly central schools, there was a tendency for higher voluntary staying-on rates.[49]

The school-leaving age remained a prominent political issue, as was made clear by a deputation to the prime minister describing itself as the School Age Council (SAC) in February 1935.[50] For this meeting, MacDonald was accompanied by his secretary of state for Scotland Godfrey Collins and president of the Board of Education Lord Irwin. In total, the SAC brought 31 representatives including a mix of leading figures representing a spread of educational, social, religious, and industrial interests embracing both Conservative and Labour-held parliamentary constituencies. The chairman of the SAC, Colonel John Buchan MP, stressed the nonpartisan nature of the council, and insisted that all of the difficulties relating to implementing ROSLA outlined by Lord Halifax could be overcome. Both the FBI and the Trades Union Congress (TUC) were present in the delegation. The churches, represented at this meeting by prominent figures, strongly favored raising the leaving age to 16 as both an educational and a social issue. The ubiquitous Sir Percy Jackson, who chaired both the West Riding Education Authority and the County Councils Association of England and Wales, pointed to the unanimous support for ROSLA among his colleagues in all districts and authorities, few of whom could be counted as radicals.

Following this meeting, the Cabinet Committee that had been convened the year earlier to prepare an education policy for the government began to rethink the politics of raising the school-leaving age.[51] Just five weeks after MacDonald had resigned (June 7, 1935) as prime minister to be succeeded by Stanley Baldwin, he was chairing the Cabinet Committee on Education in his new post of lord president of the council, this time with the Conservative MP Oliver Stanley as president of the Board of Education. Stanley took over the planning document and sent it to the Cabinet Office by the end of June.[52] The proposals included legislation "to raise the age to 15 with exemptions for beneficial employment and without maintenance allowances," estimated to cost annually £661,125 between 1940 and 1941 and £1,322,250 "ultimately."[53]

Oliver Stanley's cabinet memorandum argued that "there is a general feeling that the ground is now ready for a further move forward." The memorandum was quite specific about what it meant, stating: "The aspect of this feeling which has been most conspicuous has been the demand for the raising of the school leaving age."[54] This initiative from within the senior ranks of the National Government met with decided political opposition from many Conservative MPs, who objected strongly to having to raise a further £5 million per annum to pay for the anticipated costs

of raising the school age to 15 without exemptions. Local business lob-
bying strengthened sentiment against the measure, especially in districts
where early employment of 14- and 15-year-olds was common. Cabinet
were invited to consider four options: ROSLA to 15 with no exemptions
and with maintenance allowances; ROSLA to 15 with beneficial exemptions; ROSLA to 15 but with provision for exempted children to attend
day-continuation classes one day per week; and lastly, retention of the age
of 14 but compulsory attendance at day-continuation schools from 14 to
16 or even to 18.

The last of these options was a revival of the provisions for day-
continuation classes in the Fisher Act of 1918. It was rejected on the grounds
of costs to employers. According to the employers' lobby, it would be disruptive, having a "seriously disorganizing effect on the labour arrangements in
their works."[55] The idea of exempted children attending day-continuation
classes on a regular basis was also rejected because of employer opposition,
which argued that it would be disruptive and unworkable in thinly popu-
lated rural districts where day-continuation provision would be difficult
to provide.

The memorandum broke with Trevelyan's view that LEAs could cope
with ROSLA to 15 in a relatively brief period, and stated that 3 years would
be the required lead-in period. Therefore, 1939/40 was identified as a target
date. Oliver Stanley (and MacDonald) preferred option two because of the
anticipated costs of the maintenance allowances. Trevelyan's maintenance
allowance scales were opposed as unworkable and the memorandum noted
that "among a certain proportion of the government's supporters the principle of maintenance allowances during any period of compulsory education is regarded with hostility."[56] Stanley expanded upon his opposition
to option one arguing that maintenance allowances could not be regarded
as serving any direct educational purpose, whereas for a fraction of that
sum, very substantial educational progress...could be secured in directions where there is a popular as well as instructed demand for advance."[57]
Stanley conceded a little on day continuation suggesting that LEAs should
have discretion in the matter of whether exempted children should engage
in some form of compulsory continuing education. Stanley opposed payment of maintenance allowances to children below the age of school leaving. Part of his reasoning was that whatever the sum was agreed upon, it
would "merely be giving the Labour Party the opportunity to overbid us
by repeating their previous offer."[58] This statement further illustrates a
growing awareness of the political importance of educational reform. One
of the points commending option two to Stanley was that there would be
a reduced need for capital expenditure on new schools especially in districts where exemptions were expected to be high "in areas where juvenile

employment was good." Here mainstream Conservative Party thinking was revealed, that the extension of schooling was best justified as a means for ameliorating the social consequences of structural unemployment among youth, rather than as being essentially an educational measure.

Stanley summed up his view of broad social opinion on the issue of ROSLA. LEAs would oppose option two preferring instead no exemptions. Parents were believed to favor allowing children to take up an offer of a job. Employers were assumed to be in favor of exemptions on the basis that it lessened interference in their business affairs. Teachers would be opposed. Educationalists held onto option one "as an article of faith." Opposition Liberals and Labour would oppose option two. His summing up omitted to mention the Church of England and trade unions, who were both key players in the SAC and both with strong vested interests in the education system.[59]

As a means of appeasing anticipated social opposition to exemptions, Stanley proposed they should only be granted after consultations at local level with either the local authorities or Ministry of Labour. He suggested that existing school medical reports should be taken into account when deciding upon a claim for exemption lodged by parents to the LEA.[60]

In an editorial comment, the *Times Educational Supplement* (*TES*) noted that the high rate of exemptions, ranging from 79 percent to 96 percent in LEAs where the school-leaving age had been raised to 15, under the provisions of the Fisher Act, would undermine the point of the legislation. In only one such district, Caernarvonshire, were exemptions relatively low, running at 37 percent for the previous year.[61] At the end of 1935, a motion was passed at the annual conference of the Association of Assistant Masters in Secondary Schools declaring that any scheme with exemptions included would prove to be administratively unworkable and that compulsion needed to be accompanied by adequate levels of maintenance allowance payments.[62] The following week, Oliver Stanley met with several delegations representing local and professional interests. At these meetings, two issues were dominant: first the proposed exemptions clause, and second the consequent problems for orderly and consistent planning that would arise should exemptions be generally conceded.[63] The SAC was concerned about pressure being placed upon locally based officers by influential local business interests, and it called for a central supervisory body to rule on all claims for exemptions. They too noted the difficulty of allocating and financing adequate accommodation for the post-14 cohort only to find that exemptions would mean few remained within the system.[64]

The *TES* pointed out that the previous blacklist of schools deemed unfit for continued use would by then be outdated because more recent specifications for secondary schools had codified improved minimum standards so should a new blacklist be compiled even more schools would need to be included.[65] It was argued that increasing capital spending on new schools was urgent and necessary in order for any extension of the school age to be practical. The inadequacies of the published bill were becoming apparent, so much so, that the usually cautious and conservative *TES* warned that any extension of the age would require a planned building program before the provisions could be implemented. Stanley realized that there was a need for him to meet with a select delegation of LEAs, which was dominated by Conservative (Independent)-led local politicians. His purpose was to appease this influential lobby within his own party. When the bill was published in the second week of 1936, the *TES* reported on Stanley trying to shore up crumbling support from within Conservative-led LEAs.[66]

This minimal program was greeted with a mixture of disdain and outright opposition from the broad cross-party interest group that constituted the SAC. The *TES* of January 18 ran a leader comment about the SAC being received by Stanley.[67] However, with a secure parliamentary majority, the Act was passed into law containing the bulk of the preferences argued for in cabinet by Stanley. The main point of contention was the insertion into clause 2.2. of the Act:

> An employment certificate shall be granted to the intending employer of the child, if the issuing authority are satisfied that the parent of the child desires the employment for the child and are also satisfied, after consultation with the local committee for juvenile employment, if any, and after consideration of the health and physical condition of the child, that the employment will be beneficial to the child.[68]

The key point of contention was the use of the word "beneficial." Additionally, the absence of any mention of education or training considerations confirmed the worst fears of supporters of educational progress that the old advocates in favor of child labor were once again in the ascendency. A date of 1940 was established for raising the age to 15 with exemptions and without maintenance allowances. With the passage of the Act in 1936, Henry Hope, a barrister, was able to publish a legal manual written for use by governors and managers of schools and by LEA officers who were charged along with the church authorities of implementing the provisions of the Act within a four-year timescale.[69]

At the same time as these developments were taking place, the Consultative Committee under its new chairman, Will Spens, was considering the issue of secondary education, leading to another carefully calibrated official report designed to arrive into the public debate at an opportune moment.[70] Spens was frank in his assessment of where the fault line in provision of secondary education lay, saying that the Consultative Committee had been left "with the general impression that the existing arrangements for whole-time higher education of boys and girls above the age of 11+ in England and Wales have ceased to correspond with the actual structure of modern society and with the economic facts of the situation."[71] The reason why ROSLA was essential, according to Spens, was to achieve less disparity between types of secondary provision, and the logic of this position led to the significant statement that "the adoption of a minimum leaving age of 16 years, which is now the rule in Grammar Schools, may not be immediately practicable, but in our judgement must even now be envisaged as inevitable."[72] A higher school-leaving age appeared to offer more opportunities at the same time as sharper proposals for differentiating pupils were being aired. The joint publication of the AEC and NUT, *The Extra Year*, emphasized the need to remove "mentally defective" children into special schools; these ideas would be repeated in the 1944 Education Act.[73] However, critics continued to pour scorn on such intentions, for instance, one contributor to the *Saturday Review* argued that raising the leaving age represented the rise of individualism and neglect of communal responsibilities as "the children of the poor can never have the same opportunities as the children of the rich, and the new proposal simply means another year wasted before the identical job is taken in the end."[74]

Britain declared war against Germany on September 3, 1939. It fell to Kenneth Lindsay, parliamentary secretary to the Board of Education and a National Labour MP, to steer through Parliament the Education Emergency Bill. Lindsay had previously supported the Tawney line of secondary education for all, but he now advocated extension of day-continuation provision.[75] Hastings Lees Smith, who was in effect to become leader of the Labour Party upon Clement Attlee's entry into Churchill's coalition government, led on the Labour Party amendment to delete the clauses in the 1936 Act on exemptions. He accepted the suspension of the 1936 Education Act until the end of the war, but noted that the Labour Party wished to be free once the war ended to propose that the clauses on beneficial exemptions should be left out to ensure a clear-cut raising of the school age to 15.[76]

The New Secondary Education

By 1941, a new sense of possibilities for the future was emerging. In a forward-looking book reflecting the new optimism, F. H. Spencer described the situation in relation to formally recognized secondary schooling that existed in the 1937/38 year, the last for which the Board of Education had full information.[77] Spencer had been a divisional inspector with the Board and had only recently retired as chief inspector of education of the London County Council, and his modest support for an expansion of day-continuation schools reflected his insider's view of the inadequacies of the existing system in relation to teacher supply and school buildings.

The long-standing LEA official and educational commentator H. G. Stead also welcomed a growing consensus in favor of creating a break between primary and secondary tiers of schooling.[78] However, Stead favored 13 not 11 as the age of transfer with the caveat that this would depend upon whether the school-leaving age was to be 15 or 16. One of Stead's principal concerns was that postprimary schooling should be founded upon closer links with the wider community. War had done little to dampen the extent and intensity of the public debate and concern over secondary schooling and raising the leaving age.

Within government, the war cabinet was beginning to discuss postwar planning, a sign of the changing military tide. The question of the leaving age was of concern to several departments and not just the Board of Education. The carefully managed planning strategy devised by Maurice Holmes within the officer corps of the Board, and other officers since 1940 was to face a rude interruption in the form of a blunt intervention from no less a figure than Ernest Bevin, minister for Labour. On September 4, 1941, Bevin outlined his thinking about the school-leaving age with a small group of senior civil servants from the Board of Education and Ministry of Labour. He outlined a scheme for residential camps for all boys and girls aged 14–16 at which they would be engaged in social, practical, technical, and civic activities. Bevin wanted the school-leaving age raised to 16 as soon as was practically possible. Indeed, he argued that if ROSLA to 16 was not achieved very shortly the opportunity would be lost for another 20 years.[79]

This intervention by an influential and senior Labour Party minister cutting across lines of departmental responsibility was not received well by senior civil servants at the Board of Education. Their efforts to contain this unwanted initiative were headed by Maurice Holmes, who in a written response to Bevin, dismissed the idea of raising the leaving age to 16 in the near future as "hardly one which a responsible person with even a nodding acquaintance with the educational conditions of today could make."[80] This view reflected the pragmatism that prevailed within the Board and throughout His/Her Majesty's Inspectorate (HMI) who were acutely conscious of the further deterioration of the service since the start of the war. Holmes gave Bevin details of numbers of schools damaged by bombing. He raised questions concerning teacher supply, something he knew that would have been of direct concern for Bevin as minister of Labour. Holmes's memorandum argued that of most concern was the issue of completing the reorganization of older elementary schools into a pattern of primary and secondary schools with a clear break at age 11. He used uncompromising terms to squash ideas of a move toward ROSLA to 16 "to compel children to remain until the age of 16 in an all-age elementary school would be a fraud on the parents and a gross injustice to the children themselves," language far removed from the usually cautious and decidedly nonpolitical tone of internal communications. Holmes pointed out the slow pace of reorganization between 1927 and 1939, by which time only 52 percent of 14-year-olds had attended specialist senior schools or departments. His note concluded with a reference to those like H. G. Stead, who were still expressing preferences for an extension of day continuation after the age of 15, rather than extending the compulsory leaving age.[81] But Bevin had an idea and was active in widening discussion, exactly the opposite of Holmes's strategy of managing both policy and politicians.

In his memorandum, Bevin argued in favor of a leaving age of 16 saying: "There is the strongest case for this on general grounds of educational and social progress."[82] Bevin felt that the value of the employment of 14- to 16-year-olds was in any event wasteful and less productive than it ought to be. His view was that upon entry into employment at 16, juveniles would be more efficient and cost-effective as employees. Bevin felt that the range of temporary accommodation already in government hands should be retained and used for the type of activities and camps he had been outlining to officials in several departments. As for trained teachers and available numbers, Bevin's view was straightforward: "It will probably be desirable to widen the field of recruitment for teachers and call upon people outside the academic world."[83] In this lay the origins of the Emergency Training Scheme through which non commissioned officers[84] could undertake one-year training and move straight into teaching. Such a view in part reflected Bevin's own experience of leaving school at 11 and working in manual occupations until he became a full-time trade union organizer. Bevin's memorandum includes the formula that was eventually to be included into the 1944 Act: "The age should be raised to 15 at the end of the war, but the legislation should stipulate extension to 16 within the minimum possible period, which should be no longer than three years."[85]

The response to Bevin from Robert Wood, the permanent secretary at the Board of Education, and from Maurice Holmes, was ready by the end of October 1941. Wood revealed in his reply of November 6 that Board policy aimed "to get away from the Fisher conception of the Continuation School and to bridge over the gap in the adolescent's life between the time he leaves school and at least 18."[86] Wood's reply highlighted the changed circumstances from the proposed implementation date of September 1939 arising from the 1936 Act, in particular the lost opportunity of the dip in the cohort. The exemption conditions also meant that in some areas far less accommodation would be required. Wood stressed the damage to over a thousand schools and the urgency of completing the Hadow reorganization of separating all-age elementary schools into junior and senior schools. He stated that legal compulsion to boarding as outlined by Bevin would be difficult to achieve and that suitable camps and hostels were unlikely to be located in places where they would be most needed. He stressed the longer-term aim of ensuring that all schools for senior pupils should become secondary schools and receive "equality of treatment with secondary schools of the existing type in such matters as accommodation, size of classes etc."[87] Thus in the bill the proposal remained as moving to an age of 15 with immediate effect and a further raising of the age to 16 when circumstances allowed.

By July 1943, when the White Paper was published, it contained a clause to raise the school-leaving age to 15 without exemptions with provision for a later raising to 16.[88] The 1926 Hadow proposals for reorganization were to be completed so that "secondary schools with varied facilities for advanced work" would be available to all over the age of 11. There was to be an introduction of a system of compulsory part-time continuation education up to the age of 18, a revisiting of the provisions of the 1918 Fisher Act.[89] In addition, a more inclusive approach to disability had been developing in the Hadow and Spens Reports and children were to be allowed to attend ordinary schools if possible. This was only partially realized at a time when judgments about "types" of children were proliferating and 11 categories of "handicap" were introduced by the 1944 Act.[90]

When the Education Act of 1944 Act became law, Section 35 outlined the proposed revision of the compulsory school age as well as the mechanism for a further raising to age 16 designed to mollify advocates of moving directly to an age of 16:

> Provided that, as soon as the Minister is satisfied that it has become practicable to raise to sixteen the upper limit of the compulsory school age, he shall lay before Parliament the draft of an Order in Council directing that the foregoing provisions of this section shall have effect as if for references therein to the age of fifteen years there were substituted references to the age of sixteen years.[91]

Despite the generally positive reception of the "Butler Act" and the perception that it was a key part of social reconstruction after the War, cabinet considered postponing the raising of the school age on July 7 of 1944.

The impetus for this came from Ernest Bevin.[92] The argument was that the influx of 14- to15-year-olds into the labor force would help solve the manpower shortages across the economy. It was estimated that raising the school-leaving age would take 350,000 away from the workforce from April 1, 1945. This would be just one part of an estimated fall in the size of the national workforce of 1.63 million. It was anticipated that 1.5 million women would be leaving the workforce even though much higher numbers would remain than before the War. Despite Churchill sharing some of these concerns, nothing came of this move but it highlights the fact that at each step on the road toward raising the school-leaving age, countervailing pressure appeared to reverse direction.

On July 5, 1945, at the general election, the Labour Party, led by Clement Attlee, won a large majority of seats in Parliament. Attlee appointed Ellen Wilkinson as the new minister of education. Amid ideological controversies that conspired to place Wilkinson in a politically vulnerable position, she presented to cabinet a memorandum on raising the school-leaving age.[93] Wilkinson proposed notifying LEAs that April 1, 1947, be the date set for ROSLA to 15. This was in fact a delay by over two years as the original terms of Section 35 of the 1944 Act identified August 27, 1944, as the date for ROSLA to 15. Wilkinson was clear that her proposal implied that implementation would result in educational compromises as ROSLA "will necessitate some overcrowding of classes in some areas and the use of school accommodation (huts, prefabricated buildings etc) of a kind which could be regarded as satisfactory only as a temporary measure."[94]

Cabinet was alerted to a double problem likely to present itself regarding teacher staffing. The increase of 200,000 places required to achieve full ROSLA to 15 required an additional 13,000 teachers. But at the same time a larger-than-usual number of teachers who were still working past retirement age would be expected to move into retirement within the coming two years, so more than 13,000 new teachers were needed. Wilkinson also raised in cabinet the issue of diverting building manpower toward schools and away from transport and housing but she had the backing of the deputy prime minister and lord president of the council, Herbert Morrison, who was in charge of the legislative and government program, and this potential point of opposition was thereby lessened within cabinet.[95] Wilkinson faced several immediate problems among colleagues. One of these was whether it would be possible to release sufficient building materials and workers to bring damaged schools back into use in time for the first stage of ROSLA. Morrison presented his own memorandum to cabinet on the question arguing that sufficient supply could be released to meet the date set out in the 1944 Act. [96] However there were doubts about whether it would be possible to supply sufficient teachers even with the products of the Emergency Training Scheme that she was about to announce. Morrison described the likely overcrowding of schools and classes as "the lesser evil" when compared with delay.[97] Wilkinson was able to announce that teachers who remained past retirement age would be able to benefit from having higher pay scales reflected in their pensions.[98] The view of Wilkinson at this juncture can be judged in a letter she wrote to her Labour predecessor Charles Trevelyan:

> I am making my first major job the raising of the school leaving age to 15. This means the provision of extra classroom accommodation. We have had to do that as a war operation, putting through a global order for prefabricated huts to the Ministry of Works and letting them to Local Education Authorities on very attractive terms: this is the only way in which we could deal with that immediate programme. If it is satisfactory, it may be possible to extend it to deal with other forms of overcrowding. The question of the building of permanent schools must wait until the housing situation has eased a little. It is not only that it has taken all the weight I could bring to bear upon the Cabinet to get this extra provision for classrooms, but I should not myself find it within my conscience to take away labour from housing when we could manage quite easily with these prefabricated huts.[99]

However, for some in the labor movement, there were concerns about the delay of ROSLA to 16. Tawney reported upon a meeting that had taken place between Wilkinson and a predominantly trade union delegation:

> On May 14 the TUC is sending a deputation to Miss Wilkinson, urging her to fix now a date for raising the school age to 16...There is more behind the matter than meets the eye. Six weeks or so ago, I went with a deputation from the Council for Educational Advance to see Miss W. She horrified us all by announcing, *a propos* of nothing, not only that she *could* not raise the age to 16 (which, as far as the immediate future is concerned, we all knew), but that she did not *want* to see it raised to 16, and preferred 8 hours in County Colleges. She was in fact very wilful. The TUC has now taken the matter up, and produced a brief, but quite good, Memorandum, which probably you have seen.[100]

Tawney concluded: "It is really important to press Miss W on the matter...she is doing herself a good deal of harm by her apparent reluctance to consult people who might advise her—mainly LEA people."[101]

The proposed provision of part-time compulsory education via County Colleges up to the age of 18 was being seen in some circles as an alternative to a uniform ROSLA to 16. Fears among some were not allayed when in October 1946 in the King's Speech item 17 of 28 simply stated, "All necessary steps action is being taken to enable the school leaving age to be raised in April of next year."[102] What is highly significant is how this seemingly small item stands alone as a reform connected to social reconstruction among a government program dominated by military, diplomatic, and industrial measures.

Within cabinet, there were continuing calls for delay to ROSLA to 15.[103] Wilkinson had little choice but to confront cabinet colleagues who were supporting a four-month delay in implementing ROSLA in 1947.[104] In particular, she highlighted how virtually all of the pupils affected came from working class rather than middle-class homes, and that this was the cohort whose schooling had been most disrupted by wartime circumstances. She argued further that by virtue of staying on until 15, this group would benefit from the provisions in the 1944 Act for part-time education in County Colleges between the ages of 16 and 18. Wilkinson also stressed that this was a moment of political significance and that Labour would run serious risks with its credibility among supporters, which she described as "educational and progressive opinion in general." She argued that cabinet should avoid the situation that arose after the provisions in the Fisher Act of 1918 were allowed to lie fallow.[105]

One of the strongest points in Wilkinson's favor was that any delay would actually require legislation and this in itself would signal a political retreat by a Labour government with a working parliamentary majority. Against Wilkinson were ranged those ministers arguing from a viewpoint in which industrial reconstruction would have to take priority. The Economic Survey Working Party for the Ministerial Committee on Economic Planning produced a detailed report on the needs of industry. This expressed concern at the loss to the national labor force of an entire cohort due to ROSLA. It called for the postponement of the measure for six months, from April 1947 until September 1947, a step that would require legislation.[106]

Three weeks later, Wilkinson was dead. One outcome of this tragedy was that posthumously she carried the argument over ROSLA. Her successor, George Tomlinson, was to see implementation of ROSLA in 1947, with many pupils placed into the system-built prefabricated huts that were part of the Hutting Operation for Raising the School-Leaving Age (HORSA) program. Many others remained in unsuitable classrooms and in schools with few appropriate facilities. Set against this was the gradual opening of new schools build as part of education authority development plans, so for some the experience of staying on to 15 was a positive one. But even after the effective implementation date for ROSLA, structural problems within the system persisted. In the debates in Parliament in July 1948, the Conservative opposition pointed out that the Ministry of Works had managed to complete only 42 percent of the HORSA huts that had been ordered.[107] It questioned whether it would have been better for this task to have been undertaken by the LEAs themselves, and bemoaned the fact that for many pupils the extra year had been wasted because of the lack of practical classrooms and workshops.[108]

The school-leaving age had finally been raised to 15 despite a wide range of obstacles and continuing resistance. Nonetheless, it was far from clear that ROSLA had won over public opinion as a popular cause and a basis for further developments. In 1948, an early survey of public opinion on current politics was able to put this to test, and more than one-half of those questioned disapproved of the idea that the leaving age should be extended further to 16. Supporters of all political parties appeared to have similar views on the subject, although men were slightly more favorably disposed to the idea overall than were women.[109] There were many other priorities than ROSLA, and there remained a great deal of public indifference and even opposition to the goals of the Education Act of 1944.

Chapter 5

Forward with ROSLA 1951–1964

Over the 13 years of Conservative government between 1951 and 1964, the position and prospects of the ROSLA project were transformed. At the beginning of this period, at a time of acute shortages, there was a strong reaction against the raising of the school-leaving age (ROSLA) to 15, which had been achieved in 1947 but was compromised by the partial implementation of secondary schools for all. ROSLA could appear to be an expensive mistake and many groups looked to other educational priorities rather than follow up on the commitment that had been made in the Education Act of 1944 for ROSLA to 16. By the end of the 1950s, though, the general indifference and suspicion of ROSLA had changed to widespread enthusiasm for this cause. This was largely due to the efforts of the Central Advisory Council for Education (England) (CACE), which led to a strong endorsement of ROSLA in the Crowther Report, *15 to 18.*[1] Over the following five years, reservations remained across the political spectrum and even within the government itself, over both the financial cost involved and the educational implications of such a commitment, but at the start of 1964, Sir Alec Douglas-Home's brief tenure as prime minister was marked by an undertaking that ROSLA would go ahead by 1970–1971, with all the preparations that this would involve. This debate was of clear significance educationally, for example, in terms of assumptions about ability and arguments concerning selection and common schooling. ROSLA also connected with broader social and cultural issues in relation to youth and welfare. In coming to terms with an expanding "welfare state," education played an essential role for the Conservative Party in the postwar years. Strategists and opportunists within the party sought to make education a Conservative issue as part of a worldview based upon individualism, enterprise, and social mobility.

Going Back on ROSLA?

The Conservatives were returned to office under Winston Churchill at the end of 1951. Under continued economic pressure, now redoubled because of the expense of involvement in the Korean War, the new government considered reducing the school-leaving age back to 14, and increasing the age of school entry from 5 to 6. Churchill himself was especially keen to reduce the leaving age in order to achieve economies, and raised this as a serious proposal at a number of cabinet meetings between 1951 and 1954.[2] Other ministers, including R. A. Butler who was now chancellor of the Exchequer and thus eager to find savings, nevertheless responded by pointing out that reducing the leaving age would not save money unless teachers were sacked, which was unlikely to happen because class sizes were too high.[3] "No substantial economies" would be possible by lowering the school-leaving age unless they dispensed with a significant proportion of teachers.[4] Churchill clearly remained unconvinced by this logic.

The Conservatives' lack of commitment to the extended leaving age did not go unnoticed. As early as December 1951, the *Manchester Guardian* had returned to the fray with a stern warning that "the gravity of the country's economic situation is not in dispute. The question is whether the only or the best way of escaping economic wolves is to throw our children at them."[5] The school-leaving age was therefore an uncomfortable issue for the Conservative government in the early 1950s, and generally drew defensive responses well as skepticism about the economic and educational value of raising the age. Education was still being accorded a lower priority in the new welfare state than health and housing.

The CACE was indeed requested in 1952 to examine what the impact of shortening the period of compulsory school attendance would be, but argued strongly that such a move would "do more serious injury to education and to the nation than is appreciated by those who advocate it."[6] It judged that if the leaving age were reduced to 14 at least a quarter and perhaps a third of the age group would remain in school voluntarily.[7] Such an approach might achieve a partial relief from the "overcrowding" of classrooms, but at the price of a year taken away from their education.[8] The CACE was highly dubious as to whether any substantial savings would be made, but was emphatic about the potential rewards to be garnered from a continued investment in a higher school age. It set this in the historical context of the efforts made earlier in the century to increase the leaving age to 15, and argued that raising the leaving age was "generally regarded as the most important result of the 1944 Act."[9]

Furthermore, the CACE added, while reducing the leaving age might bring some short-term savings, longer-term effects on the economy had to be considered:

> the more efficient industry reasonably to be expected from higher standards of education might yield even higher values to the nation, reckoned in pounds, shillings and pence, apart altogether from the human values confidently to be looked for from better education—satisfaction in work, enjoyment of leisure, widening of interests and the many other rewards that education has power to bestow.[10]

It also expressed concern that "many who hold positions of influence and whose opinions carry weight" were insufficiently aware of these issues.[11] These strictures were highly significant, not only for the CACE's stout resistance to reducing the school-leaving age, but for the contribution that it made to a reasoned case for extending the leaving age as both an economic and social investment, following on from the arguments made in the Hadow Report 30 years before. Moreover, it was beginning to recast the curriculum of the secondary modern schools for the large majority of pupils around the extended demands of a four-year secondary school course.

These convictions did not necessarily lead the CACE to be enthusiastic about enforcing a higher leaving age. The Gurney-Dixon Report, entitled *Early Leaving*, was produced in 1954 on behalf of the CACE, and looked for ways of avoiding what was described as "early wastage" from secondary education.[12] It observed that on the whole, boys tended to stay at school longer and to do better academically than did girls, and that many parents continued to place a higher priority on the education of their sons than on that of their daughters. It argued that there was too little incentive for pupils to remain at school in terms of the difference that this would make to their careers and life outcomes, and that greater inducement should be found to encourage them to do so, perhaps in the form of maintenance allowances. However, it was lukewarm about the principle of a higher leaving age for all pupils. Its findings and recommendations highlighted enduring conceptions about youth and gender-based differentiation that remained pervasive throughout the 1950s and beyond. Indeed, these ideas would resonate widely and eventually feed into renewed calls for ROSLA to 16. In Essex, the local authority would become concerned about the "poor showing" of the county's students in entering university reflecting a lack of "ambition" and "knowledge" about opportunities. It was claimed, that girls, unlike boys, divided according to interests rather than ability.

Their choices tended to be based upon a sober appraisal of their expected life course usually involving early marriage:

> Quick training that will give them earning power before marriage so that they can save for a home, and after marriage if they want to work when they are middle-aged. Many see shorthand typing as having a better market value than a degree.[13]

Educationists aimed to challenge these assumptions "making the idea of professional careers attractive to the very brightest children." Crucially this had to be achieved "before they are too set in their ideas...when the excitement of having secured a grammar or technical school place makes parents and children receptive to suggestions." Such concerns about "wastage" were mainly directed at selective schools although the concept would come to be applied much more widely in the following years. Those staying on from secondary modern schools would increase from 12 percent in 1958 to 17 percent by 1962 and, increasingly, students preferred to remain in their school rather than transfer to a selective one in order "to remain in a community where they were already known,"[14] indicating changing social attitudes to education.

In 1954, however, the tone of the debate within the government was increasingly looking forward to building on the achievements of the Education Act of 1944. David Eccles, the new minister of education, agreed with the CACE that reducing the school-leaving age would have been "a major retreat from the Act of 1944." Moreover, according to Eccles, in political terms this was hardly a viable option for a Conservative government: "If we, who mostly send our children to boarding schools, encouraged early leaving from county secondary schools, we should present the Opposition with a first-class Election issue."[15] This apprehension reflected a heightened sensitivity to social-class differences and a growing emphasis on equality of opportunity in the 1950s. Eccles was also keen to respond to the Labour Party's growing opposition to grammar and public schools and increasing support for comprehensive schools by recognizing that education would need to be treated as "the most urgent of all social problems" over the next decade.[16]

A further area of growth in education, stimulated by ROSLA, was in school building, now under the guidance of the Architects and Building Branch (A&B Branch) of the Ministry of Education created in 1948. This began the task of administering a major building program for secondary schools designed to accommodate larger numbers of pupils including those staying on after 15. Over 3,000 new secondary schools were build between 1947 and 1965. However, these were confined by tight cost limits instituted within the Ministry. This regime restricted scope for flexibility and led in many localities to a second spate of "temporary" hutted accommodation being erected in secondary schools, often to house growing numbers of 15- and 16-year-old pupils.[17]

At the same time, although there was economic growth and full employment during the second half of the 1950s, the government remained concerned about the rapid growth in the education budget and the prospects that it would grow still further in future years. As late as the summer of 1956, the Treasury entertained lingering ideas about lowering the leaving age to 14, although this notion was by now vigorously opposed by the Ministry of Education. Following a further Treasury request to estimate the savings that would be achieved by reducing the school-leaving age, it was pointed out by Ministry of Education officials that Eccles would strongly oppose any such move:

> It would involve legislation, which, because it would mean amending one of the most important and generally accepted sections of the 1944 Act, would be bitterly contested. It would be a serious inroad into the principle of "secondary education for all" and it would be a damaging blow at the secondary modern schools just at the time when the Minister is doing all he can to build up these schools in the face of continued denigration of them by members of the Opposition and other proponents of the comprehensive school.[18]

This argument echoed that of the 1952 CACE report, which now seemed to be widely accepted and ROSLA provided an opportunity to defend the Conservatives against charges of elitism.

Despite this, there continued to be concerns about whether rises in education spending could be sustained. In May 1957, for example, it was pointed out that the total net expenditure by the Ministry of Education and local education authorities (LEAs) had climbed from just under £300 million in 1950–1951 to almost £500 million in 1956–1957 and was likely to pass £1,000 million by the end of the decade. A Conservative committee asked, "Is it too much to expect that some fee shall be charged for pupils in attendance at State schools, to help to meet the rising cost of education?... If education is to cost more, is the increase to fall wholly on the rates and taxes, or can some parental contribution be expected at a time of full employment and sufficient wages?"[19] Free and compulsory education as a universal right had not yet been fully embedded in Conservative thinking with different interest groups oscillating between identifying education as an investment on the one hand and as an unacceptable cost in a burgeoning welfare state on the other. For instance, Lord Hailsham, who briefly succeeded Eccles as minister of education in 1957, argued for increased educational spending and sought to persuade his cabinet colleagues that Britain compared unfavorably with many other countries in terms of its educational structure and expenditure on education. However, the chancellor of the Exchequer, now Peter Thorneycroft, insisted that no further increase in expenditure on education could be considered in current economic conditions.[20]

At this stage, ROSLA to 16 was a low priority in Conservative education policy. The main issues in education were seen as the defense of grammar schools and public schools while reducing class sizes in primary and secondary schools. Where school leaving was discussed, it was generally felt that staying on at school after 15 should be developed on a voluntary basis and many Conservatives were wary about increasing compulsion. Hailsham sought to encourage parents to keep their children at school after the age of 15, and was even willing to consider financial incentives for this, but resisted a statutory increase in the school-leaving age that would, he warned, "be sure to throw out all his plans."[21] It continued to be argued in 1958 that a policy of providing "varied opportunities for the able and the keen" would produce "worthwhile gains in a measurable time," whereas

> sweeping measures such as raising the age of compulsory schooling by a year would cost far more and would lead to a lowering of standards for years to come.[22]

This view suggested that voluntary and localized measures might be more effective, as well as less expensive and more in tune with Conservative values, than universal and compulsory reforms. The aim of social policy in general, it was argued, should be to switch the emphasis of state spending away from the services that people ought to be able to provide for themselves, a principle upon which welfare services appeared to be encroaching.[23] Those children who did not benefit from staying on at school should be released earlier.[24]

In predicting educational plans for the next five years, therefore, the permanent secretary of the Ministry of Education, G. N. Flemming, argued as late as June 1959 that the government should "continue to emphasise their belief in the voluntary principle," supporting the provision of smaller classes and encouraging pupils to stay on at school voluntarily "before embarking on any further measures of compulsion."[25] In spite of these restrictions, the government was increasingly willing to endorse further educational expansion in order to continue the advances made under the 1944 Act. It accepted the need to "swim" with a "tide of opinion" among the public in terms of a growing interest in education and an increasing belief in its value.[26] These shifts were spurred on by enthusiastic and opportunistic characters in the Conservative Party. Geoffrey Lloyd, the minister of education in 1958, confided in Butler that an "amazingly keen popular interest in Education" had arisen due to the 1944 Act.[27] In Lloyd's view, further educational progress was not merely "essential in the national interest," but was "the type of social reform that fits most perfectly into a general Conservative theme."[28] Moreover, Lloyd, argued, further reform would not necessarily be very expensive: "If we act quickly, we can do so without spending much more money than will be spent simply to continue existing policies."[29] Since the number of pupils in secondary schools would fall by about 250,000 in the early 1960s, he pointed out, there was "a great opportunity to reinforce by positive action an improvement in standards which will take place anyway."[30] Indeed, he proposed, "If we are seen to be taking such action, the general public will give us credit for the whole of what could be a quite spectacular raising of the educational standards of our school leavers within a few years."[31] It was this hope that lay behind the publication of a new White Paper on secondary education toward the end of 1958.[32]

Meanwhile, the Labour Party in opposition was identifying key priorities for education while also attempting to contain costs. Under Hugh Gaitskell, Labour was trying to improve its public image and moderate its commitments in the area of social policy.[33] The Trades Union Congress (TUC) at its annual conference in 1956 passed a resolution calling for ROSLA to 16. Anthony Crosland's influential work *The Future of Socialism*, in 1956, argued that as part of the further development of comprehensive principles in secondary education, "perhaps the most important step, directly in fostering 'parity of esteem,' and indirectly in encouraging these other reforms, would be the raising of the school leaving age to 16."[34] By contrast, the veteran socialist intellectual Margaret Cole privately complained to the new Labour Party leader about "the very airy cloud-cuckoo-land talk of many in our Party—and the TUC spokesman—about what we would do in 1960, without any real conception of (a) finance, (b) manpower."[35] Cole accurately identified what became a key political contradiction of postwar politics, between public promises to increase spending and the economic realities that prevented it. Yet the emphasis upon practicality and cost certainly curtailed the vision of what was possible.

The Labour Party's new spokesman on education, Michael Stewart, agreed with Cole that there was a need to identify clear priorities. In a joint memorandum in 1957, Stewart and Cole insisted that reducing class sizes would do more to improve schools and raise their prestige than raising the school-leaving age.[36] As a more practical alternative to raising the school-leaving age, Stewart suggested that part-time day education might be made universal for all children up to the age of 17, which would involve training for 700,000 adults and 9,000 full-time teachers as well as part-time instructors drawn from industry.[37] Thus, he proposed, a future Labour government could not undertake to raise the school-leaving age further within the lifetime of its first five years after gaining office. In the light of these suggestions, the Labour Party's study group on education agreed in July 1956, after considerable discussion, that a Labour minister of education should first concentrate on a reduction in the size of classes, especially in the primary schools, with an undertaking being given to raise the school-leaving age to 16 as soon as circumstances permitted.[38]

Many Labour politicians clearly had qualms about this decision to defer further the ROSLA, and returned to discuss the implications of this on several occasions over the following six months.[39] Such anxieties were eased however by a survey of educational attitudes that the party commissioned in 1957 as part of its first nervous steps toward opinion polling. As the earlier survey had discovered in the later 1940s, this also found that a small majority of all parents were actually against ROSLA, and that 54 percent of working-class parents disapproved of such a measure. ROSLA in fact appeared to be more popular as an idea among middle-class parents than among working-class parents. Those who disapproved of the idea felt that for the average child the additional year would be wasted, while another widely held view was that the ordinary child should be earning his or her living by the age of 15.[40] According to the polling expert Mark Abrams, who administered the survey, only a minority of parents viewed education as a means of obtaining a better job in later life, and most were not interested in social or egalitarian arguments about education.[41] Such long-held educational and social attitudes were clearly most tenacious. Labour's study group concluded from this that a decision not to raise the school-leaving age "will probably be accepted without demur by the majority of the population."[42] Such prevarication was to be overturned by subsequent events.

The Impact of the Crowther Report

A key shift occurred with the publication of the Crowther Report, *15 to 18*, soon after the Conservatives' return to office under Harold Macmillan in October 1959. This was a report produced by the CACE, which was then chaired by Sir Geoffrey Crowther, the deputy chairman of the *Economist* newspaper. It had been requested in March 1956 to investigate the education of boys and girls between 15 and 18, and reported in December 1959. The Crowther Report strongly supported ROSLA and set the tone for the debate that ensued during the Conservative government of 1959–1964.

Part three of the Crowther Report enthusiastically endorsed ROSLA to 16, on the grounds that it would realize the vision of the 1944 Education Act of secondary education for all, giving it priority over another provision in the 1944 Education Act for part-time county colleges for those finishing compulsory education. While both were judged as "important" and "overdue," it insisted that ROSLA would benefit individuals and the nation as a whole, economically and socially.[43] It also proposed that ROSLA should be introduced between 1965 and 1969, which lay in a "valley" after the numbers of pupils at school had peaked and before they began to rise again.

This was perhaps the most significant of a number of major recommendations made by the Crowther Report, which it estimated would add £200 to £250 million a year to the present cost of education (£134 million for ROSLA on its own), although it saw these as a national investment that was small compared with the total national annual outlay for its capital infrastructure of £3,514 million.[44] While the nation's annual outlay on alcohol and tobacco had increased between 1950 and 1957 by some £228 million, ROSLA was viewed as an investment in national efficiency,

> We find it difficult to conceive that there could be any other application of money giving a larger or more certain return in the quickening of enterprise, in the stimulation of invention or in the general sharpening of those wits by which alone a trading nation in a crowded island can hope to make a living.[45]

Education was coming to be regarded as having a positive economic impact and this was reflected in the spread of the term "human capital" during the late 1950s and early 1960s. It was believed that education provided the missing link in accounting for unexplained economic growth.[46] In the 1960s, when economic and social expansion appeared feasible, Walt Rostow's best-selling *Stages of Economic Growth* resonated widely in claiming that education helped to lay the groundwork for economic "take-off".[47] Politicians willingly gravitated to the notion in attempting to juggle the contradictory pressures of stimulating economic growth while promising social benefits.

Economic growth also fuelled the emergence of "youth cultures" and Crowther referred somewhat nervously to the hyphenated "teen-ager," a concept rapidly rising to prominence amid growing commercialization and privatized modes of living. Although ROSLA was a universal policy, it had differing implications across society and heavily gendered assumptions pervaded the report. Commenting upon the last two years of schooling, it was argued that

> there can be no doubt that boys' thoughts turn most often to a career, and only secondly to marriage and the family; and that the converse obtains with girls. It is plain, then, that if it is sound educational policy to take account of natural interests, there is a clear case for a curriculum which respects the different roles they play.[48]

These divisive assumptions about "natural" abilities and interests would unravel further in the coming years.

However, the Crowther Report was warmly received by most newspapers and professional journals. The journal *Education* suggested that its immediate impact reflected the "forward march of public opinion."[49] But there was an undercurrent of dissent to these ambitious plans. This was partly due to the cost of the proposals, which would involve a commitment to finding 20,000 extra teachers in addition to new school buildings. As well as the financial implications, however, many queried the educational and social dimensions of ROSLA. Some argued that county colleges were more important, while others preferred to prioritize a reduction in primary school class sizes. William Alexander, secretary of the Association of Education Committees (AEC), stated a case for continued education, but not in schools, to respond to "the desire for independence, financially and socially...a sense of maturity, and...a desire to be out in the real world."[50] The AEC itself came to argue that schools themselves would require "a major shift of emphasis" in order to provide "a setting and a curriculum" adequate to convince pupils of "the value and importance of their education."[51] Meanwhile, the letters columns of newspapers and educational journals began to fill with the complaints of teachers and head teachers in secondary modern schools who did not welcome the prospect of extending education for pupils who were already bored and alienated with a leaving age of 15.[52]

It was David Eccles, reappointed for a second term as the minister of education, who responded to the Crowther Report on behalf of the new government. Eccles had anticipated the importance of the report as a major educational document that he compared to the Hadow Report of 1926.[53] Eccles also understood the broader political context of educational reform, that his powers as the minister were mainly "powers of persuasion," and he had to take account of "some very influential independent bodies" in "the world of education."[54] Despite these limitations, Eccles argued that the government should give education top priority among the social services such as it had never previously been accorded. Growing interest in education and rising expectations for the future had been demonstrated at the recent general election, and this presented both an opportunity and a challenge. Building upon the earlier arguments of Lloyd, Eccles held that "education was the open door for erstwhile Labour voters to the Tory Middle-Class." But there was a danger that the public might "forget our splendid record and demand an ever growing rate of quantity and quality."[55]

Thus, Eccles concluded, if the Conservative government were able to extend previous achievements, there would be enduring political advantages to be gained no less than lasting social improvement:

> It fell to us to carry out the major part of the Butler Act—a Tory measure—and to set our seal on Education as the undisputed "Tory" social service. In the same way as the name of Lloyd George was associated in the public mind with Old Age Pensions, or Aneurin Bevan's with the National Health Service, the Conservatives were now presented with an opportunity of once for all establishing their image in the field of Education, such as was not to be missed.[56]

Education therefore represented not only a tangible social benefit but also a political investment for the Conservatives who now had an opportunity to claim the credit for ROSLA as a Conservative measure. Nevertheless, within the Conservative Party, Eccles had to contend with a wide range of views on ROSLA. The Conservative and Unionist Teachers' Association was hostile to the proposal, and there were many party activists in local authorities who had other priorities. Eccles himself was conscious of the difficulties around compulsion, hesitated about the cost and continued to see class sizes as the top priority.[57] With the knowledge that other countries devoted a higher proportion of their GNP (gross national product) to education, Eccles argued that educational expenditure was coming to be seen as an "essential national investment."[58] Overall, he counseled caution in responding to the Crowther Report's key recommendation of ROSLA to 16, but urged his party to stand by the provisions of the 1944 Act and "retain the valuable political initiative which they had won in education."[59]

These potential political and social gains were less obvious to an interdepartmental committee of officials established to investigate the costs of implementing the main recommendations of the Crowther Report. This reflected the concerns of the Treasury, and aimed to avoid commitments to new spending or to defer budgeting decisions.[60] It warned that educational expenditure, excluding universities, was expected to increase from 3.9 percent of GNP in 1959 to 5 percent by 1974 and that the Crowther recommendations would add to the burden. The cost of ROSLA to 16 was estimated at about £42 million per year in addition to £92 million on new school buildings and a reduction of GNP of about £125 million as a result of removing 15-year-olds from the labor force.[61] R. A. Butler, now at the Home Office, stoked up these fires by proposing that the government should commit itself to providing 8,000 extra places in teacher training colleges in order to either eliminate oversize classes, or make it possible to raise the school-leaving age by 1970.[62] However, even with the decision on ROSLA being deferred, the chancellor of the Exchequer, Derick Heathcoat Amory, pronounced himself "shocked" at the prospect of the government announcing these additional commitments to education. He argued that, on the basis of existing policies, the cost of education would increase by over £650 million, or 80 percent, by 1974: "Clearly we cannot undertake more: the question is whether we can do as much."[63] Other commitments, for example to defense, economic aid, the National Health Service, a roads program, the railways, pensions, housing, space research, and civil aviation, were also pressing on one another, and against this background he insisted that additional educational improvements could not be justified.[64]

The government attempted to address this conundrum at a meeting of the cabinet on March 17, 1960. In terms of the general economic situation, Heathcoat Amory stressed that while he did not wish to reverse the government's spending policies for growth, it was necessary to restrict the steady rate of expansion. In spite of Heathcoat Amory's reticence about spending, prime minister Harold Macmillan feared losing public support without it. Finally, after an extended discussion, it was decided to avoid making an explicit pledge to increase teacher numbers, and instead to "blur the edges" and make it an "aim."[65]

In responding formally to the Crowther Report, therefore, Eccles's statement to the House of Commons on March 21, 1960, reaffirmed the principle of ROSLA but resisted calls to announce a date for ROSLA to be implemented. This was an important speech that was to become famous in education policy circles for its use of the term "the secret garden of the curriculum." It also expressed in definitive terms the government's indecision over ROSLA.

Eccles' speech acknowledged the growth of the "public appetite for education" reflected in the number of children voluntarily staying on after the age of 15: "Each year we shall gain more experience in how to make the last years in a secondary school worthwhile, and each year the number will diminish of those who would stay on only if they were compelled to do so." He set four conditions for setting a date for ROSLA. First, school buildings had to be adequate to accommodate the extra pupils. He estimated that £80 million would be needed in England and Wales, and that if resources were available for this, four years' notice would be required before ROSLA could be introduced. Second, schools must have the confidence that they could hold the interest of the 15- to 16-year-olds, and for this there was a need to provide satisfying new courses for them. Third, more teachers would be needed—not only the 18,000 teachers that would be required just for ROSLA but also the many more to cut down oversize classes in primary and secondary schools, which remained his major priority. He pointed out that since 1951, over 4,000 new schools had been completed, 2 million new places provided, the number of children in maintained schools had risen by nearly a million, or by one-sixth; the number of teachers had risen by about 50,000, or nearly one-quarter. But in January 1959, one-quarter of primary school children were still in classes of over 40, and two-thirds of seniors in classes of over 30. The high birthrate, the increase in voluntary staying on, high wastage from the teaching profession for example when women left to get married, and the new three-year training course for teachers, compounded this general problem, so that, according to Eccles, teacher supply was the most urgent problem to be addressed. Rather optimistically, he anticipated that oversize classes could be eliminated by 1970 in order to enable ROSLA. Finally, he pointed out, public opinion had fully to support such a step.

Eccles was in no doubt about the financial implications of ROSLA and realized that, even without Crowther's recommendations, education spending in England and Wales would grow by one-half by the end of the 1960s. Yet, still he concluded that the government was convinced "that even if it means sacrificing in other directions the money must be found for education," with a greater slice of the national income, as a commitment to investing in the future. One Ministry official noted that this created an "unsettling" situation for the government which would "get no credit by accepting the principle and denying its application."[66] It is worth noting also that Anthony Greenwood, in replying to the debate, committed the Labour Party to ROSLA at the earliest possible date, which it set, following Crowther, as 1968–1969.[67]

An Act of Faith and Courage?

The lines of argument over ROSLA were now clearly established and the political and economic dimensions of ROSLA became the subject of protracted debate over the course of the government. Eccles's stance avoided an immediate government commitment, but it placed the onus on the government to make its position clear before the next general election, which was due to be held by 1964 at the latest.[68] It also permitted the Treasury to develop an argument that ROSLA to 16, however attractive it might be politically, was unaffordable on financial grounds.

In educational and social terms, there remained significant underlying doubts about the wisdom of proceeding with ROSLA. These were reflected for example in the findings of a committee of Conservative MPs exploring problems facing young people and responding to Crowther and the Albmemarle Report on the youth service, which was published at the start of 1960.[69] It reported that young people had greater leisure time, were healthier, matured earlier, and were better off financially than earlier generations had been, leading to a growing sense of independence and security. In coming to terms with these wider social changes, the proper approach for the Conservatives was to invest in this new generation and encourage individual and local freedom and variety. The committee supported the general stance taken by the Crowther Report but was lukewarm about the proposal to raise the school-leaving age, pointing out that 15-year-old pupils had a changing attitude to authority and life in general, and suggesting that voluntary staying on at school might be encouraged as "a very good second best."[70] Such an approach "would have all the advantages of a natural process of selection," and would ensure that pupils staying on at school would have support from their families and teachers, without the "distracting influence" of those who would resent another year of compulsory schooling.[71] This view was shared by the Conservative and Unionist Teachers' Association, which insisted that the existing length of school life was sufficient for a large proportion of children in secondary modern schools, who "appear to have neither the ability nor the desire to absorb more of the curricula which are at present normally available to them."[72] These attitudes reflected entrenched assumptions that ability was fixed and clearly differentiated between an elite of the academically able, and the mass of pupils who could not benefit from further educational provision and would inevitably resist it.

For a few years, the government could defer further consideration of ROSLA. As it approached its fourth year, after Edward Boyle had succeeded Eccles as the minister of education in July 1962, officials again became active in discussing the next moves forward. One argued, adapting the American John Dewey, that it remained necessary to formulate a "basic philosophy" on the issue, on the basis that "we ourselves—that is, broadly, parents of the professional or managerial class—do not let our own children leave school under 16 even if they are not doing very well."[73]

In recognizing the growing maturity of young people, assumptions about differing ability groups were being both challenged and reconfigured. The growing maturity of young people affected by ROSLA was often articulated in terms of "sexual and emotional interests" in addition to an early entry into the labor market, which required "an education with a different focus from that provided for more intellectually able pupils."[74] Such forms of separation went hand in hand with a widening recognition that ability levels had been consistently underestimated in the past. Paradoxically, it was noted that "handicapped" and "educationally subnormal" pupils already had a leaving age of 16 and it made sense to extend provision:

> It is not self-evident that the dullest children should leave school earliest... There are strong arguments for the view that pupils not quite ascertainable as educationally sub-normal need a higher leaving-age more than most; and the same arguments might have some force quite a fair way up the scale.[75]

Changes in the workplace were also demanding higher levels of education, a process that was set to continue and, according to one official in the Ministry, the country was at an "economic turning point":

> A longer school life is not only important in that we need better educated employees, but also because we shall find it difficult enough to find enough work to go around... the length of school life will in the near future be inseparable from problems of employment generally... the government is involved on a wider front than many of them appreciate.[76]

This created the need for a major shift in attitudes to education and schooling among those unaccustomed to a leaving age of 16. Civil servants feared that "conflicts" might arise within families as better-educated pupils "begin to adopt middle-class manners, attitudes and values."[77] Schools in "slum areas" of Sheffield and other cities were "acting as a kind of first aid clinic against the bruises that the youngsters get from the harsh outside world."[78] ROSLA was becoming the "central problem of secondary education" and necessitated a process of long-term cultural change:

> The more education which parents have the more education they want for their children. Thus, raising the s.l.a. for this generation of children will really benefit mostly succeeding generations, who will as a result be suitably motivated towards education and find themselves in a more satisfactory home background... compulsion in this generation provides the basis for the voluntary principle in the next.[79]

Yet there were continuing anxieties about going forward. H. H. Donnelly of the Scottish Education Department saw "great difficulty" in contemplating any firm commitment on the lines of Crowther because of the problems of teacher supply, which still appeared to be a significant difficulty for ROSLA.[80] Teacher supply was even described as the "major" problem in comparison with the "minor" issue of building supply. The valley of the 1960s identified by Crowther was rapidly disappearing from view.[81] Toby Weaver, an official at the Ministry of Education, agreed that it was not going to be at all easy to make a case for the compulsory raising of the age, and was "by no means certain that our Minister will be in favour of any commitment on it."[82]

By the summer of 1963, these negative opinions had hardened. According to one, on the basis of current progress with expanding the training colleges and universities, ROSLA was "just not a practical proposition," and the primary schools would suffer if it were introduced. Crowther was dismissed as "archaic," parents were said to be doubtful of the merits of ROSLA, and it was argued that higher education might be a better investment: "To put the matter with intentional crudeness: is it better to enforce an obligation upon the unwilling or to extend opportunities for those who are both willing and able."[83] Meanwhile, the worsening economic prospects of the country also served to highlight the potential cost of ROSLA. The economic prosperity that had blessed Macmillan's government in its early years had been replaced by a downturn that brought with it a growing pessimism about future financial prospects. As chancellor of the Exchequer, Reginald Maudling's budget in 1963 responded by reducing income tax and planning for further expansion.[84] ROSLA was a commitment too far, and the Treasury began to assert itself again to avert this threat.

The educational context of the debate had radically changed. In terms of education, the state was slowly moving into the "secret garden of the curriculum," first with an abortive announcement of a Curriculum Study Group in 1962, leading to a further debate and the development of a Schools Council for Curriculum and Examinations in 1964 that would make it possible to develop new courses in areas of national need. At the same time, two heavyweight reports were about to be published, both years in the making, which would further sharpen the issues around ROSLA. The Newsom Report, a further product of the CACE, was published in October 1963 under the title of *Half Our Future*, on the education of pupils aged 13–16 of "average and less than average ability."[85] It insisted that ROSLA was necessary and urgent on social and economic grounds,[86] and thus increased further the pressure on the government to set a date.

Herbert Andrew, the permanent secretary at the Ministry of Education, responded to these new developments by proposing that the advice provided by officials for the minister should favor ROSLA, on the basis that this represented a long-established policy, which should not be reversed without clear cause.[87] The key Ministry official responsible for drafting this advice, L. R. Fletcher, was especially positive in setting out the case for ROSLA. Encouraged by Andrew, Fletcher pointed out that international competition drove up the demand for educated manpower, and that in this respect the practices and plans of other Western countries were ahead of those of Britain. In the United States, for example, every state had a leaving age higher than 15 and 10 higher than 16, while France, Sweden, and Norway were also raising it to 16.[88] Another Ministry official, H. F. Rossetti, clearly anticipating Treasury resistance, argued that political considerations should override economic issues even if, as he felt, "there is an insufficient case on educational grounds for raising the age to justify doing this at a cost of something between £50m or £70m a year."[89] Andrew finally approved the advice to go forward to the minister, acknowledging as he did so that "since the 1944 Act educational thought and policy has been to a very large extent geared to the idea that 16 and not 15 or 17 is the magic age."[90]

At the end of October, the Robbins Report on higher education was published, urging the further expansion of higher education to all those able to profit by it.[91] This raised the stakes on how best to invest in young people for the future. It increased the potential expenditure for educational expansion and suggested a deployment of funds that might be an alternative to ROSLA. By the same token, in political and social terms, it sharpened a debate between an emphasis on higher education, which would benefit a minority, and an extension of compulsory schooling, which would provide for all. The Treasury envisaged that the ten-year program envisaged by Robbins would involve an increase of more than 100 percent in the cost of higher education by 1973–1974, which would mean giving it priority over other areas of activity.[92] Andrew was also conscious of the electoral implications of supporting the Robbins' proposals for higher education while remaining inactive on ROSLA:

> There is a considerable section of thoughtful and articulate opinion which will be very critical of any suggestion that we believe, as a Government, in increasing opportunities for the ablest boys and girls while neglecting the average and below average.[93]

For the children who currently left school at 15, he observed, secondary education was "a building only half finished and doubtfully worth the money we are spending on it," so that, as he concluded, "the completion of the building would enable us to get better value for the money we are now spending and would enable the educational world to go ahead with the necessary improvement of the content of secondary education."[94]

Nevertheless, despite this clear advice, the educational, social, and economic issues around ROSLA remained unresolved.

At this stage, as the Conservative government entered the final year of its five-year term, the political dimension of the debate increasingly overshadowed both education and economics. The Labour Party had elected a capable and popular new leader, Harold Wilson, after the death of Hugh Gaitskell in January 1963. Macmillan's government had become very unpopular, and it became mired in a scandal that led to the resignation in June 1963 of the war minister John Profumo. Finally, in October 1963, Macmillan was himself forced to resign as prime minister for health reasons. His replacement, after a controversial and contested process to choose a new party leader and prime minister, was Sir Alec Douglas-Home, who was selected in preference to the presumed heir apparent R. A. Butler. Douglas-Home's government, from the end of 1963 until October 1964, has usually been dismissed as marking the tired end of a long Conservative period of office. Nevertheless, it was this government that took the decisive step to raise the school-leaving age to 16. Moreover, it did so against all of the financial and economic advice from the Treasury, and in the face of threatening economic indicators for the future. The Treasury continued to be highly alarmed at the prospect of ROSLA adding to the many other calls on the education budget, and argued vigorously against it.[95] These tensions maintained the political disputes that had opened up with the resignation of Macmillan and the succession of Douglas-Home as prime minister.

It was a measure of the significance of the issue and the unresolved nature of the arguments that Douglas-Home found it necessary to meet personally the chairman of the CACE, John Newsom, in order to sound him out on educational prospects and gain some reassurance.[96] Newsom admitted that some children were bored with school at 15, "or indeed even earlier," but declared that it was worth keeping all children at school for an extra year: "There was an increasing demand throughout the community for competence, and experience in the United States and on the Continent of Europe showed clearly that extra time at school developed the abilities that were required."[97] He suggested that the curriculum for such pupils should be not narrowly academic, but related to their future work.

Newsom pointed out that although an increasing number of 16-year-olds were now staying at school voluntarily, most of these were in the southern half of the country, and he thought it "regrettable that there should be 'two nations' educationally as well as in other respects."[98] His report had visibly segregated a section of young people but Newsom was clearly questioning ingrained assumptions about the fixed nature of "ability," while also pointing out the significance of ROSLA in relation to issues of social equality. The social implications involved underpinned the verdict of the journal *Education*, which pointed out "the risk of appearing to underwrite an elite educational system," and concluded ringingly: "This is a matter of faith about the kind of society Britain wants to be."[99]

ROSLA was referred to the Education and Research Policy Committee, but although a majority of this group supported ROSLA to 16 in 1970, the secretary of state for Scotland argued that this date was too soon for the plan to be implemented properly and the chief secretary of the Treasury was opposed to the proposal in its entirety.[100] The chancellor, Reginald Maudling, intervened personally to warn of the potential consequences, and reminded colleagues that the £150 million of capital expenditure that would be required for ROSLA was equivalent to the whole of the money needed for the Channel Tunnel (including the French contribution); or the Victoria Line tube with another tube of the same magnitude; or two years' construction of motorways and trunk roads at the same rate; or two new towns of about 50,000 people each; or six new universities of about 7,000 each, all with 100 percent residential accommodation. He worried that "we are fast pre-empting the future growth of economic resources ahead, right into the 1970s."[101] Treasury ministers were resolved to oppose any commitment to raise the school-leaving age in the near future, even though it was recognized that "the political arguments in favour of the change are strong (especially as Mr Wilson has committed the Labour Party to the raising of the age 'before the end of this decade'), and the Cabinet may therefore wish to go ahead despite the cost."[102]

These economic arguments were compounded by the continuing uncertainties over the educational and social merits of ROSLA. These were unsettling in their implications even at this late stage. As the cabinet was preparing to make a decision about whether to confirm the implementation of ROSLA, for example, a provocative article appeared in the national newspaper, *The Guardian*, which the cabinet secretary, Burke Trend, forwarded to the prime minister as "an interesting statement of one point of view."[103] The author was Arthur Barton, a history teacher in a secondary modern school, who insisted that a large proportion of his pupils should leave school at the age of 15 or even earlier because they were not capable of benefiting from a longer school life. A typical case in his view was a pupil who he called "Wilkinson"—"a stout, stupid, rather insolent lad of 14." According to Barton, such pupils were "reasonably teachable in their limited way up to about 12 or 13," but after that it was better for them to leave as soon as possible.[104] Such a view might have been calculated to persuade Conservative politicians that ROSLA was neither an educational nor a social priority, and a poor investment of funds.

Thus, ROSLA came to cabinet with the matter still undecided. It was noted at the cabinet meeting on January 17 not only that the proposal would be very expensive to implement, but also that "on the basis of previous experience, the compulsory retention of a large number of unwilling children would tend to increase juvenile delinquency without yielding any educational benefit."[105] The minister of education, Edward Boyle, was strongly in favor of announcing a clear date for ROSLA, but the secretary of state for Scotland, Michael Noble, was less sympathetic and argued that such a decision would require more vocationally centered courses for nonacademic children. After an extended discussion, the matter remained unresolved.[106]

A further, strongly worded memorandum from the Treasury emphasized the financial risks involved that "the limits of prudence and financial probity have now very definitely been reached and that any net addition would be economically unsound and politically unwise."[107] The final estimates of costs were debated vigorously at a meeting between Boyle and the chief secretary to the Treasury, John Boyd-Carpenter, prior to the decisive meeting of the cabinet. Boyle raised the possibility of deferring the normal program of school improvements in order to help pay for ROSLA, but it was agreed that this would disadvantage the pupils who were now to stay on at school to 16. The notion that ROSLA might be introduced in 1972, rather than in 1970, was also entertained, with the educational, social, and political arguments for and against each date again finely balanced.[108]

The cabinet meeting of January 23 followed a general analysis of government expenditure led by the Treasury team. Maudling pointed out in this prior discussion that even on the optimistic assumption that the country could achieve a rate of growth in the GNP of 4 percent, by 1968 public expenditure would be absorbing over 41 percent of the national income, with continuing high pressures on expenditure in the following years. However, the prime minister in his summing up observed that it was not possible to measure the future capacity of the economy in a precise fashion, and also that if new projects were justifiable on social and economic grounds, they could be endorsed in principle, "on the basis that, when the expenditure which they entailed reached significant proportions, the necessary steps would be taken to keep public expenditure as a whole within acceptable limits."[109] On this hopeful note, the debate over ROSLA resumed. Boyle insisted that failing to announce a date for ROSLA in the forthcoming debate on education would expose the government to criticism "on the ground that they were showing insufficient concern for the education of the majority of the country's children." Most of the capital expenditure, he added, would fall in the years after expenditure on the Channel Tunnel was at its heaviest if this project were approved; and the decision would still be subject to additional buildings and teachers being available. He left open the possibilities that the change might be deferred if either the capital resources or the necessary teachers were unlikely to be available, and also that the age of entry to schooling might be raised. It was eventually agreed that raising the school-leaving age in 1970-71, "while not constituting a firm commitment, represented the Government's deliberate aim," and Boyle was authorized to announce this in the forthcoming Commons debate on education.[110]

In the view of *The Times*, the government's decision was "an act of faith and courage." Apart from educationists and interested politicians, it opined, there was little sign in the country of popular demand for this reform, and it would have been easy to find a way out. Many teachers remained anxious about the likely consequences for their classes and schools, while among parents "there is no great wish for a move which postpones the entry of extra earnings into the home."[111] Yet now that the decision had been made, there remained the still greater task of preparing for it and implementing it successfully. This was to prove more difficult than even the most skeptical of Conservative ministers could have anticipated.

Chapter 6

Waiting for ROSLA 1964–1968

With the key decision having been made to proceed with the raising of the school-leaving age (ROSLA) to 16 by 1970–1971, active planning now went forward to a new phase. Enthusiasm was expressed that the measure paved the way for the full realization of secondary education for all. At the same time, there were significant underlying difficulties that hampered preparations. One key set of issues was around the curriculum, and the new Schools Council for Curriculum and Examinations set out to establish guidelines in this area. It had limited powers in comparison with teachers and local education authorities (LEAs) but there was a widespread expectation that a new curriculum would address the problem of disaffection among young people. Providing sufficient buildings and space for the additional pupils also sparked considerable debate. In the general election of 1964, narrowly won by the Labour Party, ROSLA had received relatively little attention, and moves to encourage comprehensive education were most prominent at this time. Yet there continued to be hesitancy over ROSLA. Traditional allies such as the *Guardian* newspaper began to show ambivalence over the measure, and in Scotland in particular there was open opposition. These doubts and reservations came to the surface by 1967 as economic problems grew, leading to the decision by the Labour government at the beginning of 1968 to delay implementation of ROSLA until 1972–1973.

The Newsom Curriculum

The proposals in the Newsom Report, on "average and below average" pupils of 13–16 years of age, for ROSLA to be implemented, toward the end of 1965, had been accompanied by suggestions about the kind of curriculum that would be most suitable for the pupils who would benefit from it. It emphasized that "much fuller use should be made of the natural interests of older boys and girls in the work they will eventually undertake and that this fact should be reflected not only in the content of the curriculum but in the method of teaching and, above all, in the attitude of the teacher to the pupil, when the pupil is, after all, a young adult."[1] It recommended that all schools should provide a choice of fourth- and fifth-year programs, including a range of courses broadly related to occupational interests, that provision for extracurricular work, for the arts, for religious instruction, for sexual guidance, and for careers advice should be reviewed and developed further, and that the school program in the final year "ought to be deliberately outgoing—an initiation into the adult world of work and leisure."[2] Provision for all practical subjects, it continued, should also be reappraised, and workshop and technical facilities extended.[3] Part two of the Newsom Report made detailed proposals on subjects, and in particular practical subjects, science, mathematics, and the humanities. These were intended to promote "self-conscious thought and judgement," which it regarded as fundamental to the idea of secondary education. There was to be an emphasis on being practical, realistic, vocational, and involving choice so that schools "send boys and girls out into the world literate and able to perform simple calculations with confidence and accuracy."[4] Opportunities for personal fulfillment were to be developed "for the good life as well as for good living."[5] This was an inherently contradictory project. While the growing maturity of young people was being recognized, schools were continuing to treat them as children. Assumptions about fixed ability were being challenged at the same time as they were reinforced by the very notion of "average and less than average ability." The report adopted an anthropological lens in analyzing its target group:

> They will have to begin to learn how to manage more complex human relations...They will need guidance on social manners...They will need to acquire some awareness of a wider world beyond the limits of themselves and their jobs. They will need to be helped to understand, at whatever level of comprehension is possible to them, some of the issues of our time.[6]

In this account, schooling was conceived as an agency for the promotion of culture, discrimination, and civilization.

These were highly ambitious and visionary plans for the school curriculum associated with ROSLA but could not be easily brought into being. The teachers, schools, and LEAs were directly responsible for the curriculum and were fiercely defensive of their position.[7] It was a Ministry of Education official, Toby Weaver, who noted in 1961 that there was "no centre of power where differences can be resolved" and that "strong arm tactics" would provide no alternative to the "patient working out of syllabuses by teachers."[8] One boost to reform came in 1964 with the emergence of the Schools Council for Curriculum and Examinations, which was a broad-based consortium involving many teachers. It was to be responsible for providing a practical way forward and ROSLA became a key responsibility.

The Schools Council's approach was partly modeled on the work of a national project in school science and mathematics carried out by the Nuffield Foundation, a charitable trust. This was initially at least a plan that would promote curriculum change for academically able pupils in grammar schools, but it also pioneered a mechanism for promoting curriculum innovation in schools by involving individual teachers and groups of teachers in local trials and regional associations, supported by LEAs and experts based in the universities. This strategy of supplying ideas at the center but encouraging experiments and adaptation at the local level, provided a formula for the Schools Council to develop a curriculum suitable for ROSLA.

The first Working Paper produced by the Schools Council, *Science for the Young School Leaver,* focused upon the teaching of science to all pupils of average and below-average ability, with a view to forming part of a national program of activity in preparation for ROSLA.[9] The project was designed to "provide all pupils with a liberal insight into the character of science to serve both as a preparation for adult life and a foundation for vocational education."[10] This was a starting point for detailed development work involving extensive field trials and systematic testing in some 30 schools over the next 3 years.

The early discussions within the Schools Council also revealed the significance and ideals that were attached to the implementation of ROSLA, which represented "another stage along the road mapped out in the Education Act of 1944, leading to secondary education for all."[11] The decision to go forward with ROSLA was described as a "bold act of faith" that would mean retaining some 60 percent of the age group in school for an extra year who would otherwise have left at 15; it was feared that many of these "below average" pupils would lack motivation and resent staying in school.[12] A memorandum expanded with some eloquence on both the challenge and the opportunity involved in engaging such pupils:

> A pessimistic view of the problem would see it as the doubly difficult one of seeking to enlighten those who have rejected the very means by which they

can be enlightened. An optimistic view would regard any act of rejection as the symptom of a readiness on the part of the pupil to begin to examine critically the world of the adult, and therefore as an opportunity for the teacher to take as his starting points those aspects of life which vicariously interest, annoy, disturb or bewilder the adolescent pupil.[13]

Teachers were not always confident about an emerging situation over which they appeared to have limited control. Many felt they were entering a new era for which past educational traditions offered little guidance. As ideas of developmental psychology seeped further into educational thinking, it was believed that the growing maturity of young people in a changing society was creating new problems:

> Personal development is very rapid between the ages of 15 and 16. The contemporary pace of social and economic change is also very fast. The schools therefore face a difficult task. They must prepare to meet the needs of pupils whose personal maturity will be, in many cases, outside their direct experience. They must also help these pupils to find their place in a changing society. And there is no clearly expressed consensus of view on objectives.[14]

A feeling of stepping into the unknown pervaded the increasingly urgent preparations for ROSLA. This sense of trepidation led to the commissioning of a major survey of school leavers, which was to consider their attitudes to school and staying on. In addition, the humanities were envisaged as providing a crucial means for conveying an understanding of the basic responsibilities of citizenship in the new context of an extended secondary education.[15]

The expansive vision for ROSLA was elaborated further in Working Paper number 2, entitled *Raising the School Leaving Age: a Co-operative Programme of Research and Development*. It asserted that the Schools Council's role was simply to provide schools and LEAs with information in a convenient form about likely needs, expectations, and problems, together with material on experiments, proposals, and implications relating to the new situation.[16] Nevertheless, it took its opportunity to wax lyrically about the prospects for a new approach to secondary education:

> More of the same will not bring success. It is not the "extra year" that makes the difference; the opportunities of a five year course are totally different from those of a four year course. They require new assumptions, attitudes and understandings, and a new approach to the development of a five year course which will be truly secondary in character.[17]

Warming to this theme, it proposed that secondary school pupils needed a "telescope" in order to look back and understand the choices made in the past, and also forward, "in order to acquire some vision, albeit personal, of where they themselves, and humanity in general, are heading."[18] At the same time, they needed a "microscope" in order to gain insights into their own experiences and choices.[19] These ideals brought with them a number of implications for the curriculum but it remained unclear just how far the existing content and methods of the schools would be jettisoned.[20]

The specter of ROSLA led many to believe that the roles of the teacher and social worker were fusing with one another.[21] Welfare professionals saw a great potential in ROSLA to expand their own responsibilities while simultaneously fearing a schools takeover. In the process, "ROSLA pupils" were further demeaned. Education welfare officers in Yorkshire and Lincolnshire warned of an "acute attendance problem" that would result from an increase in the number of children "suffering from a social handicap...emotional and psychological disturbance."[22] Similarly, one youth counseling worker claimed to find young people agreeable but argued that schools had to accept responsibility for "a large number of problem cases, the 11+ failures, misfits in society, delinquents and potential delinquents, the mentally retarded and physically handicapped."[23] Such categories reproduced a deficit view of young people. Moreover, it was often assumed that these pupils would be addressed in emotional rather than intellectual terms. For instance, one project reported that abstract thought was beyond the reach of many children who, instead, might progress through "emotional" aspects of learning.[24] Connecting home and school was becoming more important as a result of ROSLA. But in introducing wider social problems, young people were also being positioned as receptacles of wider social changes rather than as agents of change themselves. A group of home economics teachers situated their subject in the context of technological innovation, immigration, poverty, and the welfare state while arguing that

> teaching the subject...now includes not only the skills, but education in human relationships, home management, nutrition, money management, consumer education, the development of good judgement in relation to buying for the home and of critical faculties in relation to advertising...the preservation of the family as the stable factor in a changing community.[25]

The theme of privatized lifestyles, in which individuals learned to make sensible choices in the commercial marketplace, would prove to be a continuing theme of many ROSLA projects in the coming years.

A subsequent Working Paper produced by the Schools Council explored issues in relation to the humanities for the "young school leaver" in greater depth. As with the earlier work on school science, this program was also developed in collaboration with the Nuffield Foundation as a preliminary study of the form that courses in modern humanities and social studies might take. After visiting over a hundred schools, further education (FE) colleges, and other educational institutions, it confirmed that it was indeed feasible to develop a new curriculum in the humanities for such pupils. In addition, it proposed, somewhat prescriptively, that the content of this curriculum should be about mankind itself, about its immediate environment, and about the worldwide community; that there would be less emphasis on the barriers between traditional subjects and more on their interrelationships; that learning would be based on things that pupils themselves experienced; that courses would tend to exploit local resources and conditions; that teachers would form local groups to develop their own ideas and measure them against each other's experiences; and that many groups and teachers would find it helpful to have a central development team to explore the ideas involved.[26] Following on from this project, Lawrence Stenhouse led a humanities curriculum project that aimed to develop curricula appropriate to all pupils, not just the "non-academic," by exploring "the adolescent's encounter with the adult world."[27] From a similar perspective, a Schools Council English project argued against "class teaching of isolated subjects defined by examination syllabuses." Whereas examinations were seen as divisive, new educational approaches were being designed to start "from individual learning based on experiences related to needs and interests."[28]

However, this impulse to make education open to all led to varying interpretations, which could take on a directly vocational purpose for specified employment in which ability levels were demarcated. Anthony Crosland himself confirmed in Parliament that ROSLA would favor "general education rather than vocational training," but he also conceded that there was scope for connecting work to school.[29] By contrast, the chief executive of the Construction Industry Training Board upset some ministry officials by making some "outlandish statements about the lowness of quality of school leavers,"[30] but couched his case in a language that was more palatable to his audience:

> Not just... "adding an extra year," but rather...refashioning the educational content and treatment of the whole post-primary period...The major problem will concern the boys and girls in the broad average range of mental abilities, for whom leaving school at 16 to commence employment is accepted as the natural situation.[31]

Thus, segregation based upon vocational training could be hatched from within a notion of transforming education for all. ROSLA also gave rise to widespread discussions on work experience, which seemed to provide an answer to the problem of recalcitrant pupils. This appeared to be justified when the Schools Council commissioned survey of school leavers found that a high proportion of young people saw education as a means to achieve vocational goals as opposed to many teachers who were more likely to talk about their aims in relation to a notion of liberal education.[32] Some "over-zealous" headmasters had already been found breaking the law by allowing children to be employed during school hours.[33]

In its organizing strategy, the Schools Council aimed to galvanize schools and teachers through an eclectic range of initiatives, funding, working groups, publications, and general exhortation—a "baker's dozen" approach.[34] Initially it was hoped to reach a peak of activity by September 1967, but the time involved was severely underestimated given the consultative and devolved methods of working.[35] Following an initial flurry of projects that focused upon a range of issues including both integrated studies and subject-based projects, the Schools Council began to discuss how full-scale development work should be commissioned.[36] At one point, it envisaged organizing five national centers that would be able to coordinate work in collaboration with local teachers' centers and schools, but this proposal was withdrawn as being overprescriptive. In the event, only one center was created in the northwest of England, based at the School of Education at Manchester University.[37] Hundreds of teachers and specialists from the Schools Council, colleges of education, government, local inspectorates, and the university would take part in 13 local development centers in the northwest of England, with teachers forming local working groups and providing support for a regional curriculum development group.[38] Elsewhere, the proliferation of teachers' centers and a range of projects funded by the Schools Council constituted the staple of curriculum development for ROSLA. However, even at this early stage it is noticeable that there were murmurings of discontent with this nondirective and persuasive approach that would feed into later calls for more coordination and planning.[39]

Against the desires of some in the Department of Education and Science (DES), the Schools Council also organized a conference on the educational implications of social and economic change.[40] Contributions from teachers were to complement those of philosophers Paul Hirst and Richard Peters and the sociologist Frank Musgrove among others. It was hoped that this event and subsequent publication would help those involved in curriculum planning and development to "see their work in its social, economic and philosophical setting."[41] In terms of curriculum, it was argued that little had changed since the early twentieth century but that educators now stood on the precipice of a revolution:

> To-day, not only in England but throughout Western Europe the curricu-
> lum is on the move...intellectual attitudes to the curriculum and to the
> child have changed; assumptions about the limits of knowledge, the social
> worth of education and the capacities of children which were minority
> views even a decade ago have now almost swept the board.[42]

Despite these high aspirations, informal reports from the conference revealed divides between "teachers" and "academics" who were accused of "arrogance and dogmatism." One civil servant noted that its contribution to planning for ROSLA was limited and many contributions from the floor were "harangues, 'cris de coeur,' bursts of methodist enthusiasm or merely extended anecdotes, rather than constructive steps in a dialogue."[43]

By 1968, the Schools Council began to evaluate its progress and this exposed the difficulties of having responsibility for curriculum development without the power to implement change directly. One review argued, "To cohere, the programme has to establish some connection between its parts: this so far has not been attempted."[44] The aim of generating peak activity by September 1967 rapidly appeared to be over-optimistic as 100–200 schools were expected to become involved in September 1968. In order to reduce the "disparateness" of the Schools Council work, more coordination and publicity were called for.[45] Tensions were also reported between teachers and local authorities, with each not always clear about their respective responsibilities. A small band of enthusiastic teachers appeared to be holding the fort in teachers' centers and little had been achieved with those who were "indifferent to curriculum development."[46] But such teachers were not necessarily the best at communicating ideas to others.[47] Changing attitudes was to be a precursor to wider shifts in approaches to curriculum, which often meant that "open discussion and exchange of views" predominated over "planned local experiment."[48] There was criticism of the northwest project that progress was slow and that many centers tended to specialize in particular subjects and so only involved a small number of teachers.[49] The coordinator, Professor Stephen Wiseman, denied the charges and noted that there had been "no recognition of the very considerable difficulties inevitably involved in creating a large, co-operative venture of this kind, and the patience and persistence necessary to achieve concerted action by a large number of local authorities."[50]

Furthermore, tensions around inequality continued to reverberate with one evaluator noting "a risk of widening the gulf between more and less able children." This became particularly clear in debates over the nature of "compensatory education" and whether new approaches tailored to the "socially handicapped" were needed.[51] H. E. Egner, the head of a boys' school in South Shields, suggested that the principles for working out courses for the "less bright" or "non-traditional" pupils over 16 years of age had still to be developed. He argued that much more attention would be needed for "remedial" and "redemptive" studies for such pupils and that an "agreement about a new minimum educational requirement for all children" was necessary.[52] Such continuing concerns, even at this stage of preparations, belied the officially expressed confidence that ROSLA would usher in a new era of secondary education for all.

Accommodating ROSLA

Curricular preparations for ROSLA were further hampered by the lack of suitable buildings. In 1967, one civil servant scribbled a note warning about a "lack of success of curriculum development for RSLA if buildings not hurried up."[53] Similarly, A. G. R. Britten, the headmaster of Catford Boys comprehensive school, in discussing ROSLA, was quoted in the *Daily Telegraph* asking whether "'many of our existing out-of-date schools', with their crumbling walls, lack of playing space and 'medieval sanitation' are to be forgotten in the march of 'progress?'"[54] It had been the Newsom Report of 1963 that had also outlined what became the accommodation requirements of ROSLA. Roughly 50 percent of the surveyed schools in the sample revealed deficits in what were described as "practical subjects."[55] The only explicitly mentioned "practical" subject targeted for girls was "housecraft" with no mention of typing or office/secretarial training facilities. Deficits were identified in rural studies, woodwork, and metalwork and specialist subjects tended to be less provided for in girls' schools.[56] The Newsom Report surveyed secondary modern schools and concluded starkly that four fifths "fall short of the currently accepted standards, and these are the standards which we regard as inappropriate to the needs of the pupils with whom we are concerned."[57] It argued unequivocally that "the nature of the new educational solutions that are needed will involve major alterations in current school design."[58]

In contrast, future ideas were previewed in a diagram that showed a center designed to house up to 120 "young adults" consisting of

> a central entrance space and snack counter; to the right the lavatories (with a powder room for the girls), and lockers for all personal belongings; to the left, three common rooms. Two of these are connected by sliding folding

doors so that a larger space can be made available for a dance or a lecture. Each room has window seats in bays for small conversational groups, shelves for books and magazines, individual study or writing places, comfortable chairs, carpets and curtains.[59]

Here is a vision of self-directed and motivated young adults cooperating on various types of ongoing project in an environment that is more or less separate and freed from the regime of the wider school, which is for younger pupils. In responding to the maturity of young people, the lines between learning and recreation blurred in a quasi-professional setting signified by soft furnishings, carpets, and magazines.

These ideas overlapped with the burgeoning movement for comprehensive schooling that was marked so publicly with Circular 10/65. However, less noticed, the following year, was the Circular 10/66 on school-building programs that made clear the government's intention to use ROSLA as a means to help achieve comprehensive reorganization:

> The Secretary of State will not approve any new secondary projects...which would be incompatible with the introduction of a non-selective system of secondary education...authorities are asked to describe for each secondary proposal how it will, or could, fit into a comprehensive pattern.

This caused a sharp intake of breath especially among LEA officials who favored selective schooling and asserted their independence from central government. F. Lincoln Ralphs from the Norfolk Education Committee complained to William Alexander that the secretary of state was undermining the "principle of freedom for the local education authorities" in a way he considered "repugnant to the concepts of liberty."[60] However, Crosland was aware that ROSLA and comprehensive reorganization were both large-scale reforms that could not be easily molded to each other in a short timescale and that it would not be possible to adapt buildings for comprehensive purposes in the envisaged timescale. The building program would only cover increased numbers resulting from ROSLA and demographic changes.[61]

An attempt to solve some of these contradictions was found in the crucial *Building Bulletin* no. 32 published in 1967 entitled "Additions for the Fifth Form," which presented to head teachers, governors, and LEA officers a series of developed ideas for special units to accommodate the new cohorts of 16-year-olds.[62] These came to be known as "ROSLA blocks." The designs contained within the bulletin were advertised and promoted for being cheap given the cost limitations that were being imposed within an overall budget of £100 million between the years 1967 and 1971. In

October 1965, J. A. Hudson, the joint head of the Architects and Building Branch (A&B Branch), had prepared a 13-page memorandum that out-lined the potential for the national co-ordination and delivery of prefabri-cated units to school sites for assembly in the shortest time possible. This was sent as a letter to all education authorities and associations that, he argued, might work in broader consortia to deliver ROSLA.[63] It was begin-ning to look like a replay of the financial and administrative arrangements of 1947, and Hudson explicitly recognized the similar situation facing LEAs in the 1940s and the 1960s, but he argued that

> changes in educational ideas over the last twenty years would call for buildings a good deal more sophisticated than the HORSA hut: and the difficulties arising from the probable variations in the pattern of school organization between authorities may well make the job of devising stan-dardized buildings a good deal more complicated than would otherwise be the case.[64]

The solution would therefore be handed over to the architects within the branch headed by William Lacey. The fear within the department was that LEAs would "take the easy way out and, ignoring the educational require-ments...put up rows of huts."[65] Such was the scale of work required of LEAs that it was felt that "a central organization" might be the only viable solution.[66] While this was considered "extreme," it was also felt that the scale of the problem required such a solution.[67]

> If the matter is left to the unaided efforts of local education authorities the more fortunate and the more efficient will solve their own problems. But in many areas the result will be a makeshift assembly of expedients which, from a building point of view, will bring about a deprecation of standards which will be regretted for a generation.[68]

The urgency of the situation was highlighted by a survey of schools located in London, Southampton, West Suffolk, Lancashire, Surrey, and Leeds where 16-year-old pupils were found staying on to follow examinable courses, "studying in all sorts of cubby-holes; in cupboards, under stairs, in stores, along corridors, and so on."[69] The A&B Branch was coming to the view that the problems ROSLA presented would require a fundamental response rather than a piecemeal approach, with new larger comprehensive schools offering courses up to 18 rather than as an addition to the second-ary modern school.[70]

Therefore nearly two years after the decision to move toward ROSLA to 16 had been taken, it is clear that government and local authorities had

not managed to come fully to terms with the scale of practical and implementation issues that such a move would create. As it stood, the existing
system that had been growing since the mid-1940s was not equipped to
absorb yet another full cohort, especially of reluctant older pupils who,
it was believed, would have little interest in or commitment to the more
traditional curriculum.

Doubts and Divisions

Despite the active preparations that were now taking place, there were continuing reservations about the plan for ROSLA to 16 being implemented
in 1970. In an economic context that was steadily worsening at a national
level, these concerned not only the financial implications of the measure
but also touched upon the effects on the schools and teachers as well as
the pupils themselves. As a result, a number of different interest groups
identified ROSLA as a threat to their interests and sniffed an opportunity
to campaign for additional resources.

One sign of disquiet emanated from the columns of the *Guardian*, the
liberal newspaper, which had been associated closely with R. H. Tawney's
educational campaigns in years gone by. Tawney was now dead, and the
newspaper's approach to the topic had become more equivocal. At the
start of 1966, it reported that Sir William Alexander of the Association
of Education Committees (AEC) and the Conservatives' education
spokesperson Sir Edward Boyle would both be speaking at the North of
England Education Conference and were "expected to put pressure on
the Government to will the economic ends as well as the means, or to
postpone the problem." The AEC was indeed carrying out a concerted
campaign threatening that it might withdraw support for ROSLA unless
adequate resources and buildings were in place, and it attempted to draw
in other bodies to this battle including the County Councils Association
and Association of Municipal Corporations.[71] The *Guardian* acknowledged that the Schools Council was leading an "impressive programme"
of research, experiment, and assessment, but felt that economic pressures
were likely to undermine ROSLA and the "harsh decision to postpone this
reform may have to be considered, however disappointing and unwelcome
it may be." Instead, 500 primary schools might be built for 140,000 children.[72] Three days later, the newspaper suggested that plans were being
taken forward "based more on faith than finance" and that there was
"genuine doubt" as to whether it would be possible to introduce ROSLA
by 1970 in view of "the doleful state of economic prospects."[73]

These publicly expressed doubts, from such a source, prompted an immediate protest from one of Tawney's old allies, Lady (Shena) Simon. She wrote to Alastair Hetherington, the editor of the *Guardian*, to complain that the newspaper was rallying opposition to ROSLA rather than seizing the opportunity to bring it about. Tawney, she reminded Hetherington indignantly, had always considered this issue "the acid test of our sincerity in believing in equal opportunity."[74] Simon urged that despite the difficulties involved, ROSLA must be implemented immediately:

> Of course, we cannot have all the new buildings by 1970. But we have never had perfect conditions for raising the age. We have had make-shift schemes at first, temporary classrooms in playgrounds, over-crowded classes, lack of equipment for the older children, yet, after a period, things have settled down, and from the beginning young adolescents have been protected from the labor market for another year.

Moreover, she declared, "Looking back to 1947, can you deny that, on balance, the children profited?"[75] Nevertheless, as economic difficulties increased during 1966, the debate over ROSLA continued.

Sympathizers continued to feel dismayed that so many teachers appeared to oppose ROSLA. The Labour MP and parliamentary private secretary, Ernest Armstrong, found it "shocking" that he received so many letters from aggrieved teachers who vented their frustrations about ROSLA. It appeared plain that ROSLA would provide a better educated and more equal population: "The Newsom child needs the extra year just as much as the high flyer. I cannot believe any teacher can seriously suggest that 'children who will present exceptionally difficult discipline problems' would be better served by being thrown to the labour market and compelled to join a hotchpotch scheme of half-time further education."[76] However, many teachers did indeed feel that they were shouldering an increasing burden of wider social problems. For example, in Nottingham, teachers were reluctant to work in some primary schools and there were calls to rectify deficiencies in buildings given that their initial ROSLA allocation had been minimal. Although the population had not necessarily increased in number, it had certainly changed with issues of "race" coming to the fore:

> The influx of coloured immigrants, who now number 2,570 out of approximately 7,000 pupils in these central areas... is creating overcrowded conditions in bad buildings with the result that it is becoming increasingly difficult to persuade teachers to stay in these schools. Yet the great need of such children is for a stable teacher/pupil relationship... there is a very real danger that... we shall create in the quality of our provision as between the

city centre schools and those in the suburbs a separatism more vicious than anything that has occurred in the field of secondary education.[77]

Moreover, one group that had never been convinced about the case for ROSLA was the National Association of Schoolmasters (NAS), representing the majority of schoolmasters in nonselective secondary schools. Its annual conference in 1966 held at Douglas in the Isle of Man at Easter urged the government to delay ROSLA until staffing and accommodation allowed such a step to be taken and further research could be undertaken on how to provide worthwhile education for less able children over the age of 16.[78] It insisted that county colleges or technical colleges should be used as an alternative to schools for many pupils.[79] The NAS attempted to persuade the Conservative Party, now firmly in opposition after the general election of March 1966, that ROSLA should be postponed. However, Edward Boyle remained unconvinced, partly in order to stay in line with international competitors such as France, which was also raising the school-leaving age to 16, and the United States, where it was already 17 in most states.[80] Other Conservative MPs were much more sympathetic to the NAS position, including Michael Shaw who appealed to Boyle on its behalf: "They claim that the profession was not consulted on the matter and that there seem to be no preparations being made."[81] This protest against ROSLA was maintained at the NAS's annual conference in March 1967, when it carried a motion opposing the measure.[82]

There were particular signs of discontent in Scotland, where the challenges involved in implementing ROSLA were greater than they were in England. Following the initial confirmation of the decision to go forward with ROSLA, the Scottish Education Department (SED) had consulted with LEAs before making a definitive statement on its plans in Circular no. 562, issued in June 1964. This pointed out the need for further study to estimate the number of pupils likely to be affected by ROSLA, the means of developing appropriate courses, and staffing and accommodation requirements. It estimated that out of 82,000 pupils, by 1970–1971, about 20,000 would remain at school for an extra year while another 10,000 would proceed to full-time courses in FE colleges. Therefore, a further 52,000 children in Scotland would require additional facilities with ROSLA in 1970–1971 in addition to the increasing number who would remain in school voluntarily after 16. It proposed that LEAs should make more detailed estimates.[83] It was vital, according to Circular 562, that "effective and satisfying courses" be developed by radically recasting the existing three-year course, for example, by making FE facilities available.[84] Alongside extra buildings, it judged that about 4,000 additional teachers would be required in Scotland with exceptional measures being required to recruit them.[85]

Responses from LEAs in Scotland were lukewarm at best, and in some cases signaled outright opposition to these plans. The education committee of Dumfries County Council discussed the circular and agreed that financial restrictions meant that the proposal to raise the school-leaving age in 1970 should not be implemented.[86] Undeterred, the SED proceeded with detailed plans for a coordinated building program to accommodate ROSLA. Well over one-third of Scottish secondary schools were housed in buildings that had been built or brought up to standard since the War, and many of these would have permanent additions completed by the end of 1970.[87] It envisaged permanent structures based upon industrialized components although, as in England, rejected a return to the Hutting Operation for Raising the School-Leaving Age (HORSA) and its plans would be "very much bigger, rather less standardised, of a higher standard of design and performance and certainly more acceptable in appearance."[88] They would provide multipurpose accommodation designed to meet the needs of vocationally based courses such as engineering, building, retail distribution, and catering, with a range of facilities for formal activities to suit a wide variety of age groups and courses.[89]

These ideas again gave rise to some skepticism and hostility. Fife County Council objected not only to the idea that it might be compelled to comply with a proposal from the SED, but also suggested that temporary wooden buildings should be considered.[90] It was acknowledged that ROSLA to 16 was a "political decision," and that the government "would not dare to undo the measure passed by their predecessors," so that it was unrealistic to suggest such a move.[91] Nevertheless, some continued to counsel a delay in these plans, especially on the grounds of a shortage of teachers in specialist areas.[92]

The discontent being voiced around Scotland found its way back to Westminster. For example, Edward Boyle, the Conservative spokesperson, received a cutting of the *Dundee Courier and Advertiser* in March 1967 criticizing Boyle and the Conservatives for their support for the plan for ROSLA. It claimed that pupils who left school at 15 had usually absorbed all the formal book-learning that they could take and declared: "The Conservatives certainly introduced the plan for the extra year. It was a mistake. They should admit it, and join the growing opposition to the scheme."[93] Boyle remained unmoved by this kind of "ill-informed excitement." He pointed out the disparity in the proportion of pupils leaving school at 15 between different regions, and insisted that ROSLA was "a step towards levelling up opportunities." He added wryly that he was "surprised and rather sorry to see that such a remarkably meretricious and ill-informed piece should appear in a Scottish paper. We have great respect for Scottish education, South of the border."[94] Such lofty sentiments, and the commitment to ROSLA that accompanied them, were soon to be sorely tried.

Delaying Tactics

In 1966, the Labour government was firmly committed to implementing ROSLA within the timescale that was envisaged, as part of an ambitious program designed to expand and modernize all stages of education. During the year that followed, its enthusiasm waned and faltered, as the potential expense of the program came to be scrutinized in the context of a serious economic crisis that affected all areas of public spending, and undermined the government itself.

The education secretary, Anthony Crosland, stood by the commitment that had been made to ROSLA as the Labour government prepared for a further general election at the start of 1966.[95] More children in the south of the country than in the north stayed on at school voluntarily beyond 15, and more middle-class children than working-class children did so. Thus, Crosland claimed, "If we postpone the reform we are penalising the Newsom children. We are further exaggerating the gulf between children who get on and children who don't."[96] Yet it was noted that Crosland failed to provide a public commitment to providing extra money to finance raising the age, while predicting "a very considerable pressure on our resources for as long ahead as I can see."[97] After the general election of March 1966, which Labour won comfortably with a parliamentary majority of more than 100 over the Conservatives, Crosland expressed optimism that within five years there would be virtually no oversize classes in British schools, and that by 1976, the problem would be solved forever through the expansion of colleges of education; the "mirage" of classes of a reasonable size would "become a reality at last."[98] Moreover, in June 1966, in a rare public intervention into the area of education, the prime minister, Harold Wilson, promised that the government would give priority to teacher supply and the provision of school buildings.[99]

These public reassurances concealed growing tensions that were discussed within the government. In February 1966, Crosland shared his anxieties with his cabinet colleagues about the likely financial effects of a growing school population being encouraged by the spread of comprehensive schools and ROSLA to 16. But he remained committed to comprehensive schools and did not "regard it as either politically or educationally

possible to postpone this reform."[100] He proposed to allow LEAs to determine for themselves whether to allow transfer of pupils from primary
schools to secondary schools at the age of 11 or 12 in order to meet targets
for an educationally better comprehensive system and a more economic use
of buildings. Yet such diversity would not by itself go far in meeting the
economic costs of ROSLA or of educational expansion as a whole.

Such worries became increasingly acute in the months that followed.
Growing industrial tensions in the summer of 1966 were followed by visible economic difficulties at a national level. Since the early years of the
Wilson government, there had been the prospect of devaluing the pound
as a currency as a way to restore international confidence in the British
economy, but steps to reduce the deficit and restore the balance of payments were becoming increasingly urgent. Outwardly at least, Crosland
remained bullish about the prospects for education. At the end of June
1967, he enthused at the AEC's annual conference that buildings were
improving, class sizes were being reduced, the level of attainment of school
leavers was rising, and increasing numbers were entering higher education, and the government was committed to "advance on every front at
once."[101]

Yet, even as Crosland voiced these convictions, the assumptions underlying them were being effectively dismantled by the chancellor of the
Exchequer, James Callaghan. In mid-June, he circulated a Treasury review
with a range of cost-cutting options including postponing of ROSLA,
by four years in England and Wales, and by two years in Scotland even
though this might cause "considerable confusion and some waste."[102]
Moreover, it freely conceded that large numbers of pupils still left school
at 15 who could profit from continued education and that postponing
ROSLA would prolong social and geographical inequality.[103] Nevertheless,
Callaghan had identified that significant savings could be made from the
education budget by postponing ROSLA—approximately £45 million by
1970–1971. Other possibilities included charges on school meals and milk,
and reductions in spending on universities.[104] The education secretary was
expected to make proposals to achieve this.

Crosland refused to accept the logic of the chancellor's calculations
and dismissed his recommended savings on education as "unacceptable"
and "totally unreasonable."[105] With regard to ROSLA, he was especially
emphatic:

> I would regard it (quite apart from the merits) as politically out of the ques-
> tion to go back on raising the school leaving age in 1970–71 and break a
> pledge first made by the Conservatives which we have repeatedly endorsed
> (as has Mr Heath [the Conservative Party leader] only a fortnight ago).

Moreover the [Labour] Party would hardly think the leaving age less urgent than colour TV or BBC pop or P1157 or Concord or the Channel Tunnel, all of which we seem to be able to afford.[106]

At a full cabinet meeting to discuss public expenditure held on July 17, Crosland pointed out that spending on education would necessarily increase over the next few years until the early 1970s because of the increase in the number of pupils. Despite his public utterances of the summer of 1966, he accepted that "only slow progress was being made in the reduction in the size of classes and we were unlikely to reduce the average size to 30 until the 1980s."[107] He reiterated his opposition to postponing ROSLA as "politically indefensible." The secretary of state for Scotland, William Ross, also opposed a postponement to ROSLA. In further discussion at this cabinet meeting, strong opposition was expressed to any postponement to ROSLA that might carry long-term risks by strengthening the hand of critics and "there would be a real danger of indefinite postponement."[108] One minister, Richard Crossman, regarded the arguments involved as being finely balanced, as he confided in his diary:

> There's no doubt that most schoolteachers would find the postponement a great relief since they don't know how to handle the crowd of reluctant students they will get and they've no idea how best to use the extra year. There aren't enough teachers or classrooms for it. Of course, socially it's true that this means giving a continuing advantage to the child whose parents decide that he should stay on voluntarily.[109]

Confrontation was clearly looming against a background of failing economic indicators, and ROSLA was to be a prominent and divisive issue in this, just as it had been for the Conservative government in 1963–1964.

An important development took place that was to help to shape this process at the end of August, when the prime minister moved Crosland to another ministerial post in a different department. Crosland's successor as education secretary, Patrick Gordon Walker, was to prove rather more accommodating to Treasury requests than Crosland had been. Nevertheless, ROSLA was not simply a dispute between education and the Treasury, but an issue that affected the government as a whole. It divided ministers because of its bearing on social-class inequalities. First, it illustrated the social differences between counties in the south of England and those in the north where pupils were most likely to leave school at 15. Second, it highlighted the competing priorities between spending on universities, which remained largely the preserve of the middle classes, and spending on "Newsom pupils" who were more likely to be working class. Gordon Walker, like Crosland and Wilson, was a graduate of the University of Oxford, and a large number of ministers in the Labour government were products of elite private schools and prestigious universities. ROSLA was to become a litmus test of social priorities at a time of maximum economic stress.

By autumn, the government was even more deeply embroiled in economic crisis, and finally decided to devalue the currency in order to restore international confidence in sterling. It also aimed to reduce the deficit in the balance of payments including a reduction of £55 million in civil public expenditure; much of it was to be met through postponing ROSLA from 1971 to 1975. While the cabinet agreed to devaluation, it was reticent about cutting expenditure, including the postponement of ROSLA. According to Crossman,

> There was no Cabinet paper. Everything was announced verbally and so fast that there was only just time to write it down. When he'd finished I blew up. I said I'd never seen business done in such a deplorable incompetent way. Roy Jenkins [home secretary] backed me up… "why do it on education? We can't have these decisions taken in a split second." This interjection seemed to hold things up.[110]

It was finally decided that there should be no reference to this measure in the announcement after devaluation, but that the cabinet should reconsider it at an early date.[111]

Callaghan decided to resign after devaluation was announced, leading to a further rapid shift at the highest levels of government as he was moved to the Home Office. In Callaghan's place at the Treasury arrived Roy Jenkins, previously an opponent of harsh reductions in social spending but now responsible for a review of expenditure following the devaluation of the currency. Jenkins was initially hesitant about ROSLA. According to Crossman's diary, he considered giving up the attempt to postpone it until Crossman reminded him that ROSLA's postponement was necessary as part of a package that would also include cuts in the defense budget, such as the scrapping of the F/111 aircraft.[112] ROSLA had again become a significant bargaining counter in a dispute over competing priorities at the highest levels of government.

By the start of January 1968, Jenkins had made up his mind, and was now prepared to estimate that up to £1,000 million was needed from taxation and public expenditure reductions in order to ensure that devaluation would be successful. Moreover, he was insistent that postponing ROSLA would be a key means of achieving these necessary reductions, since it was "one of the few self-contained and coherent decisions that could be taken at once to restrain expenditure and reduce public borrowing and pressure on the construction industry."[113] Indeed, he continued, "I cannot impress on my colleagues too strongly the overwhelming need to take this unpalatable decision."[114]

Jenkins reasoned somewhat tendentiously that nearly everyone now took it for granted that ROSLA would be postponed, and that therefore if it were not to be delayed "we shall cause a double and very serious loss of confidence."[115] A three-year deferment would not only save well over £100 million, but it would be "objected to by few, welcomed by many."[116] At the same time, it would also be necessary to take other measures including the withdrawal of free milk in secondary schools, reducing capital expenditure planned for FE, libraries and the youth service, reducing the increase due for student awards, and raising the price of school meals. However, Jenkins concluded in an uncharacteristically clumsy double-negative, "I must emphasise that there is no substitute in money or in confidence for not deferring RSLA."[117]

If this final statement was open to question, the sentiment behind it was unambiguous. Yet this was still not the end of the matter. The minister of technology, Anthony Wedgwood Benn, was certainly not alone in being strongly opposed to cuts being imposed by the Treasury.[118] At the next cabinet meeting, on January 5, ROSLA was the basis of an "extremely tense discussion."[119] According to Benn's diary account, Gordon Walker introduced it by "more or less agreeing to what Roy [Jenkins] had asked for," rather than concede to cuts in university spending.[120] At this point, the deputy prime minister and foreign secretary George Brown made a dramatic intervention:

> George Brown exploded, "May God forgive you. You send *your* children to university and you would put the interests of the school kids below that of the universities." It took some time to restore order. George Brown then continued his attack, in which he said that education was the basis of class in Britain and if we denied these kids the opportunity of staying in school for an extra year, we would be perpetuating class distinctions.[121]

Several other ministers also declared themselves against postponing the measure, including James Callaghan, who as chancellor of the Exchequer the previous summer had strongly endorsed postponement but who now, as home secretary, opposed it, in Benn's words, "on the grounds of his own experience."[122] Benn himself argued that ROSLA was important because "for the first time ever, school teachers throughout the country would have to take seriously the extra year and wouldn't just be able to shovel the majority of children on to the labour market at fifteen."[123] Crossman, another

diarist at the cabinet table, found Brown's speech "unpleasantly class-con-
scious...strongly implying that no one except the middle-class socialist who
had never felt the pinch or never had a child at a state school could dare to
suggest postponement of the raising of the school-leaving age."[124] Crossman
did not himself take sides in the debate but noted privately: "I don't know
which I disliked more—the pathetic weakness of Gordon Walker or the
outrageous cynicism of Callaghan, who as Chancellor of the Exchequer
had urged the postponement and was now joining the working-class battle
against it."[125] A compromise position emerged in which ROSLA would be
postponed not until 1974–1975 but for only two years, that is, until 1972–
1973. Eventually, the prime minister concluded the argument by judging "a
balance of view in favour of deferment by two years, subject to a firm public
undertaking that there would be no further postponement."[126]

Meanwhile, the hapless secretary for education, Gordon Walker, openly
derided by his cabinet colleagues, was obliged to continue engaging in the
public debate about the future of the school-leaving age. In an interview
with the *Guardian* newspaper, when asked whether the school-leaving age
would be raised, he replied: "I cannot answer that,"[127] although he later
hinted that ROSLA might be a victim of the "heartbreaking decisions"
that were needed over economies in education.[128] In the view of the journal *Education*, he "lacked any spark of enthusiasm, any capacity to show
he cared, any sign that in him education has a fighter who knows what
he believes and loves what he knows."[129] These indications of delay and
indecision spurred advocates of ROSLA to defend the cause. One keen
proponent, Tyrrell Burgess, protested that it would be "ignorant and short-
sighted" to defer the measure.[130] The Assistant Mistresses Association
(AMA), National Union of Teachers (NUT), Trades Union Congress
(TUC), and London Labour Party led attempts to persuade government
ministers to support ROSLA, while the Conservative spokesman Edward
Boyle was reported to be steadfast in his view that this commitment should
be honored.[131]

The final step was taken by the cabinet to delay ROSLA at its next
meeting on January 15, although even this did not pass without incident.
The former education secretary, Anthony Crosland, took this last chance
to urge colleagues to reconsider. The normally impassive formal minutes
of the cabinet for once reflect the tone of the argument:

> Of all the measures decided on this was the one which most obviously con-
> travened the basic principles for which the Government stood; it would be
> damaging to the economy in the long term; and was most likely to provoke
> very strong opposition. It would increase social inequalities, and would
> mean that education was bearing a disproportionate share of the cuts.[132]

Wilson asked whether other cabinet members wished to reopen the issue and nine did so, just short of a majority. This meant that the decision to postpone for two years was confirmed. A frustrated Benn complained afterwards: "The scandal of it all was that if Gordon Walker had voted to reopen it, that would have been ten and we might just have done it...It really was rather disgraceful. Still, that is politics."[133] Even Jenkins later noted in his memoirs his "unease" at the decision, especially given that within the "ludicrously Oxonian Cabinet...it was those deprived of a university education—Brown, Callaghan, Gunter—who protested most."[134] This verdict did not take into account the fervent resistance of Crosland and Benn, both Oxford graduates, nor perhaps the flexible political judgment demonstrated by Callaghan.

The decision to postpone ROSLA until 1972–1973 was announced as part of a range of other measures in the House of Commons the following day. The leader of the House of Lords, Frank Pakenham, another Oxford graduate, resigned in protest. This was a severe setback for ROSLA and critics quickly returned to the fray. Arthur Barton, a long-standing opponent of ROSLA, chose this time to declare that "I'm not crying." According to Barton, "At classroom floor level, a wave of relief swept through, cooling brows that if not exactly fevered have been knit in some perplexity for some time now."[135] Anxious teachers wrote to support Barton's contribution. This reaction raised fears as to whether ROSLA to 16 would take place at all especially in the context of growing political and economic problems. For now, with issues of curriculum and building also still unresolved, the waiting for ROSLA would go on.

Chapter 7

Preparing for ROSLA 1968–1972

Having delayed the raising of the school-leaving age (ROSLA) for two years, conflicts resurfaced in debates on readiness. Opponents held out the hope that it might still be rescinded, or at least delayed and diluted further. Some preparations briefly came to a halt as it remained far from certain that ROSLA would be introduced on time. Continuing problems over buildings and teacher supply also hindered plans for this development. Nevertheless, significant progress was made in a number of key areas that reflected the potential importance of ROSLA as both an educational and social initiative. This continued after the Labour government was defeated in a general election in 1970 and a Conservative government was elected. Debates over ROSLA were closely related to broader issues of social change, democracy, and citizenship. In addition, the prospect of an extra year in school encouraged new ideas for the school curriculum and challenged entrenched assumptions about ability. An expanding vision of providing a real secondary education for all underpinned these developments.

Following through with ROSLA

At the start of 1969, the *Times Education Supplement* lamented that "having put off the raising of the school leaving age for two years, we are still apparently no better prepared for it."[1] Doubts were expressed that the measure might never be implemented at all. This created a space for criticisms by conservative papers such as the *Daily Telegraph*, which even in April 1971 castigated ROSLA as "little short of lunatic."[2]

Such sharp denunciations drew upon broader forces that were impinging upon education. An educational storm was gathering during the 1960s and the 1970s and, from 1969, the Black Papers on Education held education to account for a sense of breakdown and decline.[3] Widening political and social divisions emerged as the educational system received higher levels of government expenditure and public attention. The symbolic moment of James Callaghan's speech to launch a self-styled "Great Debate" at Ruskin College in 1976 marked this shift very publicly, but he was also responding to a previous chain of events. The visibility of ROSLA can be understood in this context.

Prevarication over ROSLA continued as the date of implementation came closer. As late as April 1971, William Alexander at the Association of Education Committees (AEC) noted that there remained "several matters" concerning ROSLA that the Department of Education and Science (DES) "cannot very well leave unresolved for very much longer."[4] In 1964, it had not been clear exactly what the extra year group would be doing in their final year, and a cloud of indecision still hung over the issue. Many were enticed by continuing calls for greater levels of vocational education related to life outside the school. Earlier in the century, proposals for continuation schools and county colleges had been submerged beneath the priority accorded to the school-leaving age. Now the motivations behind them surfaced in new ways. A desire to avoid the negative consequences of compelling unwilling teenagers to remain in schools had given rise to the possibility that the fifth year might be spent in further education (FE) colleges. A number of people had flirted with this idea, including Edward Boyle, and it found expression across the political spectrum. In 1968, for example, the Conservative Education Policy Group noted that "careful consideration" should be given to "the types of institution in which the last year of compulsory education should be spent."[5]

Edward Short, the secretary of state for education and science from 1968 until 1970, also courted the idea that a final year of compulsory education could be spent in a further education college in appropriate cases. This appeared to square with the lowering of the age of majority from 21 to 18 following the Family Law Reform Act of 1969. Accordingly, he sent the proposal out for consultation with educational representatives. William Alexander was fully supportive, arguing that FE colleges should not be too restricted: "I have no doubt whatever that our people will welcome the suggestion."[6] However, consultations sparked counterarguments in favor of retaining pupils in schools. Alexander later noted that his own committee was in fact wary of the proposal, in part because of the difficulty of guaranteeing equality of services between schools and FE colleges, which might "reduce the good effects of raising the school leaving age."[7] Schools feared that FE colleges or parents would choose which students attended colleges. Mutual anxieties arose that colleges would be allowed to run Certificate of Secondary Education (CSE) and 'O' level courses or, conversely, that schools would develop vocational qualifications.[8] As in the past, the bout of enthusiasm for diversifying educational routes in the final years of schooling proved short-lived. Rather than offering a bridgehead to a more varied education system, limited forms of cooperation between schools and FE were developed through linked courses that helped to manage temporary shortages and allow schools to access the vocational resources of colleges.

Outside the world of education, the school-leaving age could appear to be a pliable reform that might support plans in other areas. In 1971, the *National Institute Economic Review* recommended bringing forward the implementation of ROSLA by one year to help address a potential increase in unemployment.[9] Flustered civil servants predicted "chaos" given the sizeable numbers of teachers and buildings still required, let alone that the "conscripted 15–26 year olds... might well feel aggrieved at the unexpected compulsion."[10] Less than half of the additional building for ROSLA would be ready by September 1972, and there remained a shortfall of 150,000 school places. In Scotland, the proposal was described as "political suicide" in view of the greater shortage of teachers.[11] The permanent secretary William Pile was caught unawares that this proposal had even been made although he rapidly questioned its practicability.[12] The episode was indicative of the way in which education was commonly viewed as playing a secondary role to other areas of policy.

Employment issues also became central to debates on school-leaving dates. Anthony Crosland had noted the "powerful arguments" in favor of a single leaving date as opposed to the Easter and Summer leaving dates that had been established by the 1962 Education Act.[13] The Manchester Education Committee was typical in favoring a single date on the grounds that "too many young people too easily write themselves off educationally at an early age."[14] However, the minister of labour Ray Gunter countered that those who would suffer from a single leaving date would be "the less able, the 'Newsom' children, and the handicapped." He elaborated that a process of "natural selection" helped the "more able" to remain until the summer and take advantage of apprenticeships, whereas the "the less able, many of whom are liable to pose placing problems, are able to enter employment at Easter."[15] Against his own better judgment, in 1969, Edward Short decided against introducing a single date.[16] One Inner London Education Authority (ILEA) document noted presciently that schools would face considerable difficulties in enforcing a summer leaving date once the school-leaving age had been raised.[17] Changing the leaving date would have impacted upon the intricate negotiation of building allocations for

ROSLA, and there was no desire in the DES to bring this to the attention of the Treasury.[18]

While the gestation of these ideas was hastened by ROSLA, material constraints were limiting the scope for action. The condition of school buildings was a crucial structural factor in both enabling and inhibiting educational plans for ROSLA. From 1964 to 1972, the implications of ROSLA for the school building program came under detailed scrutiny. By 1968, the problem had become acute and was compounded by the two-year delay. Following Circular 6/68, problems arose from the restriction of school building, starts which fell from 101 in 1968 to 83 in 1969 and 79 in 1970. Postponing new starts resulted in the largest building expenditure for ROSLA falling in the same year that it was to be introduced. Herbert Andrew, the permanent undersecretary at the DES, confirmed to the secretary of state: "In effect we should start the year with a backlog of projects to be started almost as big as the announced programme."[19] Pressures on local education authorities (LEAs) were ratcheted up in the face of these squeezed timescales. The hutted provision that Architects and Building Branch (A&B Branch) had been so concerned about became an option to be taken up alongside the designs contained within Building Bulletin 32. Cheap units that would separate older students from the main school, manufactured off-site and assembled in a matter of days during school holidays, could be rolled out in much the same way as the Hutting Operation for Raising the School-Leaving Age (HORSA) program of two decades earlier.

The effect of delay was judged to be "particularly serious" for schools that tied ROSLA to comprehensive reorganization.[20] ROSLA building allocations were intended to help nurture comprehensivization by providing additional specialist facilities, by enabling the enlargement of schools and by providing middle schools.[21] But the delay in the leaving age provided a pretext for inaction on comprehensive secondary reorganization, and Herbert Andrew suspected LEAs of using ROSLA as an excuse to further delay their reorganization plans.[22] Solutions to the perceived threat to selective schooling were indeed bubbling under the surface in areas where a strong body of opinion favored the retention of grammar schools.

The desire for centralized solutions to building problems came across clearly in the complaints of P. S. Litton at the DES who argued that local authority attitudes were "not conducive to the efficient planning and execution of building work." He bemoaned "a disinclination to use the R.S.L.A. units (which involve careful overall planning and pre-ordering)...This is not logical, but betrays a passive 'wait and see' attitude."[23] However, as secretary of state from 1970, Margaret Thatcher proclaimed that she was "delighted by the imaginative response" from LEAs that had adopted ROSLA units.[24] In March 1972, the DES was able to report on a varied pattern of preparedness that arose not only from short-term expediency but also reflected local political, social, and economic environments. A&B designs proved popular in Nottingham and Redbridge, while locally devised variants were developed in Surrey with an emphasis upon practical, craft areas and flexible spaces. Early assumptions about building for ROSLA had been to include adaptable rooms of varying sizes that would enable small group work alongside social areas where more mature fifth formers would "cast off the schoolboy or schoolgirl image and encourage their own feelings of adult-hood."[25]

Smaller and more southern areas tended to be less affected where existing staying-on to 16 rates were, by the late 1960s, already somewhere between 50 and 60 percent. By contrast, larger authorities such as Lancashire received building grants for ROSLA in excess of £6 million, which made detailed planning difficult and was conducive to the uptake of ROSLA blocks. The ONWARD consortium and a single builder provided a series of ROSLA units at a cost approaching £3 million.[26] By contrast, across the Pennines in West Yorkshire, it was claimed that the majority of ROSLA units were "designed individually to suit the differing requirements of each school" although, in reality, requests for varying the design and layout of these units had met with financial obstacles.[27]

Debates on preparation for ROSLA regularly focused upon the other key tangible issues of teacher numbers. In the early 1960s, this had appeared to be a major stumbling block to reform. It was a small number of optimists who were confident that enough teachers could be trained in time and teachers warned of oversize classes packed with recalcitrant pupils,[28] while Conservative Party leaders were alarmed at the prospect of "severely oversize classes."[29] The National Union of Teachers (NUT) also complained of DES "complacency" over teacher supply, which would "retard the expansion of educational opportunities resulting from ROSLA."[30]

In the event, considerable progress was made in recruiting and training additional teachers prior to 1972. While overall numbers in public debates could appear drastic, the actual impact on many individual schools was more limited. For instance, in Eastbourne it was expected that an additional 250–300 pupils would require an extra 14 teachers despite a claim for additional numbers to handle the "considerable stress" of teaching ROSLA pupils.[31] In any case, ROSLA was part of general increases in the school population. In Essex between 1970 and 1975, there was an expansion of 24,000 pupils, of which only 6,500 were due to ROSLA. Some areas, such as Cheshire, Nottingham, Manchester, and Bristol, pursued an active policy to "stockpile" teachers prior to 1972, which created more time to devote to ROSLA.[32] In 1970, it was considered tolerable that ratios might rise albeit temporarily from 17:1 to 18.1:1 by 1973–1974.[33]

Indeed, Edward Short was able to proclaim confidently in Parliament that "the schools will be able to take the strain without any difficulty."[34] In 1969, the DES argued that the overall numbers of teachers had increased from 283,000 in 1963 to 360,000 by 1969 and would reach an expected 445,000 by 1975/76.[35] However, this situation was not equally distributed across the United Kingdom and warning signs remained in Scotland, where a 3,000 shortfall in teacher numbers was predicted.[36] Reflecting these pressures, the Education Institute of Scotland, supported by many LEAs, requested a further two-year delay in ROSLA.[37] In addition, the effect of pupil numbers impacted differentially across schools where pupil growth rates could vary drastically. Shortages were felt in specific subjects, a typical example being Haringey where posts for crafts, vocational, and "leisure" subjects remained unfilled.[38]

After 1968, in a period of moderate improvement in the national economy, cross-party support for ROSLA finally helped to ensure that there were no further delays. Despite a large number of vocal critics, abandonment was judged to be too risky. International developments helped to convince doubters as both France and Denmark raised their leaving ages by 2 years to 16. ROSLA helped address concerns about equality of opportunity. A DES publication argued that investment in higher education had benefited the middle classes but ROSLA "should redress the balance in the interests of the entire school population."[39] In addition, ROSLA was to equalize regional disparities. The *Daily Express* argued that ROSLA would help the north, because pupils in the southeast were twice as likely to stay on until 16 as those in the north.[40]

From 1970, Margaret Thatcher, as the incoming secretary of state for education and science, maintained a commitment to ROSLA despite harboring fears about truancy and discipline in schools. The Conservative government claimed to be honoring a pledge originally made in the Education Act of 1944, which was reaffirmed in January 1964 by Douglas-Home's government. At an education seminar in London in March 1971, Thatcher argued that the problem of the "really disruptive child" did not justify a further postponement of ROSLA.[41] In June, Lord Belstead, the parliamentary undersecretary of state at the DES, acknowledged that many pupils and parents were still to understand the advantages of ROSLA but confirmed that the government believed

> that in the long term the advantages to be gained both individually and nationally are very great indeed...one of our many objectives must be to try to meet the educational needs of older children by providing a five-year course for all secondary pupils with the opportunity for staying on longer if they wish.[42]

Thatcher defended ROSLA even in the face of late challenges from political allies. In Scotland, where there remained strong concerns about staffing, it was proposed that permissive legislation might be brought in across Britain to allow LEAs to defer ROSLA if they faced an impossible staffing situation.[43] Hasty telephone calls to the DES permanent secretary, Wilma Harte, at the DES in London found no enthusiasm for such a course of action, nor for a specifically Scottish Bill to this effect.[44] Harte let it be known that Thatcher did from time to time show impatience with the idea of ROSLA, especially when she was "got at" by grammar school teachers and head teachers, but that she had no intention of "reneging" on this commitment.[45] Representatives of the three main teachers' organizations in Scotland met the undersecretary of state at the Scottish Office, Edward Taylor, in June 1971 to hand him a petition with 16,752 signatures—more than 80 percent of all the secondary teachers in Scotland—demanding a further postponement of ROSLA.[46] The government remained unmoved.

At the start of 1972, when prime minister Edward Heath asked Thatcher about plans for the curriculum following ROSLA, she explained that the government had no power to dictate the school curriculum, but that the Schools Council was providing useful work in this area and that there were clear educational benefits for those who stayed on at school for an extra year. She noted that at present 91 percent of those who left school at 15 had no General Certificate of Education (GCE) or CSE qualifications, but that this was true of only 7 percent of those who left school at 16.[47] Accordingly, she went on to report to the House of Commons that preparations had generally been thorough and that "resources are being applied effectively and sensibly," truancy and discipline problems had been exaggerated, over 60 areas had built ROSLA units, 100 areas were actively publicizing and promoting ROSLA, and 102 operating link courses; 480 teachers' centers had been established and Schools Council projects formed the basis of preparations in 80 local authorities. Thatcher considered that this provided a basis for optimism: "All told, there are grounds for confidence that the reform will be constructively and effectively implemented."[48]

ROSLA had become a significant aspect of the government's general program of reform in education. As the economy continued to grow, Mrs Thatcher felt able to proceed to a ten-year strategy with the publication of a White Paper, *Education: A Framework for Expansion*, at the end of 1972.[49] This was a "sensibly progressive" program, in the words of the *Guardian* newspaper, that was to constitute the high-water mark of the postwar expansion and reform of the education service.[50] The achievement of ROSLA to the age of 16 was made at the very same time, and would have proved more difficult if it had been left any later.

Social Change and Democracy

Building programs, although significant, on their own, did not constitute adequate preparations for ROSLA but were tied into wider social needs. In 1969, a government press release on the ROSLA building program spoke of the need to help the young school leaver establish "a relationship with his society." Two elements were identified—"the stress on values, attitudes and expectations" in addition to ensuring that pupils are "better equipped to earn a living, and to use their leisure in a satisfying way." An integrated secondary course was needed to help young people become more critical, articulate, and mature.[51]

The emergence of secondary education for all was part of a wider story of social change in British society, which, in the 1960s, became engulfed in tensions over modernity and tradition. Assumptions about discipline, authority, and order came under pressure from a number of quarters, and debates on ROSLA were closely tied into perceived economic change. For example, *The Times* supplemented its moral promptings for greater equality of opportunity with economic and social argument about the new skills and greater adaptability that would be required in future conditions of fast technological change.[52] These ideas were widely shared. The Labour MP Arthur Davidson argued in *The Accrington Observer* that ROSLA was responding to a "fast-moving age of technological change," which had undermined many assumptions across society. The "bogy of a new average competence," he observed, was "outstripping us," not only in commerce and industry but also in "the law, the trade unions, the factories, and even in social welfare."[53]

ROSLA incubated new challenges to a sense of traditionalism in education reflecting a need to shift from "giving information and precepts by which to live" toward "providing children with the ability to look at a problem, work out a number of possible solutions, evaluate these and chose the best solution."[54] According to the Schools Council, values and attitudes and the ability to learn were to be exalted over memorizing an exact body of knowledge.[55] Even among supporters of ROSLA, the rate of social change created a "degree of anxiety" about the future.[56] The exact implications of these changes were not clear although they unleashed a general willingness to countenance change that directly affected the role of teachers, pupils, and parents. Edward Short, the secretary of state for education, noted that the effect of war had "turned our society upside down," and he criticized schools that thought that "anarchy is the only alternative to the cane."[57] Schools were expected to become "a more integrated part of life" and to foster educational relationships based upon active inquiry and mutual respect. They faced the difficult task of recognizing the growing maturity of school pupils, as "more than school children," while also treating them as not ready for full-time work.[58]

In Brighton, a group of teachers faced multiple pressures, not least from the mass media and commercial forces that were putting pupils "at the mercy of the entrepreneurs of instant teenage fashion,"[59] and undermining the "moral fibre" and traditions inherited from the grammar and public schools. ROSLA appeared to be maintaining discipline by a "confidence trick," whereas an "educational revolution" was required:

> The young adult of average ability is asking to be educated more than ever before, but probably, for the first time is seeking a purpose previously demanded only by the most intelligent. The negative picture is dismal. If these trends and desires are not acknowledged then conflict must follow and the first to suffer will be the child and the teacher.[60]

In this sense, ROSLA unleashed democratic forces: "We can no longer teach children only what we as teachers think is good for them. Consideration must be given to what they themselves feel is relevant."[61] At the very least, pupils had to be "consulted about their own programmes."[62] Underpinning these debates was the wider diaspora of student dissent and circulation of radical ideas about the necessity to reconfigure education from the position of the learner. From 1968, student protests became widespread and would involve some school students, although relatively few direct references to this upsurge can be found in debates on ROSLA. Even Her Majesty's Inspectorate (HMI) thought it "disquieting" that, at a time of widespread student discontent, voluntary stayers on revealed "a near-conformity of view about school, examinations and life, and a constellation of associated attitudes," reflecting an over-paternalistic and formal attitude on the part of the school.[63] A professor of chemical education crossed these boundaries in arguing that

> if we are genuinely to train people to think and act independently, we must be prepared for them to act against the educator and, logically, not be surprised if they act against society...whatever we choose as education objectives—pupils must be brought into the picture or we shall be "Sorbonned."[64]

This problem could not be resolved in the short term given existing assumptions and educational structures where the inertia of educational thinking lagged behind such hopeful ideas. A survey on ROSLA in West Yorkshire, where the progressive Alec Clegg held sway, lamented that no evidence could be found that "this provision would involve the pupils in more choice about their education, more consultation about its objects, or more participation in carrying out the programme."[65]

The example of Lancashire helps to illustrate the way in which democratic impulses were in fact redirected into a concern with personal relationships. Some schools gave pupils "a large measure of self-government" in organizing their social life.[66] But, given the pressures on buildings, such social spaces were being squeezed and this was only going to be a short-term measure. Nevertheless, it was claimed that changing social attitudes, pastoral care, and guidance represented a transformation "fundamental to the educational process."[67] Informal relationships between staff and pupils, particularly through clubs, residential activity, and nonclassroom environments were considered essential to "recover relationships." In a survey of schools in the Midlands, flexible courses that respected pupils' maturity led to them becoming "less self centred as they attempted to communicate their own feelings and tried to understand how their contemporaries felt."[68] According to this viewpoint, surface alternations in curriculum and pedagogy were inadequate unless they operated as a vehicle for deeper pupil-teacher relationships as one survey revealed in West Yorkshire: "Pseudo realism abounds often dictated by the apparent refusal of the teacher to look beyond his own experience for the motive influences in the child's culture and day to day activities."[69]

Preparations for ROSLA highlighted the imputed passivity of pupils in constructing a vision of the future lives of children. For instance, home economics pilot projects revealed tensions over home life, consumerism, and social change. One study found that fourth-year pupils tended to see the personal aspect of home economics in terms of good grooming and being treated as an adult, while to the older pupils it was linked with their own sense of identity as acceptable individuals in society.[70] In Lancashire, courses offered "realistic tuition in home ownership, management of money, social and family relationships, consumer education, child care, and so on."[71] This was at a time when approximately 50 percent of homes nationally were owner occupied, and the percentage for Lancashire ROSLA pupils, one would expect, was much lower.[72] Outward-looking courses were often popular with pupils who "respond to tasks which they see as being of benefit to the community as well as being of benefit to themselves."[73] But public participation and citizenship were sharply contained in terms of leisure, volunteering, and helping others, rarely breaking out, for instance, into trade union activity or forms of collective community action. In this way, ROSLA contributed to wider social changes. The Thatcher revolution in the 1980s built upon changing social expectations that had been developing in previous decades. Despite the open critique of consumerism entailed in preparations for ROSLA, many of the new courses confirmed a particular form of privatization that would later harden into a social assumption. The idea that pupils might actively mold the world through economic, political, social, and cultural means registered much less clearly.

Changing relationships further impacted upon new forms of teacher involvement as a result of ROSLA. Collaboration among teachers helped counteract their traditional isolation and "loneliness" through fostering cooperative teaching, discussions, and joint production of materials at teachers' centers.[74] Faced with "a sense of isolation and inadequacy," one group of teachers argued that "it is only by sharing ideas, experiences and problems in a co-operative effort with colleagues in their own and other schools that teachers can hope to solve in a professional way the difficulties posed by ROSLA."[75]

The perceived social problems that came with ROSLA meant that greater levels of communication and support were required, for example between house tutors, heads of years, heads of department, careers advisors, and others.[76] There were increasing calls for teachers to sit on governing bodies. Yet teachers were not a coherent force and ROSLA stimulated discord:

> One of the biggest obstacles to achieving success in any ROSLA programme will be the division amongst staff...in their attitudes to ROSLA itself; on relationships with children; on patterns of school organisation; on content; on integration; on modes of teaching and learning.[77]

Strong leadership was often required to overcome these schisms and plan "the total direction of the school."[78]

Moreover, in preparation for ROSLA, there was a realization that the support of parents was becoming essential. In Haringey, it was found that "a complex pattern of choices...necessitates close consultations with the parents."[79] Negative reasons included the desire to diminish absenteeism and antisocial behavior, which it was believed many parents condoned.[80] However, as with teachers, this was far from settled.[81] The issue temporarily ignited the tense relations between the DES and local authorities. When, in 1971, the DES proposed a leaflet on ROSLA to parents to be distributed through local authorities, the response to this evidence of central government encroachment was "hostile."[82] LEAs found the leaflet "condescending" in its claim that "staying on at school means staying on at *school.*" These strong reactions indicated the rising status of parental opinion in education as a result of ROSLA.[83]

The New Curriculum

Harnessing the commitment of pupils, parents, and teachers, all reflected the need for detailed planning, a feature very evident in curricular preparations for ROSLA. The expansion of comprehensive reorganization created further planning issues. Both ROSLA and comprehensive schools were commonly viewed as innovative, groundbreaking reforms that responded to the growing pace and complexity of social change. At times, the two blended intimately and it proved hard to extricate them from each other. In Cornwall, a rural county with a dispersed population, reorganization allowed "positive forward planning for all pupils rather than as an RSLA appendage."[84] In some cases, comprehensivization had supported the establishment of larger departments that cut across subject headings and facilitated plans for ROSLA.[85] Some schools in West Yorkshire used ROSLA as a means to change the whole secondary course in ending banding systems—so-called package deals—or introducing integrated studies.[86] Moreover, many LEAs were adamant in their desire to avoid two groups of students: Bournemouth was to distribute the new fifth year into various CSE groups; Ealing and Dudley adopted a common core curriculum, while Richmond had opted for block timetabling, integrated courses, and team teaching. In Haringey, it was felt that great benefits derived from the fact that the Borough had gone comprehensive before ROSLA and was now able to concentrate upon "compensating for the difficult home and cultural circumstances of the children,"[87] a view that revealed prevailing ideas of educational deficit. Paradoxically, conservatism could also lead to inclusive approaches. In Huntingdon and Peterborough, where comprehensive plans were being developed, some schools had already developed options systems and an apparent lack of preparation for ROSLA revealed a quiet confidence in their capacity. Rather than viewing ROSLA as a revolutionary crescendo in education, it was argued that "they can handle any problems that arise without any fundamental change of methods."[88]

ROSLA significantly accelerated the pace of curriculum reform to such an extent that it almost became synonymous with particular changes. The Schools Council had problematized subject divisions and integrated studies were to break down these barriers and offer the right level of relevance and maturity for 15-year-olds. In Scotland, it was argued forcefully that for nonacademic pupils there should be a move away from separate subjects in favor of themes such as preparation for leisure and employment, social and moral education, which would support "the basic skills of communication and mathematics."[89] Small group work, flexible timetabling, and blocked-off periods allowed some of these needs to be met. A senior inspector,

Murray White, estimated that an additional teacher would be needed for each group of 11–12 extra pupils, otherwise ROSLA pupils would be forced into "CSE courses inappropriate to their needs and capabilities."[90] Given the autonomy of schools and teachers, preparations for ROSLA were built around the enthusiasm and relationships of teachers and resulted in a striking diversity:

> INTEGRATION of separate disciplines into new areas is a main feature: community studies, technological studies, cultural studies (Norwich); health education, domestic studies, social education are part of the special courses devised by the NW Curriculum Development Project in use in Manchester; design, environmental studies, community studies are examples from Bucks; personal relationships from Nottinghamshire.[91]

Outward-looking courses with a strong practical element were proliferating with visits to hospitals, play groups, and work places, urban environment projects as well as residential courses.[92] New technologies were seen as part of a ROSLA response. In order to appeal to students and widen their horizons, one school judged that "all the media of popular culture—music, films, theatre, journalism, sound broadcasting and television" would be necessary.[93] One ROSLA block was, typically, kitted out with a cine projector, overhead projector, slide/loop projector, record player, and tape recorder.[94]

In constructing a balanced and rounded curriculum for the "less able," preparations for ROSLA aimed to break free from the constraints of examinations. A sympathy for wide-ranging nonexamination courses led, in some cases, to eulogies for the disappearing secondary moderns. According to one HMI survey of non-selective secondary schools, for example, these

> have a fine, liberal tradition of education and Her Majesty's Inspectors would wish strongly to support head teachers and staff in maintaining and developing that tradition. Sometimes this will mean protecting the pupils and the curriculum against the narrowing effects of outside pressures including examinations.[95]

By capturing the strengths of liberal education, especially in practical and aesthetic subjects and tied to citizenship, such a tradition might still be adapted to the needs of ROSLA. Indeed, the essence of ROSLA was at times conceived as the development of nonexamination courses.[96] Some schools began to reduce the number of examination choices in order to nurture social, cultural, and craft activities.[97] Certificates were developed to recognize social and personal qualities. Burton on Trent had a "passing out" certificate, Norwich a "certificate of endeavour," and Swindon a "record of personal achievement," where it was claimed that exams were becoming "meaningless and irrelevant."[98] According to one head teacher, employers did not want to know "where the pupil fell on the road to a medieval ideal of scholarship," but about specific aptitudes, social, emotional, and physical, as well as about intellectual skills.[99] Southend on Sea was judged to be "examination ridden" and its "internal certificate of achievement" included "any achievement, such as ability to work a projector."[100] HMI favored this development and noted that "persistence, punctuality and integrity are at least as important as intelligence quotient in achievement."[101] These alternatives were placed alongside existing exam structures and responded to a perceived "less able" ROSLA pupil.

This was a contradictory development as examinations continued to play a significant role in preparations for ROSLA. The introduction of the new CSE exam in 1965 attracted many teachers to develop internally examined versions of the new exam under the Mode III category and schools commonly expected that examination enrolments would increase as a basic effect of ROSLA.[102] In some cases, the double entry of pupils into CSE and 'O' level exams created an "extreme pressure."[103] A revealing survey in West Yorkshire found that schools were happy to make exams available to increasing numbers of pupils but were less sympathetic to the idea of offering broad nonexamination courses for the more able.[104]

The restraining influence of examinations on ROSLA also highlighted other problems. Critics pointed to problems with integrated blocked-off courses: the difficulty of grasping the "intellectual notions of integration,"[105] the unbalanced curriculum, insufficient expertise in teaching, lack of liaison between subject departments, and the need to choose between "two entirely different routes at the end of the third year—examination and non-examination."[106] The claim that one school was "more concerned with the development of pupils than the content of their studies" proved difficult to put into practice because the heavy demands of Nuffield science projects left only scarce resources for nonexamination science pupils.[107] Integrated courses were not always the panacea as some held them to be, especially when subject-based approaches offered greater depth and consistency.

These voluble criticisms were related to many undercover acts of resistance and prevarication over ROSLA that were motivated by personal impulses and feelings over what it meant to be a teacher. In West Yorkshire, a sharp distinction was perceived between teachers who elevated "academic values above individual pupil needs" and "the less subject-orientated teachers (usually in temporary roles—probationers, part-timers, unstable) who often lack status and responsibility but try to hold the fort."[108] In Southend, over a three-year period, subject-working parties of teachers produced a report that stimulated a lot of talk but little action, which HMI found "very disappointing."[109]

Curricular weaknesses and contradictory approaches to examinations also correlated with a lack of planning. By the early 1970s, planning for ROSLA was gaining force, but many schemes remained at a rudimentary stage, notably where schools were not familiar with planning for the future. A rising level of reform was seen to be squeezing out space for thinking ahead on ROSLA:

> Some schools who wished to make innovations had a multiplicity of other problems—building programmes, rapid expansion, going comprehensive and so on—to resolve, and had to spend more time on the problems of the moment and less on those of the future than they would have wished.[110]

HMIs continued to discover schools, head teachers, and LEAs that were still at an early stage in their planning and vague about their intentions.[111] Even in East Sussex where younger pupils were "already being prepared to accept the value of a five year course," the director of education wrote to the DES as late as January 1972 that by experimenting over the following few months "schools hope to have developed courses capable of sustaining the interest of pupils who would formerly have left school at the age of 15."[112]

The London Borough of Barking had developed 36 courses but only involved a minority of teachers and "have not been well prepared."[113] This was worrying since the Borough had a "tradition of early leaving."[114] By contrast, neighboring Redbridge enjoyed a high rate of staying on, at 60–65 percent, yet this also gave rise to "complacency" on ROSLA and working-party meetings had met with a "tepid response."[115] The tardiness of these actions and aspirations struck an ominous chord among curriculum reformers in the Schools Council who realized that a more proactive line might be needed. As one Schools Council statement observed, "Evidence continues to accumulate that the Council ought to try to formulate some advice to heads about how to assimilate Council projects in planning their curriculum."[116]

Schools Council ideas took time to proliferate. Much of the readiness for ROSLA depended upon the work of individual teachers, but this proved difficult in a divided system in which schools and teachers guarded their autonomy. For instance, tensions arose over the pace and level of progress and coordination of the North West Curriculum Development Project.[117] Block courses for "slow learners only" were based on much "opportunism rather than planning." Long-term approaches were needed to avoid repetition and fragmentation: "There are grave dangers in continual improvisation and opportunism."[118] Such forebodings did not augur well for the implementation of ROSLA.

The new ideas emanating from ROSLA underestimated the inertia of educational ideas and entrenched institutional structures. In a number of areas, ROSLA was tamed and caged within inherited structures and assumptions about different needs and abilities. At St Anselm's Catholic School in Canterbury, an extreme version of this developed when expansion was viewed in terms of two diverging streams of activity, with the sixth form students needing two seminar rooms "with all the facilities required." By contrast, "to meet the requirements of the pupils with the lower I.Q. it would be useful to have a large shed where they can have some instruction in such activities as car maintenance, cement mixing, brick-laying, gardening etc."[119] The chief education officer for Canterbury further exposed these priorities in responding to DES circular 8/71, when he was not immediately able to locate any outward-looking courses although, upon searching, he found a number of community service schemes, recreational and residential experiences, careers work, and those of general teenage interest, all focused upon the "non-examination child."[120]

The debate on "divisive and non-divisive courses" was a vexed issue that generated debate and experimentation. Many educationists who were sympathetic to ROSLA retained fixed assumptions about differing abilities. The desire not to foster an "undesirable dichotomy" between students existed alongside a contradictory determination to tailor the curriculum to needs and abilities. Brighton teachers, while noting that "ROSLA/Newsom" courses carried the stigma of being suitable only for the "chuck-outs," nevertheless themselves focused upon "the average and below average children."[121] This tension was apparent in one school where a "separate but equal" policy seems to have been prevalent: "There is no 'sink' in this school. Non-academic pupils, especially those taking the humanities course, are clearly receiving a degree of attention to match that given to the academic, and attitudes are good."[122] Throughout the 1950s and the 1960s, it is possible to chart these continuing but partial attempts to break away from ideas of fixed ability that ROSLA helped to bring to a head. HMI offered a telling example when it expressed a sense of pleasant surprise at the enthusiasm and "industrious application" of students, tempered by their "lesser natural ability," which resulted only in "moderate success."[123]

The crucial definition of ability was extremely variable in different schools and regions. Disparities in understanding among head teachers meant that their estimates of nonexamination pupils varied from 25 percent to 50 percent of the total.[124] The increasing success of many pupils had the effect of aggravating the residual status and sense of failure of early leavers, for whom courses were becoming "essentially palliative,"[125] and a form of "compensation for the under-privileged."[126]

These impulses drew from the ideas of Jean Piaget who argued that young people developed through stages of learning and, by 13–15 years, should have become capable of abstract thought and "formal operational thinking." Preparations for ROSLA blended such ideas with notions of ability, for example, in a history teaching context, giving rise to a distinction between mental and emotional forms of learning.

> These difficult mental operations are beyond the abilities of some children; but for them the emotional experiences involved in learning through history are a necessary part of their education…explicit effort is needed to ensure that understanding is deepened and a measure of confidence acquired in the use of dates and conventions associated with the recording of past time.[127]

This echoed the Newsom Report that had argued in favor of a "psychological sensitivity and intuitive awareness rather than rational fact-finding…an enlarging of the spirit for our boys and girls to meet great men and respond to them as men did and still do."[128] New ideas about ability and teaching were thus being grafted onto more traditional notions and limitations faced by the ROSLA student.

Assumptions about differential ability mutated with other inequalities surrounding race, gender, and disability. One head teacher, in facing multiple and tangled inequalities, argued that ROSLA exacerbated the need to find ways of reducing the segregation of pupils by sex and ability and to apply "principles of equality of opportunity and education of the whole personality of the child in a technological community."[129] Separating boys and girls in education and work came to be viewed as a problem that denied personal opportunities for girls and held back economic development through unmet needs in the labor market. But it is a paradox then that ROSLA simultaneously problematized and fostered sharper gender distinctions. In so far as new forms of curriculum were developed, optional courses often led to the separation of boys from girls.[130] Some did this in an obvious manner, as with many single-sex schools or in courses on "women's subjects" and "girls' grooming."[131] More subtle means of differentiation were becoming apparent whereby girls chose supposedly expressive areas of the curriculum and were guided away from, for instance, science courses. These choices were enhanced by stereotypes, such as that expressed by one member of the National Association of Schoolmasters (NAS) that "girls tend to be more of a problem than boys—they want to get dolled up and go out on the town. They just want to earn enough money to enjoy themselves."[132] While opportunities for employment were opening up, they were also curtailed by hierarchical assumptions within and about the labor market. In areas where employment opportunities were limited, priority was given to boys. In addition, it was generally expected that girls would take a long career break to have children, which confirmed their subordinate status in the workplace.[133]

Very little attention was paid to the position of black and minority ethnic students in relation to ROSLA, and this silence exposed a wider neglect of the issue. In Huddersfield, immigrants made up 7.6 percent of the population, and it was assumed by HMI that many of these would be directly affected by ROSLA and would need some form of special provision:

> As yet, no special consideration has been given to the needs of the young immigrant school leaver. While the primary concern must be to ensure that each pupil has a useful command of English, thought may well need to be given to the provision of special courses which will provide these particular pupils with a greater understanding of the world into which they soon must emerge.[134]

Assimilationist approaches mingled with compensatory expectations. ROSLA raised awareness of the perceived new needs of immigrants who required not only language support but also an additional form of education to understand the society in which they found themselves. The first report of the Select Committee on Race Relations and Immigration, established in the wake of the 1968 Race Relations Act, did focus upon the "Problem of Coloured School Leavers," but repeated previous assumptions about the need for special FE courses to "help them catch up with those who have had a full British education."[135]

Fears began to focus upon education in the inner city, a newly imported term from the United States. At the annual conference of the NAS in April 1971, Donald Macleod, a teacher from Hampshire in the south of England, lamented that the "inexorable advance of blackboard jungle schools" put increasing stress on older teachers and even reduced their life expectancy. The same conference again followed NAS tradition by rejecting ROSLA after what the *Guardian* described as "a debate boiling with references to the 'bloody-minded, disruptive, violent' minority of children who would be kept at school after 15."[136] The autonomy of schools, teachers, and education authorities meant that varying approaches were developed according to local circumstance. A DES press release in 1969 echoed the Schools Council in claiming that "more in the end will depend on local initiative than on materials produced by national projects," although the two were interconnected.[137]

In relation to disability, it is interesting to note that the focus upon the separateness of ROSLA pupils, that had been particularly significant since the Newsom Report, began to blur the distinction between "normal" pupils and those with special educational needs. The diffuse and variable notion of "social handicap," which could even include teachers who did not know how to organize a humane environment in schools, gained some usage as a result of ROSLA.[138] Specialist teachers started to "come out of the broom cupboard" and played a wider advisory role in schools that wanted to develop nonexamination courses.[139]

An element of falseness pervaded preparations for ROSLA given that courses were being piloted with existing fourth-year leavers and those who were voluntarily remaining at school.[140] As Edward Boyle had warned earlier, only when the new leaving age became a reality could curriculum changes be tested in practice.[141] Nevertheless, there was a sense in which, as another commentator closely involved in ROSLA claimed, that it was "almost certainly the most prepared for event...in English educational history—heralded by Crowther, conceived by Newsom and weaned by the Schools Council."[142] It had certainly managed to survive a difficult and protracted birth, although it was still to be tested for effectiveness and longevity. At the same time, ROSLA was not an isolated event but part of an ongoing program of educational and social reform, which would continue after 1972.

Chapter 8

Achieving ROSLA

The raising of the school leaving age (ROSLA) was achieved in England and Wales from 1972 by the simple means of an Order in Council that brought into law what had lain on the statute book since the 1944 Act.[1] In Scotland, the statutory instrument comprised the Raising of the School Leaving Age (Scotland) Regulations of 1972. In England and Wales, two fixed school-leaving dates at the end of the spring and summer terms had been set by the 1962 Education Act. There was more flexibility in Scotland where 3 dates could be decided upon by local authorities and 35 had varied their leaving dates.[2] The Order in Council also marked a deeper and more substantial kind of achievement, as it heralded a new phase of ROSLA as readiness was translated into practice, and the legal compulsion of the whole new year-group took effect. The attempt to reform a diffuse educational service, "a national system locally delivered," in which the central government, LEAs, schools, and teachers each jealously guarded their autonomy, meant that a variety of responses emerged. The extension of compulsion, resulting from ROSLA, on top of comprehensive reorganization and an already rising school population, meant that new developments were stepping into an already moving stream of activity. The difficulty of separating out ROSLA from other educational changes, including issues such as building, curriculum, examinations, welfare, and employment, was widely remarked upon.[3]

Buildings and Curriculum

Even in areas of activity where ROSLA was considered successful, variations and limitations persisted and made for a diversity of experiences. Senior Inspector D. G. Lambert undertook a review of the first year of

ROSLA in 1974 and found that many building schemes were adequate for schools to implement their curricular plans. However, he noted problems caused by industrial action among building workers, late arrival of pre-fabricated accommodation, rises in the costs of materials, and continuing problems arising due to the contemporaneous nature of school reorganization and ROSLA. A lack of facilities and space for the social needs of older pupils was also recognized.

Difficulties arose in implementing reform based on a hasty and tardy building program, and certain schools had to adopt short-term measures. In West Yorkshire, 22 schools experienced a delay in addition to another 18 where buildings were being completed in the summer of 1973. Protracted negotiations with builders, attempts to develop individual designs suited to the needs of schools, and rising inflation all contributed to such delays. One head teacher from Sowerby Bridge lamented the late arrival of a ROSLA block: "I have seldom felt sadder during the whole of my teaching career...it is heart breaking to find the united effort of an entire staff placed in jeopardy by the lack of walls."[4] Others complained that, after being encouraged to make time-consuming preparations, "not only the teachers...but the parents and public...are going to feel completely deceived and let down."[5] The aspiration to make a success of comprehensive schooling in West Yorkshire was being undercut by the rushed building program for ROSLA.

Elsewhere, sympathizers of selective schooling saw an opportunity in ROSLA to obstruct change. In the 1960s and the 1970s, Labour governments actively used building programs to nurture nonselective forms of schooling, but planning for a comprehensive future could be undermined by stubbornly selective assumptions that cut across the grain of this intention. For example, in Canterbury, the DES confirmed that ROSLA building allocations were for projects "solely because the age is to be raised...compatible with a non-selective system of secondary education."[6] The reform created logistical problems for the expanding secondary modern population of the city and, in 1969, the chief education officer reported that he was engaged in some "contingency thinking" on this issue.[7] Ultimately, the ROSLA building allocation of just over £100,000 was divided between temporary classrooms (3–4%), a ROSLA block for an existing secondary modern (30%) and the bulk, about two-thirds, to be spent on the Simon Langton Girls' Grammar School due to a supposed "shortage of selective places for girls in north-east Kent."[8] The claim that it might become an upper secondary school for all never came to fruition because political control in the county remained with Conservatives who were staunchly in favor of grammar schools. In such ways were funds for ROSLA siphoned off to benefit selective secondary schools.

This defensive recoil on the part of proponents of selective education was repeated in other parts of the country. A similar situation arose in Great Yarmouth where it was "hoped" that ROSLA would coincide with comprehensive reorganization. Accordingly, the ROSLA allocation was spent largely on 340 places at 3 grammar schools, "purpose-designed 5th form accommodation...in permanent construction." However, reorganization plans were then put on hold, ostensibly "owing to lack of money," and 150 additional places were provided in "temporary accommodation for RSLA in the existing secondary modern schools until they are in a position to reorganise."[9] A further example was at Southend on Sea in Essex, where ROSLA money was used to provide a new sixth form block in a grammar school, which, it was optimistically claimed, was to be "shared with the secondary modern school on an adjacent site."[10]

In the 1970s, such tendencies would have appeared to be swimming against the tide of making secondary education for all a reality. There had been a great flurry of activity in curricular preparations for ROSLA, not least through Schools Council projects, teachers' centers, local authorities, and individual schools, all supported by extensive debates in the press, conferences, and educational journals. The situation changed after 1972 when it became clear that schools were still adjusting to the new context. This became visible when a civil servant noted that a draft parliamentary answer seemed to have gone "badly wrong" in mentioning "new" courses, since the relevant planning should have been completed about three years before: "Any school which left planning its courses until the year of RSLA has only itself to blame for the results."[11] More sympathetically, Ernest Armstrong, undersecretary of state for education and science, argued that "teachers must be given time to acquire experience in the building up of courses of interest and relevance to young people."[12] Such pronouncements revealed that many schools had indeed made only partial preparations.

The range of alternatives developed for ROSLA defied simple categorization. As we have seen, one significant feature of these preparations was the tendency to collapse the boundaries between subject areas that were considered by some to be increasingly outmoded. The Keele Integrated Studies project as well as the Humanities Curriculum Project were noteworthy examples of this approach, albeit with differing emphases.[13] Outward-looking and community-based education was to be tailored to specific pupil needs. At the Linwood Boys Secondary School in Leicester, experimental courses embraced a wide conception of life:

> The syllabus really does start at the beginning, with the Creation, moves through personal questions, into the family and then the family in the

community in the broader context of the country, Britain's position in the world and finally to a consideration of world problems.[14]

Teachers borrowed from thinkers such as Jerome Bruner and wider progressive trends. Other examples included the Bristol ROSLA Community Education Project, which attempted to offer "a survival curriculum for the non-academic urban adolescent" by extending schooling out into the community.[15] Similarly, *The Terrace* described a project influenced by the ideas of Dartington Hall, a private progressive school, and their application to the education of working class ROSLA pupils in Yorkshire with an emphasis on talk and respecting the experience of students. Other lower-key ROSLA developments were nonetheless significant such as that led by the "Mersey poet" Adrian Henry, who ran a poetry group for a ROSLA class in Liverpool. ROSLA helped to stimulate an already strong trend toward expressive forms of English education.[16]

Not all ROSLA plans and courses were as coherent as this. Apparently adequate preparations that had been made before 1972–1973 had to be rethought as ROSLA was put into practice. Indeed, HMI surveys took on a decidedly frosty feel as deficiencies were uncovered in the ways that ROSLA took shape in individual schools and classrooms. Attitudes, planning, and courses all seemed inappropriate for the new purpose. The initial despondency of inspectors led to broad criticisms at the range of emerging problems in schools. HMI Lambert identified "poor planning and lack of leadership but predominantly staff attitudes" as being mainly responsible for this, and blamed in particular the hostility of some teachers to the concept and philosophy of ROSLA, the unrealistic and divisive nature of courses, and the authoritarian approach that some schools continued to adopt toward their older pupils: "This may be due to ingrained traditions and habits but the youth and inexperience of some teachers and a lack of knowledge of how to deal with a reluctant learner must also have played a part."[17]

ROSLA exposed an education system in transformation and challenged the assumption that different types of pupil required varying forms of education. The "undesirable dichotomy"[18] between the proverbial "sheep" and "goats" was being challenged in schools that developed common core studies along with options that created both shared and separate pathways for students. ROSLA could facilitate comprehensive reorganization as happened at Ashton Park Secondary Modern School in Bristol, which was keen "to do away with segregation involved in having a lower band which . . . had contributed to problems of discipline and attitude."[19] ROSLA focused attention not only upon lofty notions of equality but also on the practical need to cater for growing numbers of students. Nevertheless, wider class tensions continued to have a tangible presence and the ROSLA debate about "separate or integrated provision" could not be easily solved. While mixed ability classes became relatively common in the first two years of secondary school, the scope for this was radically curtailed in the fourth and fifth years as the focus shifted to examination success. By 1974, in Bristol and Gloucestershire, schools had "grappled energetically, if not always successfully" with this issue and were still actively debating whether to offer separate courses for fear of creating a "depressed element" cut off from those taking examinations.[20] Ability groupings could easily be reestablished as when one school surveyed the "needs of pupils, parents and staff," which resulted in "courses for the able, the average and the slow learner." It was found surprising that even a few of the "more able" students chose to take social welfare and composite crafts that had been designed for "slow learners."[21]

In addition, ROSLA could heighten the visibility of lacunae in curriculum planning. One school introduced an "extremely ambitious option scheme" at a point when the fifth year contained only 4 pupils. As the number increased to 68, it created "extremely heavy pressure" and proved unworkable.[22] A Plymouth school limited CSE entries to six but neglected to provide any alternative provision, so that pupils were sent to "so-called private study" which, in some cases, amounted to 40 percent of the time-table. Unsurprisingly, "the lowest of the 5th form groups in this school were totally unmotivated and resistant to being at school."[23] Some curricular offers had been rushed so that, in practice, "rural science" was little more than "gardening"; while "motor maintenance" courses had not "been designed to capture the boys' interest."[24] Compiling folders for project work was "often badly chosen, ill-supported and involving little more than sticking in pictures and copying from books." Materials were widely considered a crucial element of meeting new needs thrown up by ROSLA, but many teachers remained unaware of this.[25] As ROSLA fell short of aspirations, the reestablishment of subject boundaries became more attractive.[26]

A further unforeseen issue that arose was the relative balance of subjects within the newly amalgamated areas of study. New options often overlapped and the combination of subjects was variable across schools. In the attempt to rework traditional subject barriers, maths and English were in theory to be relevant in all areas. However, these core subjects could be submerged so deeply that they rarely surfaced in class work.[27] Schools in Salop (renamed as Shropshire from 1980) intended that maths would "come in incidentally as part of the general science course, but there is little evidence to show that this is happening."[28] At Heanor Gate Secondary school in Derbyshire, the proliferation of small option groups and clubs drew staffing away from other areas. For example, wine making attracted

5 students, gardening 11, indoor games 15, modeling 9, and community service 10, while larger classes elsewhere were required to compensate for the imbalance.[29] In costly subjects, such as science, a similar pattern was repeated with more resources generally devoted to those expected to achieve exam success.[30] As a result of these sobering experiences, by 1978, many integrated courses had been disbanded as teachers returned to their respective subjects.

Changing the attitudes of teachers and pupils was a further feature of ROSLA. Good intentions were not always worked through in detail and half-hearted attempts at relevance could easily pander to stereotypes. HMI reported on one school where the "earnest efforts" of young teachers to discuss current social problems "fell flat" because pupils were "pretty tired of these well-meaning attempts to persuade them to share their thoughts on crime, vandalism, drugs, sex and the like."[31] A significant group of teachers remained hostile to ROSLA and ambivalent about new approaches to pedagogy, and this was reflected in the "sadly disappointing" classroom situations that HMI uncovered: "Many staff told us that they considered RSLA to have been a mistake and some expressed themselves very strongly indeed. Nevertheless, they had a strong sense of duty towards their pupils and were trying to cope as best they could."[32] At a time when a majority of teachers voted Conservative, many held fast to disciplines as a way of maintaining tradition and professionalism. Subject specialisms were perceived as "fairly traditionally defined bodies of knowledge and techniques...unsuited to the ways of working coming to be associated with RSLA."[33] Yet, one way of diffusing teacher opposition to ROSLA was to highlight how traditional approaches could be adapted to the new situation. The stark differentiation of some ROSLA courses began to break down under these pressures.

Teachers who muddled through the ROSLA maze were circumspect about the faith that all pupils might benefit from a five-year course and that everyone was educable to 16. However, rather than the widely anticipated disaffection, in their new condition, pupils were surprisingly compliant: "HMI frequently wondered at the pupils' patient acceptance of what they were being offered." Contrary to earlier and commonly expressed fears about the potential disruption that ROSLA pupils would cause, the moral panic appeared to fizzle out in unimaginative classrooms and mundane teaching. Many boys on one course were found to be "just marking time in readiness for the day they can go to work."[34] This view corresponded with a wider awareness that "apathy" was not simply an individual trait but could result from inappropriate institutionalized provision: "some poorly behaved classes...was easily explicable in terms of the unsuitability of teaching...the precipitating factor was often the ineptitude of the teaching."[35] Indeed, it proved to be a surprise finding that ROSLA did not lead to ubiquitous rioting, a welcome result that contradicted the commonplace negative stereotypes of working-class children. The experience of ROSLA for a sizable number of pupils was that they remained in unexciting schools for a longer period of time.

The interest in outward-looking courses also stimulated link courses that utilized the specialist and vocational facilities of further education (FE) colleges. In 1974, it was estimated that 77 percent of local education authorities (LEAs) had taken advantage of this scheme in a wide number of areas.[36] This new provision struggled to fit comfortably between separate institutions and was not to become a permanent feature of the educational landscape. Some link courses offered no better facilities than schools, for example, in home economics and design as opposed to electronics and motor maintenance where more specialist provision existed in colleges. Link courses caused a potential reduction in the teaching capacity of schools and led to claims for additional funding to fill this gap.[37] In some cases, pupils were expected to make a financial contribution to materials that constituted "a real hardship."[38] On the other hand, FE colleges complained they were being used as a "dumping ground for poorly motivated, badly behaved and unresponsive students."[39] On both sides there was a "mutual suspicion" and, in several cases, it was found that "liaison is tenuous in the extreme."[40] Despite the popularity of link courses, in the long run these obstacles proved difficult to overcome.

Work experience in the final year of compulsory schooling represented a further vocational reform resulting from ROSLA, which had also been recommended in the Newsom Report. It was enabled by the Education (Work Experience) Act passed in May 1973, and was generally welcomed by schools, although take-up was initially much slower than for link courses. Again, contested definitions were evident as work experience tended to be viewed by schools as taster sessions. Employers often considered it to be a way of recruiting pupils to future employment, while trade unions feared the introduction of cheap labor.

Examinations

Curriculum innovation in connection with ROSLA had arisen as an alternative to examinations and in some cases in opposition to them. For those firmly located in a "progressive" camp, who believed that ROSLA was about helping the "less academic child," a "vicious circle" of examinations exerted a "tyranny" over the curriculum to the extent that it was "not a person who leaves the schools...but a piece of paper testifying to an often arbitrary selection of skills."[41] Nonetheless, it was hoped that examinations would follow the curriculum that was "suited to the capacity and interests of staff and pupils, leaving examination work to fit into the general frame-work of their basic courses."[42] This vision of an alternative education adapted to "less able children" was undermined both by the assumption about ability and by the realities of a divided system. For HMI, the fear that exams would limit educational content was tempered by an awareness of their value in providing an incentive. Curriculum innovations associated with ROSLA struggled to provide a positive definition of "nonexamination" courses, and many of them only ran for two terms before requiring "major modification."[43] In one case, it was noted that "a narrow attack on an examination syllabus has had an adverse effect on the pupils' attitudes and achievement, despite conscientious if misguided effort on the part of the staff."[44]

These debates were overtaken by the decline in integrated and nonexamination courses that followed ROSLA. Ironically, the extension of compulsion led to their downfall. As the DES noted in 1978,

> At the time of the raising of the school leaving age some of the schools designed courses for pupils who were leaving school before the fifth year. Now that all pupils remain in the fifth year, few of these schools had retained or developed these non-examination courses.[45]

The basic assumption that ROSLA required a separate educational response for those who would be compelled to stay in school was overthrown by the actual experience of change. Special ROSLA courses for the "least able" failed to satisfy pupils and teachers and led to their abandonment or integration into teacher-led examinations, the so-called Mode III CSE.[46]

ROSLA took the educational world by surprise in that, having generated extensive activity in nonexamination courses, it stimulated a significant increase in those taking and passing examinations. The DES Report on Education reported on the surge in examinations from 1,426,000 CSE entries in 1973 to 2,356,000 in 1975; from 2,352,000 GCE entries in 1973 to 2,591,000 entries in 1975. In Nottingham, it was observed that the CSE position was transformed, as the number of CSE candidates more than doubled from 4,147 in 1973 to 8,400 in 1974. GCE 'O' level increases were considered "not dramatic" but entrants nevertheless rose by 20.9 percent to 3,254 and subject passes by 4.1 percent to 7,501.[47] There had already been indications of a growing examination culture with the introduction of CSE in 1965, which targeted the 20–40 percent of pupils below the "top" 20 percent who took GCE 'O' levels. For example, in the early 1960s, Cornwall LEA had officially discouraged examinations in secondary modern schools, but the introduction of CSE had a "bracing effect" and attitudes rapidly altered.[48] ROSLA multiplied and intensified this process in a few short years and on a national scale. ROSLA to 16 thus represented a significant historical moment when educational opportunities were raised and leveled by equalizing the age of public examinations and the school-leaving age.

A number of reasons can be identified for this growth in examinations. Historical assumptions about ability were destabilized by comprehensive schooling and related ideas of equality and equal educability. Paradoxically, the confluence of ROSLA and comprehensive reorganization was a further factor that fostered the proliferation of examinations. In Essex, the reaction against the kinds of segregation outlined in the Newsom Report found expression in a strong opposition to creating "a separate RSLA animal" or "a Newsom Chap" or "The Director of Non-Academic Studies."[49] For much of the 1960s, the Newsom Report and ROSLA had been virtually indistinguishable but, after 1972, ROSLA triggered the curtailment of Newsom courses. In a widening context of equality, it appeared increasingly obvious that everyone should have the opportunity to sit for examinations. In giving all pupils the same facilities, "reluctant stayers...are likely to be less reluctant if they can see some goal in view." [50] It also caused schools to delay separating GCE and CSE pupils for as long as possible.[51] The concern to create equality of opportunity found an outlet in encouraging more students to sit exams and this was repeated across the country, not least in Scotland.[52] A mutually reinforcing process generated discipline and enthusiasm that overcame earlier assumptions about ability: "The fact that pupils find the courses so absorbing and that attitudes to work are improved brings with it a need for teachers to sharpen their judgment of what is and can be achieved."[53] The pressure for a common examination at 16, which was not to come to fruition until 1986, was felt early on in the life of the CSE exam. Exams rapidly became an acceptable default option for schools that had not devoted too much energy to specific preparation for ROSLA. It was recorded that one head teacher "frankly admits that he has made no attempt to organise such a course, as his staffing resources are inadequate."[54]

The take up of exams was reinforced by pupil and parental pressure and wider social influences even when they contrasted with professional opinion about ability. In a city such as Plymouth, large employers including the armed forces and dockyards gave "some recognition" to qualifications,[55] while in Derbyshire "parental and pupil pressure" favored examinations. In one school where approximately 50 percent of pupils had traditionally stayed on for a further year, 97 percent of pupils opted to take at least one

examination. HMI were uneasy that ambitious aspirations might be undermined by failing pupils and confidently asserted that "the inability of some
pupils to fulfil their ambitions would become clear within 6 months if not
earlier." They advised developing a nonexamination course that the "less
able" should be advised to take from the start of the fourth year.[56] Such a
clear demarcation of ability levels became increasingly problematic. One
student attempting two CSEs convinced an inspector that an examination
goal was "eminently worthwhile" given his palpable excitement: "Do you
know, sir, if I pass CSE I shall be the first member of my family who has
ever passed an exam."[57] Furthermore, in 1978, a survey on ROSLA found
that, in 28 out of 30 schools, there was no obvious relationship between a
commitment to examinations and the type of catchment area or the previous history of the school. The emerging awareness that notions of ability
were more flexible than had been thought and could be overridden by
motivation and dedication was a nascent example of the school improvement movement as well as of broader ideals of educability.[58]

The expanding culture of examinations carried with it some negative
consequences. Exams served to narrow the curriculum, entrench hierarchies and further marginalize certain groups. Some pupils took no science
after year 3. Putting pupils on inappropriate exam courses led teachers
to adopt "excessively didactic methods directed entirely to examination
demands, with insufficient regard for individual needs or opportunities."[59]
Alternative certificates could become stigmatized with minority and subordinate status. The "search for paper qualifications" led the "most able"
away from courses geared to personal and social development and practical
and aesthetic disciplines. As exams became more popular, those considered
unsuitable for such a course could find themselves isolated. New types
of provision beyond the school gates, link courses, work experience, and
social service, were further downgraded as a result.[60] In embracing exams,
schools could intensify the sense of separateness felt by those with the least
educational status. Courses were then developed for the diminishing group
of "the least academically able and less well motivated." [61]

This situation had to be placed in context, particularly in relation to
the Schools Council. In the 1960s, great hopes for fundamental curricular
changes gave way to a gradual realization that Schools Council projects
were only preparatory and had not been immediately implemented on a
widespread basis. In fact, the short-term effect of the Schools Council was
found to be limited and only 16 LEAs were found to have benefited from
local curriculum development schemes. Sometimes this was restricted to a
single school. The exception was the North West Curriculum Development
Project that had stimulated the formation of local curriculum development
groups in Rossendale in Lancashire, and elsewhere.[62] It became relatively

easy to criticize the Schools Council as an ineffective organization as a result of the lackluster and sporadic implementation of its programs. Indeed, this very criticism would be repeated by the Trenaman Report leading to the disbandment of the council in 1984. The apparent lethargy in preparations was picked over by critics such as the National Association of Schoolmasters (NAS) which issued the dire verdict, after all its earlier protests, that schools and the teaching profession had not been ready for ROSLA.[63]

These limitations were to be expected. The Schools Council only had an advisory role in working with schools and teachers. Although the Schools Council was criticized for a lack of attention to implementation and dissemination, it had no direct control over what went on in schools. This nondirective and persuasive program frustrated some policy makers and, over time, fuelled demands for greater coordination and planning.[64] At the same time, the diffused model of development retained its influence for many years. In 1978, the DES "post RSLA Working Party" pointed to the need for local diversity in arguing that it was "unlikely that any one model could be successfully and universally applied."[65] The Schools Council represented a tentative step into the "secret garden" of the curriculum, and it was hardly realistic to expect that detailed curricular plans would be immediately effective. ROSLA was not a quick fix but, rather, necessitated widespread alterations before, during, and after implementation. In this sense, the council encapsulated tensions that ran through the whole of the education service.

The implementation of ROSLA marked a rapid change of focus from the macro to the micro level and in-service training was singled out as a crucial area that required greater attention. In Norfolk, training for ROSLA was limited to haphazard discussions in a teachers' center.[66] For curricular modifications to seep down to the classroom level, it was realized that a greater concerted effort was required. New materials and approaches could not simply be imported into classrooms wholesale but, rather, had to be adapted to particular situations. The dangers of "ready-made materials" were becoming obvious as well as the corresponding "need for a great deal of teacher preparation."[67] ROSLA was thus not simply a technical adjustment that required the cooperation of various levels of the education system, but was also tied into changing attitudes and feelings, particularly on the part of teachers. Indeed, for some teachers, planning offended the essence of teaching. Curriculum change impacted upon personal sensibilities and wider cultural understandings, which took some time to alter.[68] HMI Lambert concluded that "the enthusiasm and personal qualities of the staff are more important than the content of the courses or even than the overall curriculum planning."[69] This finding was supported by a number of studies in addition to the everyday observations of inspectors, teachers, and observers. As a result, ROSLA helped to reinforce the attention being given to in-service training that came to be understood as central to the future of teaching, a missing link in curriculum development.[70] Some LEAs made use of university training, as for example the London boroughs of Redbridge and Ealing that worked with Goldsmiths College. Such initiatives would grow into a much bigger movement over the coming years.[71]

The changing role of teachers reflected social as well as educational influences. Welfare services would be called upon to deal with the effects of ROSLA, and prolonged discussions took place between the youth service and the Schools Council. While youth workers identified a new role in schools, it was expected that teachers would need to develop some of the skills of youth workers. Projects such as the ROSLA Community Education Project actively developed new relations with welfare services. The new connections might only be temporary, but significant divides were being crossed and new skills were being learned as education took on features of the wider welfare state that also evoked some political displeasure.[72] On one fifth year general course in which over half the pupils came from "broken homes," counseling services had been discontinued. Yet the program allowed pupils to talk to the tutor and a "life and leisure" course became "a useful vehicle whereby staff can come to know of problems facing individuals."[73] Indeed, the way in which a few pupils took up a lot of time was "intensified by ROSLA." In this setting, drawing on wider social services made a great deal of sense.[74]

Public Debates

In 1972 ROSLA took place at a significant watershed as basic postwar economic assumptions came under strain. Economic recession compromised the policy of full employment. At the same time, the nature of the labor market was changing with the gradual increase in service sector and white-collar work and the corresponding decrease in "manual" and "unskilled" jobs. ROSLA was engulfed in these debates on the changing nature of work. It permanently removed 15-year-olds from the labor market and employers were encouraged to recruit more than their usual requirement the year before the measure took effect, although some employers remained unaware that the supply of 15-year-olds was to end.[75] For example, the Northern Region of the Central Youth Employment Executive (CYEE) anticipated 22,000 fewer school leavers in 1973. It was projected that the unemployed and those in jobs below their qualifications and aspirations might be needed to fill the gap, even though it was believed that such applicants "deteriorate in quality during idleness."[76]

For much of the twentieth century, educationists had argued, against considerable opposition, that withdrawing vulnerable young people from the deadening influence of the workplace was a social necessity. Both employers and working-class families had resisted ROSLA as it delayed entry into the labor market and, in the 1970s, this residual perspective continued to be voiced. Some employers warned of logistical problems inherent in ROSLA although the TUC countered that there would be "no intractable problems" as in 1947.[77] The former miner and Labour MP Adam Hunter in questioning ROSLA, argued that "working class families require the income of young members of the family."[78] In Plymouth, it was claimed that controlling fifth-year girls was especially difficult given a "considerable demand for unskilled female labour in local factories."[79] Some politicians also relegated ROSLA to the needs of the labor market. For example, in 1973 the Conservative minister, James Prior, proposed allowing pupils to leave at the end of the term in which they became 16, which, he claimed, would help "easing any overheating in the economy." Prior's suggestion was supported by the Liberal MP David Steel. The DES response was understandably less sympathetic as it "cuts right across educational thinking" for uncertain benefits.[80] These tendencies were echoes of a much stronger historical trend that had died down. In the 1970s, civil servants claimed to be confounded by the "apparent complete unanimity" in favor of ROSLA despite "the considerable hole" it would create in the labor market.[81]

ROSLA was a forward-looking measure and precipitated many new ideas about the nature of work and employment. ROSLA provided a pretext for the greater involvement of employers in debates on both the overall purpose and, increasingly, the specific details of education. Many of the industrial training boards (ITBs) set up by the 1964 Industrial Training Act welcomed the extra year as an opportunity for young people to develop knowledge and skills relevant to their future work. They argued that most school leavers were going to spend the bulk of their working lives in industry and the private sector, and that schooling should be geared to this basic fact.[82] A survey on ROSLA among ITBs revealed a range of opinion heavily influenced by wider social divisions including the Chemical Board, which favored "a strong vocational bias" for "less academic pupils." The Gas Board argued for "introductory clerical courses," while the Electricity Board went furthest in stipulating that 15-year-olds should make a "provisional selection of their future career" in order to "enable them to be put into broad streams following courses orientated towards their particular choice." By contrast, the Engineering ITB appeared to buck the trend in outlining the need for literacy, numeracy, and general education:

> A technological society makes increasing demands on the ability to communicate and comprehend. The industry in general has no difficulty in giving adequate training to its intake provided that they have the necessary general education.[83]

This diversity of opinion was contained within a shared framework that was heavily inclined toward vocational learning and the needs of the economy. "General education" was to include not only personal finance but subjects, such as "basic applied economics, civics and human relations, which would enable the school leaver to better understand the operation of an industrial society."[84] These concerns went beyond the content of the curriculum into the realm of the identity of young people. For instance, in Scotland it was argued that changing economic needs implied "the stimulation and maintenance of interest and the inculcation of attitudes rather than training in a narrow range of vocational skills."[85]

Vocational education was also caught up in contradictory pressures over class and gender. ROSLA helped to break down barriers between the education of girls and boys while constructing differences in other areas that could be sustained by policy makers, parents, teachers, and even pupils themselves. Indeed, it was realized that institutions could play an active role in configuring both difference and inequality through "an amalgam of assumptions in curriculum planning, of the availability of material and of teacher resources, and, above all, of the attitudes and aspirations of parents and the pupils themselves." [86]

Gender distinctions were particularly exacerbated in link courses, with technical subjects considered as male, and caring and office work as female. Inspectors found it "disturbing" to find so few girls on science courses although both boys and girls did choose catering, rural studies, jewelery, and computer studies.[87] Preparing pupils for life was often interpreted in fixed ways. At the Newton Abbot County Secondary Girls' School in Devon a successful leavers' course was linked directly to "future hopes of a secure job, a happy marriage and a good home."[88] In Gloucestershire one head teacher had requested freestanding fuel burners to heat classrooms to be occupied by ROSLA students, on the basis that "the girls would get experience in the handling of this type of heater, but more important it would tend to create dirt and thus the necessity for thorough daily cleaning."[89] In the event this proposal proved to be impractical, but it showed that the content of courses that aimed to prepare students for adult life very much depended upon what sort of life was envisaged. Where barriers were superficially weakening, gender differences could easily be reasserted. One inspector was sanguine that "less able boys" were more motivated in home economics than their female counterparts, but this was explained by the fact that girls "probably have to take responsibility for household duties when mothers are out at work."[90] Where schools were working to change attitudes, the world of work might resist. For instance, in the southwest, it was claimed that employers were "very conservative" and needed convincing to take boys as hairdressers and girls for drawing offices.[91]

The Northern Region of the CYEE felt convinced that those taking exams were likely to exert a new influence upon the labor market, and anticipated that there would be an imbalance in the supply of school leavers with few of "average and below average ability" available.[92] Even though qualifications were becoming a new proxy for ability, a more flexible employment situation was being prefigured. It is noticeable how notions of ability were not simply applied to an academic/vocational divide but also pervaded work-related education. Many within the ITBs argued that industry had to improve its "image" because young people and parents were becoming alert to the value of training and qualifications that benefited both the individual and the firm. Indeed, a mutually reinforcing process lauded a "versatile workforce, able to adapt quickly to changes in techniques and operations, and flexible enough to understand the importance of their own improved performance."[93]

Initial problems over the reduction in the supply of labor intensified a long-term perspective on economic change that prioritized the mechanization and automation of routine tasks and the need for increased productivity. These suggestions chimed with the fear that "able" boys would be lost for apprenticeships resulting from increased staying-on.[94] Government warned employers that the labor force was "not sufficiently flexible in its outlook to adapt to the complexity and rapid development of technology in the 1970's and beyond."[95] Indeed, in 1972, *The Times* feared further social discord that might arise from the continuing "monotony of mass production work" that would not satisfy a more educated and mature generation of school leavers.[96] However, such arguments did not prevail over the position that the quality of recruits was simply inadequate.[97] The concerns of employers blended with a number of social and educational issues. Rising examination results stimulated both fear and disbelief. The growing numbers of working-class children who passed exams dented ingrained assumptions that inequality was a natural feature of life. In addition, the crude notion of "more means worse" represented a right-wing backlash against the postwar welfare state but it also drew upon common feelings that older traditions were decaying. During the 1970s, these attitudes and fears found a target in secondary education, a shift that reflected the more general breakdown of consensus politics.

In this way, ROSLA became a major stimulant to debates on standards. When Alan S. Willmott produced a report on examination standards resulting from ROSLA, he surrounded his claim about a small decline in standards with multiple assumptions. The *Daily Mail* response to this leaked report was unequivocal and symbolic of a step-change in press reporting on education: "GCE survey shocks education chiefs. EXAMS—THE CRUMBLING STANDARDS."[98] Such invective contributed to the mounting attacks on education that had been channeled by the Black Papers. Indeed, after 1972, far from dying down, ROSLA continued to stimulate skirmishes that, at particular moments, appeared as if they might spiral out of control. Absenteeism, the segregation of ROSLA pupils, patchy curriculum development, and inappropriate pedagogy all provided ammunition for critics. Despite the broad successes of ROSLA, it continued to invoke fears of educational disintegration.[99] At times, it appeared that ROSLA was foundering. In 1973, Norman St John-Stevas, the Conservative under-parliamentary secretary of state for education, reported that 22 of the 4,870 maintained secondary schools in England had to resort to part-time schooling.[100] This became widespread in the west of Scotland, particularly in Strathclyde where there were "serious staffing difficulties."[101] In December 1973, 6,473 secondary children in Glasgow and Lanarkshire were receiving part-time education, three-quarters of them in Glasgow.[102]

A continuous bout of parliamentary questions requesting details of correspondence sent to the DES ensured that ROSLA was kept alive in Parliament. It was often aggrieved teachers who wrote in to vent their frustrations, a scenario that was repeated locally. One head teacher in Hove, Sussex, complained to the Hove Committee for Education about intolerable pressures resulting from ROSLA, which "has not worked." Her school had suffered from staff shortages, and she pointed out that staff could not be expected to shoulder this burden indefinitely.[103]

The Liberal Party politician, Clement Freud, stoked up these fires by introducing two bills in 1974 to allow children to leave school early amid "alarmingly disruptive" behavior including widespread truanting and assaults on teachers.[104] Freud was responding to stereotype and fear, and had limited evidence of growing violence in schools resulting from ROSLA but the issue of early leaving rapidly developed into a crisis. He was supported by the press. For example, the *Guardian* newspaper reported in January 1975 that four 15- and 16-year-old boys were said to have become burglars because they could not leave school to get work and that ROSLA had led to more crime. According to the counsel for one 15-year-old, "The court may wonder why it is that a boy with a good home background does nothing wrong for years, and then becomes involved in a series of offences at the age of 15. The argument is that it is all due to the compulsory extra year at school."[105] In the face of mounting criticism, the Conservative MP Nigel Lawson also initiated a parliamentary debate arguing that pupils should be allowed to leave at the age of 15 in appropriate cases.[106] The official leaving date was the end of the summer term and pupils were legally obliged to remain in school until well after examinations had finished. Teachers, pupils, and parents all questioned the value of such legal compulsion during the summer term. Nottinghamshire reflected many parts of the country and attendance in the summer term dropped to as low as 20 percent as many young people found employment in domestic work and agriculture.[107] Schools often turned a blind eye to "condoned absence" supported by parents.[108] William Alexander argued that schools were being "self-defeatist" and should be able to occupy all children in useful and liberal outward-looking education.[109] This optimistic view was undercut by the fact that most courses finished at the end of the Easter term in preparation for examinations. A further injustice appeared to be that those in approved schools, who came under the jurisdiction of the Home Office rather than the DES, could leave early, on their sixteenth birthday.[110]

A pervasive anxiety over this issue rapidly escalated into a common determination that the rule should be altered. After the first year of ROSLA, the DES found that 87 out of 96 inspection districts favored an early leaving date,[111] and, in Scotland, LEAs, MPs, and teacher associations requested leaving at age 16.[112] But the matter had to be handled delicately and admitting mistakes too openly ran the risk of fomenting more public discontent while being seen as condoning bad behavior in schools and breaking the law through absenteeism.[113] Magistrates, the police, and social services all complained about "the morality of this situation and the strain which it is creating."[114] C. K. R. Pearce, headmaster of Leek High School in Staffordshire, took the initiative to propose to the National Youth Employment Council that National Insurance Cards should be made available for issue to pupils whose sixteenth birthday fell after February 1 and before September 1 in any one year, so that these could seek work after public examinations were completed instead of having to attend school. As he related the outcome,

> I'm afraid I got nowhere. My case was received very favourably by the Chairman, but with some hostility by the DES representatives, who churned out all the old ideas, that the post-exam period provided splendid opportunities for devising programmes of great interest, taking them out and about and explaining fascinating by-ways of education. (I sometimes

wonder whether some of the HMIs have ever been in a secondary modern or comprehensive school).[115]

Officials at the DES and the Scottish Education Department were quick to point out that only a change in the law would enable some children, on whatever exceptional basis, to leave before the end of the summer term, and that there was no prospect of any such legislation being introduced in the near future.[116] The NAHT made a direct appeal to Margaret Thatcher, the secretary of state,[117] and her initial response was not encouraging.[118] R. J. Cook, the general secretary of the NAHT, opined that the DES was adopting "a much too rigid attitude towards this problem," and that it would "ignore the warnings of Head Teachers of Secondary Schools at their peril."[119] By the end of the year Thatcher had reconsidered the position, and made clear that she was willing to consult on the matter.[120]

The Conservative government was defeated in a general election in March 1974, so it was Thatcher's successor, Reginald Prentice, who had to address this issue in a new Labour government initially with no overall majority in the House of Commons. The wider context was of worsening economic and industrial problems. Prentice indicated that at such a time education could expect little in the way of further financial resources. In 1975, fearing that a rushed Bill "would smack of panic reaction,"[121] civil servants warned that "Ministers will possibly have to ride out a situation again this year."[122] New legislation could not, finally, be introduced until 1976 in the form of the Education (School-Leaving Dates) Act, which allowed pupils to leave at the end of May. The bill was introduced in the House of Lords, encouraging a number of peers to express in voluble terms their strong dissatisfaction with education in general and ROSLA in particular.[123] The effects of the change were rapidly felt in most secondary schools. One school welcomed the "peace and quiet" that ensued as staff gained more time to "think and plan,"[124] and truancy declined to a 'very small minority."[125]

Politicians, civil servants, and educationists sympathetic to ROSLA were disturbed by such controversies. Allowing critics to keep an anti-ROSLA flame alive in public debate was a hazardous course for those already unnerved by the growing unease surrounding secondary education in the 1970s. Dampening down debate on ROSLA became a priority if it was to become accepted as a permanent feature of the educational landscape. Accordingly, ROSLA was presented as a one-off specific reform from which the country needed to move on—"a once-for-all operation which took place on September 1, 1972." It was also placed within a long historical tradition, as a logical extension of previous reforms rather than an abrupt innovation.[126] In drafting the DES report on the first year of

ROSLA, it was noted that "the sooner we lose the term RSLA, the better" although, in the interests of continuity with previous reports, "The First Year after RSLA" was chosen to "establish that RSLA as such was over." The term "RSLA" was to be excised from public announcements.[127]

As a long-term and apparently permanent reform, ROSLA gradually merged with mainstream educational debate. Poor education for working-class children persisted but this became a problem of the education system more generally rather than a "ROSLA problem": "ROSLA kids" were rapidly transformed into "problem children." For example, in 1978 inspectors gained "considerable satisfaction" that ROSLA pupils were "difficult to identify" even though there remained problems with the "least able."[128] Curricular responses to ROSLA were rearticulated into what became a long line of vocational educational reforms. Indeed, ROSLA provided one important context from which vocational experiments targeted at lower achievers, grew, such as the Youth Opportunities Scheme of 1978, and the Technical and Vocational Educational Initiative in the 1980s.[129]

Despite all the accumulating evidence of problems with ROSLA after 1972, there were also grounds for hope. Alongside the trenchant criticisms made, HMI appeared relatively relaxed and hopeful about the emerging transition in the classroom context. In 1974, HMI acknowledged that schools had developed "a wealth of hopeful ideas," and that teachers were "still very much in the process of assessment and reappraisal."[130] Civil servants tended to place ROSLA within a historical discourse of incremental and progressive change in order to help make sense of the problems they faced. J. A. Hudson at the DES, for example, provided reassurance in the light of his long-term experience that "we shall move on to gradual acceptance and adaptation to the change, but that it will be several years before we even approach the full realisation of the potential educational advantages."[131] In Nottingham, history was used to allay the fears and criticisms and pupils were leaving school "better prepared." As further resources became available, so "secondary education for all will move towards its full fruition."[132] HMI reports identified many young people who directly benefited from the reform, including the "fairly able," the "less able," and "those, of varying abilities, who have gained in maturity and self-reliance in this final year of their schooling."[133]

In politics, too, the measure received support. Prentice noticed the tendency to separate pupils into two opposed camps of the willing and unwilling, a distinction that did not reflect the reality that large numbers of pupils who might have left previously were now benefiting from education. Similarly, Ernest Armstrong, the undersecretary of state for education, argued that "teachers are succeeding because the curriculum, the methods of teaching and learning, the corporate life of the school and school contact with outside communities have been adjusted and made relevant to young people."[134] All the same, there were unmistakable signs of change in national politics that would come to influence public debates about education. In March 1976, Harold Wilson retired as prime minister, and was succeeded by James Callaghan. The problems in the economy that had been growing for the past three years led to an economic crisis. At the same time, Callaghan chose to spark a renewed debate over education through a widely trailed speech at Ruskin College Oxford. This was a speech that raised doubts about the Labour government's commitment to comprehensive education. It also carried significant implications for ROSLA with its criticisms of the failure of schools to prepare pupils for the world of work and its announcement that there would be a further inquiry into the examinations system, especially in relation to students staying at school beyond the age of 16.[135] In spite of all the doubts and the initial teething problems, ROSLA had finally been achieved, more or less successfully. Its fate over the longer term would rest with the next generation of reformers, restless and discontented with the education system in general, and emboldened to act by economic stringency and social division.

Chapter 9

Raising the Participation Age: Policy Learning from the Past?

The historical processes through which the school-leaving age came to be increased, to 16 in particular, bequeathed a complex educational inheritance to future generations that intensified a number of tensions at the heart of secondary education. These were not always understood to be connected to the raising of school-leaving age (ROSLA) because the issue was rapidly subsumed under the shifts in educational policy that took place in the years after 1972. ROSLA to 16 was not simply a case of extending what was there already, but implied widespread systemic change that would eventually impact upon the policy of raising the participation age (RPA).

From ROSLA to RPA

In stimulating examination entry, ROSLA set in train a process that tied growing numbers of school students into curricular regimes that were linked to public examinations. One consequence of this was that previously tenacious assumptions about fixed ability levels became more muted. In recommending the establishment of the Certificate of Secondary Education (CSE) in the early 1960s, the Beloe Committee had argued that 'O' levels would cater for the top 20 percent; CSE for the next 20–40 percent and the significant numbers left would follow "non-examination" courses.[1] Ironically, many of the curricular projects associated with ROSLA were similarly influenced by assumptions about the differences between these ability groups. However, by creating a situation in which examination success proliferated, ROSLA heightened feelings that the distinction between 'O' level and CSE was inappropriate to contemporary needs. It would then take a number of years for this to be acted upon and although it would not be until 1986–87 that the common examination, the General Certificate of Secondary Education (GCSE), was taken by all students.

Some of the experimental work stimulated by ROSLA also came to be associated with a lowering of educational standards. To such critics certain aspects of ROSLA appeared to have more to do with experimental teaching and personal relationships than with learning and standards. This claim was not supported by evidence but, rather, reflected broader class tensions that initially became more marked with the breakdown of the postwar consensus. The *Black Papers* enabled "traditionalists" to vent their concerns over changes in the school curriculum and linked this to a perceived social breakdown. Ultimately, these debates would connect with calls for a national curriculum that came to fruition in 1988.[2]

In the 1970s, ROSLA was broadly welcomed for promoting equality of opportunity. But alternative trends were identified with new forms of discrimination being identified, particularly around race, class, gender, disability, and sexuality. The role of educationists in channeling pupils into unproductive forms of learning would be described through evolving theories, for instance, of labeling, and later, institutional racism. A significant number of pupils did not fit in well with school and actively resisted the imposition of educational discipline up to the age of 16. It was widely reported in the press that ROSLA had the indirect effect of raising the peak age of criminal activity and that it led to "rising crime."[3]

ROSLA created a framework and set of problems that could not be solved in the short term. It proved to be a convenient way of managing youth unemployment that began to increase in the 1970s and the 1980s with the decline of manufacturing industry.[4] It also encouraged a more diversified sixth form that catered to a variety of needs. One wider response to this pressure was the development of vocational education and training schemes of which there was a continuing stream including the Youth Opportunities Programme (YOP) from 1979 and the Technical and Vocational Education Initiative (TVEI) from 1983 introduced through the Manpower Services Commission (MSC).[5] "Less able" pupils were targeted through these initiatives although some courses were linked to the emerging computing industry and were broader in their approach.

With the advent of GCSE, the local education authority (LEA)-led partnerships providing TVEI courses with the MSC and further education (FE) colleges began to falter. Despite having had nearly £1 billion of

investment, this attempt at creating a national framework for 14–18 vocational education was abandoned.[6] The shift also reflected interdepartmental tensions within government leading to the closure of the MSC in 1990
and a move toward greater central powers for the Department of Education
at the expense of LEAs. Academic routes for the older groups of secondary
school students came to predominate with a corresponding diminution of
emphasis upon vocationally based options. The system gradually came to
be dominated by GCSE and 'A' level examination results, which were used
as indicators of school performance.

However, there were tensions within the conservatism of the 1980s.
Alongside the emphasis on tradition, nationalism, discipline, and hierarchy was a contradictory belief in free markets and private capital.[7] Within
education, these competing polarities played out in complex ways. Ideas
of "diversity" and "choice" became important mechanisms to undermine
and diminish the functions and roles of LEAs. As a result of the 1988
Education Reform Act, this was partly achieved through local management of schools (LMS), a measure that rebalanced the power relations
between LEAs and central government. The institution of the national
curriculum and associated supervisory regimes led to increasing the power
of central government, particularly over the curriculum.

By the turn of the millennium, the specialized notion of the "knowledge economy," which reflected the rise of industries based around information technology, had been extended to society and education more
widely. In policy discourses, the education system was tied evermore
closely to the needs of the economy with the result that the notion of
skills, competencies, and aptitudes became increasingly important alongside ideas of curriculum as a body of knowledge. Concern has mounted
in the face of international economic competition from the emerging
economies of Southeast Asia in addition to Brazil, Russia, and India.
Indeed, Britain's long-term economic decline in relation to other nations
sparked off a number of educational debates on the role of learning in
stemming the trend; the "learning society" was being seen as essential to
building social capital and economic success. From within this changing
context, the issue of compulsory education resurfaced once again into
mainstream public debates. Education has come to occupy center stage
in domestic and international policy arenas not only due to perceived
economic change but also because education has been closely associated
with social justice, personal well-being, a thriving civil society, and a
reduction in antisocial behavior.[8] It has become seen as a ubiquitous positive force across society. In 2006, the Leitch Review of Skills, emanating from the Treasury, took this evolving educational discourse forward
by arguing that economic competitiveness depended upon increased

investment in a diversified and vocationally relevant curriculum.[9] That the Treasury took the lead was itself indicative of the way that education was being reconfigured as an economic investment. The Labour secretary of state for education Alan Johnson was impressed with a reform to extend compulsory education in Canada and he publicly suggested that Britain might embark on a similar journey. Following a generally sympathetic public reaction, the process of policy formation was relatively rapid as the idea of RPA was seen to address a range of needs and a green paper was published in 2007.[10]

The 2008 Education and Skills Act extended compulsory participation in education and training to 17 years of age from 2013 and 18 years of age from 2015, and represented an important element of the Labour government's legislative program.[11] The delay in implementing the policy was to allow time for capacity building, curriculum development, new qualifications, and other related preparations. The idea of "participation" was broadly conceived to include schooling, training, apprenticeships, and part-time, certified, work-based learning. The legislation is a major policy initiative with significant educational and social implications. It represents a further addition to the system of compulsory education and is closely connected to the wider context of educational policy development and reform, in particular, 14–19 education.[12]

The past, present, and future "trajectory"[13] of this policy reveals contradictions and tensions that are closely related to the history of ROSLA. Connections between educational policy and research are complex, multiple, and, at times, fraught.[14] Placing contemporary developments within a historical setting can provide insights into policy and practice. An historical framework helps to locate the parameters within which educational practices are configured and reconfigured. However, while historical approaches have been widely recognized as contributing to our knowledge of policy, it is a commonplace that academics and policy makers regularly ignore them. "Policy amnesia" and "year zero" thinking can be a shortcut to believing that policy can achieve something new, often in a very short space of time.[15] Indeed, many initiatives of the New Labour governments from 1997 were characterized by a turning away from historical explanation and a wariness that they might become ensnared in the briars of past; instead, Tony Blair championed the idea of continuous "radical" change. At such times, history can appear as a burden, an unwelcome inheritance that constrains the scope and imagination needed for an unknown future.

Therefore, it is all the more interesting to note that the decision to lengthen the period of compulsory education did inspire historical thinking and justifications among policy makers. Government ministers themselves deployed historical arguments in explaining the benefits of RPA, betraying an element of "social learning" from past policies,[16] particularly ROSLA. It was argued forcefully that, for much of the twentieth century, there existed a widespread historical consensus in favor of raising the leaving age: "Historically as a nation, we have long believed that young people should be in some form of education and training at least up to the age of 18."[17] In vindicating RPA, ROSLA was summoned as a central feature of post-1945 peacetime society.[18] Indeed, internationally the growth of compulsory education has been closely allied to nation building.[19] Historical arguments were endorsed by the secretary of state for education Ed Balls in his 2007 speech to the Fabian Society, when he pledged the government to raise the participation age: "Now—90 years on—we are finally legislating to fulfil that 1918 commitment [i.e., 1918 Education Act] and raise the education leaving age to 18."[20] His analysis maintained that the key remaining issue was one of implementing an agreed proposal. Here also historical lessons from the past were drawn, with particular parallels to the 1972 raising of the leaving age from 15 to 16. Balls was determined not to make the "same mistake as in 1972, when there was little thought given to what young people would actually do in their extra year of schooling."[21] Although explicit historical arguments and assumptions have informed government proposals, such "policy learning" has been noticeably constrained by the political context.[22] Our own research suggests that the formation of the policy to raise the participation age has been unduly selective in its historical awareness. For instance, it is notable that the assumption of a historical consensus on the need for compulsory education to 18 ignores the long and widespread opposition to the reform and the fact that widespread discussions and preparations were made in the 1960s and the 1970s.

The policy interest in the history of extending compulsion has been matched by research interventions either keen to find out "what worked" in the past[23] or to relate 14–19 education to wider social and historical forces.[24] Educational structures have resulted from the tenacious legacies of previous policy and practice and, as a result, schools and teachers have often proved remarkably resilient to change and reform.[25] The attempts to compel successively older sections of the population to attend school also reveal some familiar arguments relating to the economy, the organization of education, the curriculum, and school building. An historical analysis lends itself to comparison and juxtaposition with RPA in a number of areas including notions of human capital, the structural organization of education, the implications for the curriculum, and the preparation for, and implementation of, change.

Human Capital, the Economy, and Finance

Economic motivations have furnished the crucial justification for RPA. Education policy and learning has been saturated by economic thinking in recent years although social justice and cohesion are often presented as secondary factors flowing from the economic. While this appears to capture a markedly modern phenomenon, it also represents a contemporary inflexion of a much older debate that revolved around the thorny issue of how education has been understood as a cost and a benefit.

For much of the twentieth century, education was seen as an additional outlay, a burden upon productive industry that had to be paid for when the country could afford it. Even this could be an optimistic view for, in the early twentieth century, grave doubts were expressed regularly about the value of educating the working class. It hardly seemed worth schooling the supposedly less-able children beyond the basic 3R's, which were seen as more than an adequate preparation for life dominated by manual work. It was in this context that arguments in favor of greater educational equality were shaped. Education came to be seen as an autonomous activity and as a broadly conceived investment benefiting society as a whole. For example, R. H. Tawney viewed education as a spiritual experience protected from the rigors of earning a living later in life and offering some immunity from the life-sapping influence of the workplace. In reflecting on the history of compulsory education, he complained of the "subordination of education to economic exigencies"[26] and argued that 50 years of practical experience reflected the wisdom of raising the school-leaving age. This line of thinking came to fruition in the post 1944 welfare state. Education gradually came to be seen as an investment within an expanding system. It would be argued that "wastage" in education, through early leaving from grammar schools, was having adverse affects across society.[27]

The Crowther Report, *15 to 18*, crystallized many of these arguments and took them further in presenting the case for raising the leaving age to 16 albeit primarily within an economic framework. The report argued that prolonged compulsory education would enrich both individual and societal fortunes.[28] Education was coming to be regarded as complementary to the economy and this was reflected in the spread of the term "human capital" during the late 1950s and early 1960s. It was believed that education played a significant role in economic expansion.[29] Edward Boyle, having announced the raising of the leaving age to 16 in 1964, later argued that the reform would play an essential part in meeting an urgent economic need for more middle managers.[30] However, it has become clear that, despite such apparently propitious circumstances, this course of action was not a foregone conclusion as it required substantially increased funding.[31] The Crowther Report attempted to justify such expenditure by identifying the "valley of the later 1960s" (1965–1969) when a population dip would help the country make the necessary financial and logistical adjustments incumbent upon raising the school-leaving age. Arguments such as this helped to build pressure for change and make the reform appear achievable.[32] In the 1960s, civil servants would struggle to recognize such a valley in working out the detailed proposals but, by then, the commitment to raise the age could not be retracted.[33] Even so, financial concerns again became paramount with the devaluation of the pound in 1967. Delaying ROSLA for two years stood out as providing "a relatively self-contained and coherent decision, while the other possible savings cover a wide variety of different educational fields."[34] Despite the widespread dismay felt by Labour politicians, a Treasury employee had noted that criticism would be subdued "compared with any package of smaller measures which could mean spoiling lots of ships for half-pennyworths of tar."[35] Thus, with a sudden economic downturn, ROSLA became a soft target, reflecting a heightened awareness of costs within government.

In the contemporary context, it is possible to illustrate the way in which these varying approaches to education and the economy have been met with sympathy in political constituencies and policy circles. The mutating notion of human capital has been a survivor from the 1960s through to its present-day neoliberal incarnation—the very elasticity of the term has contributed to its longevity. But it has become pervasive at a time when government regulation and control of the economy has been considerably weakened. Indeed, the meaning of human capital has shifted significantly so that there is now a responsibility upon us all to develop skills to be able to respond to rapid economic change while also delivering individual and collective prosperity:

> It used to be that natural resources, a big labour force and a dose of inspiration was all that was required for countries to succeed economically.
>
> But not any more. In the 21st century, our future prosperity will depend on building a Britain where people are given the opportunity and encouragement to develop their skills and abilities to the maximum; and then given the support to rise as far as their talents will take them.[36]

While there have clearly been noticeable changes in the economic context, the Leitch Review of Skills[37] presented a before and after picture that simplified the way in which education may have contributed to economic and social well-being in the past. In building upon this idea, the impact assessment for the 2008 Education and Skills Act approached the issue of costs in a way that directly echoed the Crowther Report and perhaps underestimated the balance of incomings and outgoings. Its idealized accounting models led to the following claim:

> The additional costs for each cohort of young people who participate to 18 due to RPA is £774m...Compared to the current 90% participation aspiration, the additional economic benefit of all young people participating is around £2,400m for each cohort, discounted over their lifetimes (in 2016–17 prices).[38]

Two key expectations were that 90 percent participation could be achieved voluntarily by 2015 and that the benefits should be calculated according to projected lifetime earnings. While these may or may not be reasonable conjectures to make, and the first of these may well be met, such confident assertions certainly facilitated the decision to spend additional funds.[39]

Since then, with coming to power of the Conservative-Liberal Democrat Coalition government in 2010, there has been a dramatic shift toward an emphasis upon costs and the need to find savings to reduce the national debt. The persistent oscillation between cost and investment has thus impacted, quite suddenly, upon the evolving policy in the twenty-first century. The initial vision for RPA has been diluted in the face of such pressures; the most obvious example being the canceling of general diplomas that had been part of Ed Balls' curriculum reform.[40] Moreover, the government has been criticized for abolishing educational maintenance allowances (EMA) and replacing them with a less generous system of funding that has taken a long time to implement, factors that may impact negatively upon participation in the future.[41] The focus on cutting spending has also served to diffuse initial Labour government concerns that those in "jobs without training" should be directed toward certified learning opportunities. This has not been a major issue for the Coalition government, a change indicative of an increasing voluntary take up of post-16 education and training. However, in 2011, the numbers of 16- to 18-year-olds pursuing full-time education in England fell slightly for the first time since 2001, from 68.6 percent in 2010 to 67.7 percent in 2011. Of all 16- to 18-year-olds in England, 83.1 percent were in education and training, comprising 93.5 percent of 16-year-olds, 87.0 percent of 17-year-olds, and 68.3 percent of 18-year-olds.[42] The numbers of young people who are not in education, employment or training (NEET) has been hovering between 7 and 10 percent in recent years.[43] At the end of 2011, 197,600 (9.9%) 16- to 18-year-olds were NEET although rates varied with age so that 5.4 percent of 16-year-olds, 8.4 percent of 17-year-olds, and 15.8 percent of 18-year-olds fell into this category.[44]

This is a rapidly changing context and it is by no means guaranteed that wider social pressures will all work to make RPA a smooth transition. One civil servant described how a Canadian example where jobs were accepted in lieu of training was frowned upon under the Labour government, but was later utilized as a positive example under the Coalition government. In 2012, the secretary of state for education, Michael Gove, decided not to commence parts of the 2008 Act that required employers to check that young people are enrolled on courses before employing them, nor to arrange work to fit around training as would have previously been the case.[45] In view of the erratic and changeable economic climate, challenges may well escalate in the years ahead. RPA was inherited with mixed feelings by Coalition partners who were initially lukewarm about the measure even though they maintained the policy when in power. Contradictory impulses are apparent in the decision to implement RPA while delaying its enforcement, ostensibly to allow time for adjustments and to avoid "criminalizing" young people.[46] As in the past, being seen to publicly cut such a significant commitment was viewed with some trepidation. Moreover, adverse publicity would have been compounded by the need for primary legislation—unusually, a clause had been inserted into the Act stipulating that it either had to be implemented by 2013 and 2015 or repealed through primary legislation.[47] This requirement may even have represented historical learning from the 1944 Education Act, parts of which, notably those covering county colleges, were never implemented but remained on the statute book for decades before being quietly dropped.

Structures and Curriculum

The initial vision for RPA was based upon the claim that traditional schooling may not be the appropriate track for all students. In order to achieve 100 percent participation, it was suggested, a range of options relevant to 16- and 17-year-olds would have to be offered. Diversity was perceived as the key to attracting students to appropriate learning opportunities in the workplace, FE, and other training bodies. There was to be a "learning route for everyone" with options "broad enough to enable all young people to choose a worthwhile and engaging education or training option that suits their needs and interests."[48]

Here again, historical understanding is instructive. As supporters of the policy have been keen to point out, the impulse for education to 18 has a long history,[49] not least in terms of the promised day continuation schools of the 1918 Act and the county colleges of the 1944 Act, each of them proving to be expendable ideas that failed to be implemented in practice.[50] County colleges and ROSLA were, for a long time, considered to be twin pillars of an emerging educational system. In 1959, the Crowther Report persisted with this idea by advocating that ROSLA to 16 should pave the way to county colleges although ROSLA was given priority.[51] Sir William Alexander and the Association of Education Committees were sympathetic to the policy but they "reluctantly" concluded that the school-leaving age should take precedence given the material and teacher shortages.[52] Furthermore, the proposal that the final year of school might be spent in FE colleges proved shortlived given the entrenched interests of schools.

Since the school-leaving age was raised to 16 in 1972, a profusion of terms have attempted to represent this ideal of postsecondary education: not just adult education, which has a longer history,[53] but also permanent education, recurrent education, continuing education, and, most recently, lifelong learning. In comparison with the dominant position of schooling, this educational litany of transient terms has never managed to capture a coherent set of institutionalized practices.

The participation age policy, in a different context, faces similar pressures. The creation of a 14–19 category has done little to dispel the fact that 16 remains the crucial divide because it marks the end of the compulsory school age. As the participation age rises to 18, the assumption of a variegated offering for young people in a range of different settings may be called into question. Some important and positive partnerships have been developed between schools, FE, and training providers, but it is clear that most work will take place in and around schools.[54] However, the initial vision of a diversified offer attuned to the needs of all young people will have to be channeled into what is available in any given area. In the past, the responsibilities for delivering compulsory education fell back on schools and, in the absence of an adequate number of alternative providers in the future, it appears the same pattern will be repeated. Even though there is no expectation that all work will take place in schools, their presence will continue to predominate. If diversification is to take place it will partly take place within schools as it occurred after 1972. The students who leave school may find that alternative opportunities are limited, even with targeted support, a shortage that will stimulate FE, the voluntary and private sectors to develop new provision. For some time, this declining group of young people may be unable to locate appropriate learning opportunities and find themselves isolated in unsuitable courses. It may prove difficult for students who wish to change course part way through a term to locate an appropriate alternative. These tensions were partly addressed by the Wolf Report on vocational education[55] that identified both the importance of core academic study as well as the need for innovation and flexibility in vocational education—a vision that may take some time to achieve.

There is an irony here with implications for the future development of policy. Local education authorities have been consciously undermined by successive governments so that their role is now limited to monitoring and service provision, fostering collaboration rather than giving direction.[56] They were recently offered a lifeline with responsibility for 14–19 education[57] and, as RPA comes into force, local authorities may find their remit theoretically widened. But in practice, downgrading the role of local government has continued apace and the diversifying ecology of secondary education in England, including academies, trusts, and free schools, will exert countervailing influences that impair them further. Initial powers granted to local authorities to commission new educational provision were later rescinded. It was perhaps unsurprising that the National Audit Office discovered a £100 million shortfall in the estimate of the enforcement and monitoring costs of local authorities.[58] In some areas where a range of agencies were leading RPA trials, it even proved difficult to generate the active support of local authorities.[59]

Moreover, information, advice, and guidance (IAG) will now be organized through schools although there have been widespread doubts about their capacity to provide "independent" advice to young people. Rather, evidence points to the fact that schools are likely to retain successful pupils while encouraging others to leave, further widening the divide between school and nonschool.[60] The fact that, from September 2013, colleges will be able to enroll 14- and 15-year-olds, which was one response to the Wolf Report, may have a limited impact in this context. This measure is thus occupying a zone between vocational and nonvocational routes and between schools and colleges, and may heighten tensions.[61] As a result, 14–19 education is likely to remain divided between schools, on the one hand, and a more isolated presence within a range of FE, voluntary and private training options on the other. The need for collaboration and partnership can be expected to grow further in this new context, an example of which are the calls for "middle-tier" structures.[62] Cooperative values have also been adapted to educational purposes by federations of schools in order to strengthen partnerships.[63]

Changes in the structure of education have been intimately linked to issues of content. The decision to extend compulsory education shone a spotlight upon the curriculum as a contested area bound into broader social and moral concerns. The Schools Council, from 1964, was charged with developing appropriate curricula to deal with the expansion of education and specifically with ROSLA. Following the policy decision to go ahead with ROSLA to 16, the political and policy focus shifted rapidly to curriculum development that was identified as a critical solution to the conundrum of what young people would actually do in the "extra year." It was recognized that isolating ROSLA students could easily stigmatize them. Advocates of comprehensive education also saw the raising of the leaving age as a necessary prelude to achieving a common curriculum for everyone. A five rather than four-year secondary course, ending in public examinations at age 16, had long been held up as a requirement for an educated democracy. Yet, as we have seen, wider social differences impinged upon education in such a way that low-status vocational education could easily emerge from within this framework.

Bouts of enthusiasm for vocational education in relation to ROSLA gave way to fears and prevarication. Concessions to the vocational needs of young people and society would be subsequently tempered by an emphasis upon the importance of general education prior to entering the labor market. Fears about the lack of progression or quality of some vocational proposals were compounded by trade union concerns that work experience might become a source of cheap labor. Although "vocational" often implied an introduction to issues connected with the world of work as opposed to training for actual employment,[64] in practice, many ROSLA students directly sampled vocational opportunities through courses like home economics and hairdressing for girls and motor mechanics for boys.[65] The varied permutations of vocational education did not dispel the reality that secondary education continued to reflect broader educational and social divisions. The pursuit of curriculum reform could be continually thwarted by the reality of preparing pupils for radically different futures in life and work. A sense of equality and spirituality might easily be reduced back to a material analysis based on the needs of the economy. The tension between equality and differentiation would rapidly blur in such cases. Overlapping yet distinct educational arguments appeared to separate and dovetail in unexpected ways and were indicative of the confusion and complexity in developing a suitable curriculum for all.

A congruent set of dilemmas has suffused contemporary debates over the participation age and 14–19 education. For instance, the attempt to provide an overarching baccalaureate qualification, following the Tomlinson Report, was sacrificed by the Labour government just prior to the 2005 general election.[66] The proposal for a common qualification had been partly inspired by the need to create greater equality of opportunity and ensure that all students were on commensurate tracks from which they could progress. As a result, Ed Balls was left to argue that the new diplomas would be equivalent to 'A' levels, a barely credible claim given the latter's embedded status as "gold standard" qualifications. The more recent decision by the subsequent government to abandon academic and general diplomas did little to boost a flagging response to these new qualifications in an already overcrowded educational market place; diplomas were to fend for themselves and would remain "as long as there is a demand," according to schools minister Nick Gibb.[67] The gradual undermining of diplomas eclipsed the desire for separate but equal qualifications. Although today there is a greater awareness of the need for progression routes for all learners, especially at the lower levels, the deep-set historical and curricular inequalities have been an enduring presence. It is ironic to note that while prevailing assumptions about fixed ability have dissipated over the past half century, economic and social inequality has intensified, a development that affected the education system as a whole.[68]

Nevertheless, RPA has given rise to debates over the value and purpose of examinations at 16. Michael Gove suggested that 17- and 18-year-olds will continue to strive for exams that others take at 16. His attempts to institute a restrictive and more difficult EBacc, or English Baccalaureate, had to be dropped given wide-ranging criticism. By contrast, Stephen Twigg, the Labour Party education spokesperson, has argued that we should consider replacing exams at 16 with ones at 18 as a result of RPA. This latter proposal is built upon a future projection for RPA as an equivalent measure to raising the school-leaving age rather than a limited form of participation in education or training. Such demands reflect the kinds of thinking about education systems that have been apparent since the inception of compulsory education. Once again, the long-term implications of extending compulsory education will take many years to unravel.

Preparation

The curriculum reform stimulated by ROSLA proved to be a very long-term process. It aggravated the lack of purpose felt by a section of young people and stimulated experiments in vocational education that gathered pace from the mid-1970s. In the 1960s, great hopes for fundamental curricular changes gave way to a gradual realization that Schools Council projects were only preparatory and had not been implemented on a widespread basis. It proved difficult to generate a sense of ownership among schools and teachers, many of whom were, initially, less focused upon the reform. The proliferation of teachers' centers played an important role in disseminating curricular changes and facilitating discussion but, in the first instance, they only reached a limited number of teachers and schools, a point picked over by critics of the reform. Only when the new leaving age became a reality could curriculum ideas be fully tested in practice. By

1968, Edward Boyle, watching the evolving situation from the shadow cabinet, noted that readiness was relative to the enactment of the reform itself:

> When people say "we shall not be ready for this reform" the answer is, we shall not be ready until everybody knows it's coming. We shall never be ready until we do it...it's only when people know that there can be no further postponement and this reform is coming, that we shall prepare ourselves and be ready for it.[69]

Despite its initially limited reach, the Schools Council played an essential role in fostering discussion and development that might be more widely adopted at the appropriate moment. While some LEAs asserted their confidence in preparing for ROSLA, such as Manchester and London, elsewhere grave doubts were raised about what had been done in anticipation of the change.

The Schools Council had represented an initial move into the "secret garden"[70] of the curriculum and it was unlikely that finished syllabuses could be delivered prior to widespread teacher participation. Indeed, for some teachers, planning for ROSLA contradicted the very nature of teaching; curriculum change impacted upon personal identities and cultural meanings that were resistant to new ideas.[71] ROSLA was not a technical solution and required significant change across the educational system. After 1972, many Schools Council projects had learnt from the experience of ROSLA and their impact improved, often working alongside LEA subject inspectors and targeting teacher training and newly qualified teachers.

The extended period for implementation created considerable space for interpretation and adjustment of the initial aims of ROSLA. Today, the situation is very different to that in the past, with a national curriculum and a far more centralized education system. However, it will prove difficult to fully implement the participation age policy until it has actually come into force. As we have seen, local action wil not lead to universal and coherent plans given the eclectic and widening range of semiautonomous stakeholders in education. The evaluation report for RPA local pilot projects bore this out and revealed variable levels of preparedness; for example, one recommendation suggested that LEAs appoint someone to coordinate the participation age work, a strong indication that many had not done so by 2010[72] and, a year later, most of the trial areas did not have a "fully complete plan for delivering RPA."[73] Only so much preparation was possible prior to the new participation age coming into effect and, inevitably, there was a degree of falseness about testing out ideas for a situation that did not yet exist. The staged plan for enforcement will further broaden the scope for adjustment and experimentation. As a result, the more significant moment of implementation may be revealed in the many adjustments and alterations that will take place in the years following the change. Developing long-term quality options for 16- to 18-year-olds will prove to be a considerable challenge for all concerned. In the process, the past history of the school-leaving age will continue to reverberate in the present. The way in which politicians have invoked historical justifications for RPA testifies to the fact that the extension of compulsory education as a whole represents a contested and ongoing historical project.

Chapter 10

Conclusion

The raising of the school leaving age (ROSLA) has been a crucial and substantial educational reform with wide social, economic, political, and cultural implications. At many historical points, it appeared to be quite a fragile reform that had to fight off hard-nosed opposition. If ROSLA to 16 had been delayed any later than 1972, just at the point when an economic recession would be coupled with new economic restraints, it might not have happened for many years to come.

ROSLA has been central to educational and social change and formed the basis for the emergence of a compulsory school system. For the progressive alliance of the early twentieth century, to which R. H. Tawney was so central, ROSLA provided the lynchpin of educational advance. In extending compulsion and the duration of the school year to 14 and then 15 years of age, attention was increasingly paid to the separation and specialization of different pupils, what would harden into the selective tripartite system of the postwar years. For the Conservative Party in the context of a growing welfare state, critics saw an opportunity to save money by reducing the leaving age although education was increasingly seen as one area that the party could champion. In the 1960s, the great furor stimulated by the call for comprehensive reorganization left ROSLA in the shadows but the reform was, in fact, central to the establishment of a five-year common curriculum for all. Although preparations were extensive in the 1960s, ROSLA to 16 helped to highlight the contradictions apparent in a divided system that separated out "Newsom pupils" from the rest. But by forcing all pupils into a singular school regime, a significant number of young people remained isolated and marginalized, a fact that in turn stimulated the growth of vocational initiatives during the years of the 1970s and the 1980s. The raising of the participation age (RPA) can be read as a partial attempt to respond to these educational transformations. As in the past, achievement of raising the participation age will only be a beginning point from which entrenched forms of inequality will develop into new patterns within the system of compulsory education.

Politically, ROSLA has been a major preoccupation for governments, which have rarely made the decision to extend compulsion without wide-spread debate over the value of forcing young people to remain in school for a further year. In the twentieth century, cabinet debates on agreeing, delaying, and confirming ROSLA were crucial turning points in educational history. Politicians were all too aware that, for the bulk of the population, the length of time for which pupils were to be retained in schools was often the essential fact of educational life and this applied even to the landmark 1944 Act.

Political interests have been matched by economic ones. The costs of ROSLA have been substantial and have had to be justified against sustained opposition. But the tension between education as a cost and an invest-ment was not always an either-or option and each side of this equation has shifted over time. Tawney's view of education as a means of strengthening national life in general was quite different to more recent incarnations of education tied to skills and economic competitiveness.

In addition, ROSLA had always dominated in comparison with other visions of educational development, for instance, based upon day-continuation schools, county colleges, or vocational and further education (FE) more generally. From the very inception of compulsory schooling, edu-cationists highlighted the need to rescue young people from the workplace and allow them to develop as children within schools. Employers and chil-dren themselves both challenged these practices in different ways. The his-torical priority accorded to the school-leaving age reflects the fact that the education of young people in schools has been the dominant form of educa-tion to which other, more marginal forms, have had to adjust and adapt. This historical legacy continues to underpin the many criticisms of employ-ers who feel that young people are inadequately prepared for the workplace. Other alternative models and informal modes of learning have struggled for recognition. In one sense, the advent of state education represented a neutering of existing forms of working-class education and learning.[1]

State legislation could be widely perceived as a top-down paternalistic measure. Schooling was not immediately welcomed by the working class for whom it could appear as an enforced childhood, which drew them away from the essential task of earning an income. Yet, individuals cer-tainly benefited from it, a fact that could lead to mixed feelings about the value of raising the school-leaving age in which benefits and drawbacks had to be weighed up.

In the long run, ROSLA represented both a response to and an intervention in a growing popular sympathy for education. Being perceived to be a "failure" in educational terms could give rise to a determination that one's children might be more successful in the future. It is no wonder that personal experiences of education continue to stimulate intense and ambiguous feelings. ROSLA then represents a major means through which the age and meanings of childhood have been determined—coming of age in both individual and collective terms. Extended schooling to a minimum of 16 has become a widely shared cultural assumption. The gradual extension of ROSLA can be read as a basis for the contemporary "right to a childhood" that is now sacrosanct across many societies.

Compulsory education has itself stimulated a logic of continuing expansion. Raising the school-leaving age necessarily led to an increase of regulation. As social and economic complexity has come to characterize life, an extended education has been viewed in positive terms, as a self-evident truth. An increasing number of parents who had kept their children on for an extra year prior to ROSLA continued to do so afterwards for a further year. This reflects the multiple and contradictory purposes that education serves, such as social mobility, social and educational differentiation, and social reproduction. The connection between the values of the school and the family has been a crucial determinant of the educational success of pupils.[2] As one Australian policy document noted recently, "The cumulative nature of education means that raising student achievement will require an ongoing effort across all aspects and years of education."[3] ROSLA has stimulated pressures that forced schools, teachers, and administrators to make adjustments to the content and processes of education.

The project of ROSLA has yet to run its course. While each step in raising the age must be placed in its historical context, the reform has nevertheless given rise to widespread historical comparison. From a contemporary perspective, previous steps in raising the age can appear to be part of a single coherent project related to economic growth and modernization. This has not only been an administrative issue but also one in which social, economic, and political forces have coalesced around education as pivotal to the way society operates. Extending compulsory education has provided one means of addressing a number of wider problems.

In its successive stages, ROSLA has also provided a powerful model for other countries to imitate, emulate, and adapt to their needs. While this has been a privilege of wealthier nations, it reflects political will and a faith in the educability of ever-wider sections of the population. The Millennium Development Goals for universal primary education clearly highlight the centrality of full-time schooling in the way that poorer countries are developing. The widespread extension of compulsory education across many countries must also be located within the particular national and cultural contexts that give meaning to the reform.

State formation has been closely allied to the creation and expansion of compulsory education, an area that has been subject to intensifying debates. Despite neoliberal ideas about the declining importance of the national state, governments have generally been the driving force behind educational reform albeit alongside a range of other bodies. Today, in Britain, the postwar expansion engendered by ROSLA has given way to greater central state control of education policy channeled through quangos and quasi markets, informed by a plethora of policy texts, in which an array of organizations are active.[4] Previously, and particularly in the postwar years, policy followed clearer avenues between national government, local education authorities (LEAs), their representative bodies such as the Association of Education Committees (AEC), County Council Association, as well as schools and trade unions, the Confederation of British Industry (CBI), and academic educationists, an arrangement that bore a resemblance to wider corporatist politics.[5]

Despite the great significance of ROSLA, as we have noted, there has been relatively little attention given to the measure in histories of education. In part, this can be explained by the sporadic nature of ROSLA that has risen and fallen in historical stages. At each moment in the augmentation of compulsory education, public interest has swelled and then subsided once the new leaving age became widely accepted. The staged and periodic nature of the reform meant that during the period of incubation and preparation, the policy acted as an umbrella under which many educational policy issues were gathered—curriculum, pedagogy, buildings, and so on. But this phase was inevitably short lived before the change found a gradual acceptance and ROSLA ceased to be an organizing element of education policy. In this way, broad and politicized debates over educational reform became gradually transformed into issues of educational administration.[6] Historical research into this process helps to unravel the political and social contestation inherent within such apparently neutral and benign measures. It can reconnect the interplay of politics, economics, curriculum, and educational structures that may at first sight appear to be independent of each other.

An historical approach to policy helps to identify not only continuities but also breaks with the past. In some respects, the raising of the participation age represents unexplored educational territory. RPA bears a resemblance to earlier proposals for county colleges and day-continuation schools rather than ROSLA, which was focused almost exclusively upon schools. However, it would appear likely that RPA will, to a large extent, depend upon schools taking the bulk of students given that the number of alternative institutions is limited. Clearly there will be a role for FE and voluntary organizations but these are likely to be limited to those students who do not wish to remain in schools.

ROSLA and RPA show how policy is prone to ambiguity and interpretation during an extended process of adoption,[7] a problem amplified by protracted lead-in times, intensive debate, and contested preparation and implementation. Moreover, on each occasion when the school-leaving age was raised, issues and problems have been bequeathed to successive generations, which could not be resolved in the short term. Extending compulsory education has been motivated by creating fair and equal access to education and, for many, there has been improvement. But such policies have to survive for a long time during which they may be downgraded and this can have an impact upon the quality and nature of the provision, especially during economic crises when policy can assume new shapes and directions. When the participation age is raised, it is likely to have a number of unforeseen consequences, fostering access and opportunity, as well as differentiation and inequality.

Each step in the process of extending compulsory education has also generated opposite forces and continuing reservations, and this has continued into the early twenty-first century. For example, Peter Preston, a former editor of *The Guardian* has argued that forcing teenagers to stay in education to 18 would do little to improve numeracy and literacy, and that the increase in the school-leaving age in the 1970s had been a "costly, bumbling shambles."[8] Others on the left who were suspicious of the Labour government's fondness for central control in education saw these new reforms as a further initiative in social control. Economists such as Alison Wolf[9] remained wary that these opportunities will have limited long-term impact in comparison with spending the money on early years and primary education. In addition, advocates such as Sir Chris Woodhead, former head of the schools inspection agency Office for Standards in Education (OFSTED), and Lord Digby Jones, former director of the CBI, have also argued for reducing the school-leaving age to 14 on the grounds that vocational opportunities could be provided for those not happy at school.[10]

ROSLA has represented a progressive social force in a divided society. Unsurprisingly, the extension of compulsory schooling reflected wider inequalities, particularly around social class, gender, race, and disability. The very value of ROSLA depended upon the acceptance that all children were potentially educable, a claim that had been vehemently denied in the past. The growing number of women and working-class pupils who succeeded through schools helped to convince those in positions of influence that making an extended secondary education available to all was a worthwhile pursuit. While inequality has been visible in every aspect of raising the school-leaving age, ROSLA has also represented a crucial move toward equality of opportunity that was hard won over many years. From 1870, it took just over 100 years to build an education system in which all children left school at the same age as public examinations were held. The current extension of the participation age to 18 will also give rise to arguments for common forms of assessment as well as counter claims for sharper forms of differentiation. Ensuring a quality education that supports all children and meets collective as well as individual needs thus remains a continuing and contested undertaking.

Notes

1   INTRODUCTION

1. Tom Woodin, Gary McCulloch, and Steven Cowan, "Raising the Participation Age: Policy Learning from the Past?" *British Educational Research Journal* 39, 4 (2013): 635–653.
2. David Crook, "Compulsory Education in the United Kingdom. Historical, Comparative and Contemporary Perspectives," *Journal of Educational Planning and Administration* 3 (2005): 397–414; Nigel Norris, "Raising the School Leaving Age," *Cambridge Journal of Education* 37, 4 (2007): 471–472; David Raffe and Ken Spours, *Policy Making and Policy Learning in 14–19 Education* (London: Bedford Way Papers, 2007); Robin Simmons, "Raising the Age of Compulsory Education in England: A NEET Solution?" *British Journal of Educational Studies* 56, 4 (2008): 420–439; Nicola Sheldon, "When Should Children Leave School?" Policy and Society website www.historyandpolicy. org/lessons/schoolage.html (accessed September 25, 2008); J. Kewin, M. Tucker, S. Neat, and M. Corney, *Lessons from History: Increasing the Number of 16 and 17 Year Olds in Education and Training* (Reading: CfBT, 2009). For an earlier version, see Malcolm Seaborne, "The Historical Background," in J. W. Tibble (ed.), *The Extra Year. The Raising of the School Leaving Age* (London: Routledge, 1970), 9–19.
3. G. A. N. Lowndes, *The Silent Social Revolution. An Account of the Expansion of Public Education in England and Wales 1895–1965* (Oxford: Oxford University Press, 1937/1969).
4. Andy Green, *Education and State Formation: The Rise of Education Systems in England, France and the USA* (London: Macmillan, 1990).
5. Harold Silver, "Education, Opinion and the 1870s," in *Education as History: Interpreting Nineteenth- and Twentieth-Century Education* (London: Methuen, 1983), 85–86.
6. For example, see R. H. Tawney, "Keep the Workers' Children in Their Place," in R. H. Tawney (ed.), *The Radical Tradition* (London: Penguin, 1964), 49–54, and *The School Age and Exemptions* (London: Workers' Educational Association, 1936).
7. Board of Education, *The Education of the Adolescent* (the Hadow Report) (HMSO: London, 1926).

8. AEC/NUT, *The Extra Year: A Report of the Joint Committee of Investigation Representing the Association of Education Committees and the National Union of Teachers* (London: University of London, 1938).

9. Isaac L. Kandel, *Raising the School Leaving Age* (Paris: UNESCO, 1951); W. O. Lester Smith, *Compulsory Education in England* (Paris: UNESCO, 1951).

10. Tibble, *The Extra Year.*

11. Barry Turner (ed.), *Raising of the School Leaving Age* (London: Encyclopaedia Britannica, 1971).

12. Roger White and David Brockington, *In and Out of School: The ROSLA Community Education Project* (London: Routledge and Kegan Paul, 1978); Michael Duane, *The Terrace: An Educational Experiment in a State School* (London: Freedom Press, 1995).

13. Dan Finn, *Training without Jobs: New Deals and Broken Promises, from Raising the School Leaving Age to the Youth Training Scheme* (London: Macmillan, 1987). See also Robert Moore, "Education and the Ideology of Production," *British Journal of Sociology of Education* 8, 2 (1987): 227–242; Robert Moore, "Vocationalism and Educational Change," *Curriculum Journal* 5, 3 (1994): 281–293.

14. OECD, *Compulsory Education in a Changing World* (Paris: OECD, 1983).

15. Joshua Angrist and Alan Krueger, "Does Compulsory Schooling Attendance Affect Schooling and Earnings?" *Quarterly Journal of Economics*, 106 (1991): 979–1014; Colm Harmon and Ian Walker, "Estimates of the Economic Return to Schooling for the United Kingdom," *American Economic Review* 85 (1995): 1278–1286; Philip Oreopoulos, "The Compelling Effects of Compulsory Schooling: Evidence from Canada," *Canadian Journal of Economics* 39, 1 (2006): 22–52; Philip Oreopoulos, "Stay in School: New Lessons on the Benefits of Raising the Legal School-Leaving Age," *Commentary* (Toronto: C.D. Howe Institute, 2005).

16. Alison Wolf, "Education and Economic Performance: Simplistic Theories and Their Policy Consequences," *Oxford Review of Economic Policy* 20, 2 (2004): 315–333.

17. Harold Silver, *Education, Change and the Policy Process* (London: Falmer, 1990).

18. Brian Simon, *Education and the Social Order 1940–90* (London: Lawrence and Wishart, 1991).

19. Dennis J. O'Keefe, "Some Economic Aspects of Raising the School Leaving Age in England and Wales in 1947," *Economic History Review* 28, 3 (1975): 500–516; Dennis J. O'Keefe, "Towards a Socio-Economy of the Curriculum," *Journal of Curriculum Studies* 9, 2 (1977): 101–109.

20. Roy Lowe, *The Death of Progressive Education. How Teachers Lost Control of the Classroom.* (London: Routledge, 2007).

21. Raymond Williams, "Culture Is Ordinary," in Robin Gable (ed.), *Resources of Hope: Culture, Democracy, Socialism* (London: Verso, 1989). Also, Raymond Williams, *The Long Revolution* (London: Chatto and Windus, 1961).

22. Jane Pilcher, *Age and Generation in Modern Britain* (New York: Oxford University Press, 1995), 39.

23. John Springhall, *Coming of Age: Adolescence in Britain, 1860–1960* (Dublin: Gill and Macmillan, 1986), 52.
24. Ibid. See also David Fowler, *Youth Culture in Modern Britain, c. 1920–c. 1970: From Ivory Tower to Global Movement: A New History* (London: Palgrave Macmillan, 2008).
25. Jon Savage, *Teenager. The Creation of Youth 1875–1945* (London: Chatto and Windus, 2007).
26. See, for example, Hugh Cunningham, "Review Essay: Histories of Childhood," *The American Historical Review* 103, 4 (1998): 1195–1208.
27. Simmons, "Raising the Age"; see also Robin Simmons and Ron Thompson (eds.), *Research in Post Compulsory Education* 18, 1–2 (2013), special issue on "Reclaiming the Disengaged: Critical Perspectives on Young People Not in Education, Employment or Training."
28. Anna Davin, *Growing Up Poor: Home, School and Street 1870–1914* (London: Rivers Oram, 1996).
29. Bernard Coard, *How the West Indian Child Is Made Educationally Subnormal in the British School System* (London: New Beacon Books, 1971).
30. Paul Lodge and Tessa Blackstone, *Educational Policy and Educational Inequality* (Oxford: Martin Robertson, 1982).
31. Richard Johnson, "Educational Policy and Social Control in Early Victorian England," *Past and Present* 49, 1 (1970): 96–119.
32. Ivan Illich, *Deschooling Society* (Harmondsworth: Penguin, 1973).
33. See for example Jonathan Rose, *The Intellectual Life of the British Working Classes* (Yale: Yale University Press, 2001); Richard Aldrich (ed.), *A Century of Education* (London: Routledge, 2002).
34. See Gary McCulloch, *Documentary Research in Education, History and the Social Sciences* (London: Routledge, 2004).

2 The School-Leaving Age in International Perspective

1. The term 'ROSLA' became widely used in the 1960s and 1970s. We are also using it as an acronym to describe the longer-term historical changes in school-leaving ages.
2. For example, Ellwood P. Cubberley, *Changing Conceptions of Education* (Boston: Houghton Mifflin, 1909).
3. For some international summaries, see J. A. Mangan (ed.), *A Significant Social Revolution* (London: Woburn Press, 1994).
4. For example, see Philip Corrigan and Derek Sayer, *The Great Arch: English State Formation as Cultural Revolution* (Oxford: Blackwell, 1982); Pavla Miller, "Historiography of Compulsory Schooling: What Is the Problem," *History of Education* 18, 2 (1989): 123–144. Andy Green, *Education and State Formation: The Rise of Education and Training Systems in England,*

France and the USA (London: Macmillan, 1990); Francisco O. Ramirez and John Boli, "The Political Construction of Mass Schooling: European Origins and Worldwide Institutionalization," *Sociology of Education*, 60, 1 (1987): 2–17.

5. Gary McCulloch, *The Struggle for the History of Education* (London: Routledge, 2011).

6. For example, see Mary Jo Maynes, *Schooling in Western Europe. A Social History* (Albany, NY: SUNY, 1985). James van Horn Melton, *Absolutism and the Eighteenth Century Origins of Compulsory in Prussia and Austria* (Cambridge: Cambridge University Press, 1988).

7. For example, Brian Simon, *The Two Nations and the Educational Structure 1780–1870* (London: Lawrence and Wishart, 1974).

8. Carlo M. Cipolla, *Literacy and Development in the West* (Harmondsworth: Penguin, 1969); Francisco O. Ramirez and John Boli, "The Political Construction of Mass Schooling: European Origins and Worldwide Institutionalization," *Sociology of Education* 60, 1 (1987): 2–17.

9. Francoise Furet and Jacques Ozouf, *Reading and Writing: Literacy in France from Calvin to Jules Ferry* (Cambridge: Cambridge University Press, 1982).

10. Catherine Hall, *Civilising Subjects: Metropole and Colony in the English Imagination, 1830–1867* (Cambridge: Polity, 2002).

11. John Malcolm Forbes Ludlow and Lloyd Jones, *The Progress of the Working Class 1832–1867* (London: Strachan, 1867).

12. J. F. Kett, "Juveniles and Progressive Children," *History of Education Quarterly* 13 (1973): 191–194.

13. Frank Musgrove, *Youth and the Social Order* (London: Routledge and Kegan Paul, 1964).

14. For example, Thomas Wright, "Mis-education," *Fraser's Magazine* 6, 35 (1872): 641–650.

15. See Clive Griggs, *The Trades Union Congress and the Struggle for Education, 1868–1925* (Lewes: Falmer, 1988).

16. For example, Simon, *The Two Nations*.

17. Ian Davey, "Capitalism, Patriarchy and the Origins of Mass Schooling," *History of Education Review* 16, 2 (1987): 1–12.

18. Thanks to Fabio Pruneri for pointing this out.

19. J. L. Ewing/National Commission on Education, *Compulsory Education in New Zealand* (Paris: UNESCO, 1972), 22.

20. Ibid., 30.

21. UNESCO, "Extension of Free and Compulsory Education," Second Regional Conference of National Commissions, WS 091/64, 1951. http://unesdoc.unesco.org/images/0015/001554/155412eb.pdf (accessed May 21, 2010).

22. Sascha Auerback, "'The Law Has No Feeling for Poor Folks Like Us!': Everyday Responses to Legal Compulsion in England's Working Class Communities," *Journal of Social History* 45, 3 (2012): 686–708.

23. Susan Williams, Patrick Ivin, and Caroline Morse, *The Children of London: Attendance and Welfare at School, 1870–1990* (London: Institute of Education, 2001).

24. John G. Richardson, "Common, Delinquent and Special: On the Formalization of Common Schooling in the American States," *American Educational Research Journal* 31, 4 (1994): 695–723.

25. Bernard Bailyn, *Education in the Forming of American Society* (New York: Random House, 1960); M. S. Katz, *The Irony of Early School Reform* (Cambridge: Harvard University Press, 1968); Robert B. Everhart, "From Universalism to Usurpation: An Essay on the Antecedents to Compulsory School Attendance Legislation," *Review of Educational Research* 47, 3 (1977): 499–530.

26. M. S. Katz, "Compulsion and the Discourse on Compulsory School Attendance," *Educational Theory* 27, 3 (1977): 179–185.

27. Dennis H. Cooke and Edgar G. Pruet, "Constitutional and Statutory Development of Compulsory School Attendance in Alabama," *Peabody Journal of Education* 16, 5 (1939): 330–334.

28. William M. Landes and Lewis C. Solomon, "Compulsory Schooling Legislation: An Economic Analysis of Law and Social Change in the Nineteenth Century," *Journal of Economic History* 32, 1 (1972): 78.

29. David B. Tyack, "Ways of Seeing: An Essay on the History of Compulsory Schooling," *Harvard Educational Review* 46, 3 (1976): 355–389.

30. Harold Perkin, *The Rise of Professional Society: England Since 1880*, 2nd ed. (London: Routledge, 2002); John G. Richardson, "Variation in Date of Enactment of Compulsory School Attendance Laws: An Empirical Inquiry," *Sociology of Education* 53, 3 (1980): 153–163; Ira Katznelson, Kathleen Gille, and Margaret Weir, "Public Schooling and Working Class Formation: The Case of the United States," *American Journal of Education* 90, 2 (1982): 111–143.

31. UNESCO, "Extension of Free and Compulsory Education."

32. IBE, "Compulsory Education and the Raising of the School Leaving Age (1934)," in *International Conference on Education. Recommendations 1934–1977* (Paris: UNESCO, 1979).

33. ILO, *Child Labour in Relation to Compulsory Education* (Paris: UNESCO, 1951).

34. J. Majault, "The Transition from the Primary to the Secondary School and Its Influence on the School Curriculum," Summary Report of International Advisory Committee on the School Curriculum (Paris: UNESCO, 1956). http://unesdoc.unesco.org/images/0014/001459/145906eb.pdf (accessed July 10, 2010).

35. UNESCO, "Extension of Free and Compulsory Education."

36. Ibid.

37. Ewing, *Compulsory Education*, 89.

38. Ibid., 92.

39. J. S. Pischke and Till von Wachter, "Zero Returns to Compulsory Schooling in Germany: Evidence and Interpretation," *Review of Economics and Statistics* 90, 3 (2008): 592–598.

40. Fabrice Murtin and Martina Viarengo, "The Expansion and Convergence of Compulsory Schooling in Western Europe, 1950–2000," *Economica* 78 (2011): 501–522.

41. On Soviet education, see Mervyn Matthews, *Education in the Soviet Union* (London: George Allen and Unwin, 1982); Joseph Zajda, *Education in the USSR* (Oxford: Pergamon, 1982); Dora Shturman, *The Soviet Secondary School* (London: Routledge, 1988).
42. Jonathan Kozol, "A New Look at the Literacy Campaign in Cuba," *Harvard Educational Review* 48 (1978): 341–377.
43. Costas Meghir and Mårten Palme, "Education Reform, Ability, and Family Background," *American Economic Review* 95, 1 (2005): 414–424.
44. John McNair, "Education in Spain, 1970–1980: The Years of Compulsory Schooling," *Comparative Education* 17, 1 (1981): 47–57.
45. Charles K. Woltz, "Compulsory Attendance at School," *Law and Contemporary Problems* 20, 1 (1955): 6.
46. Haile Yesus Abeje, "How to Provide Universal Schooling," *Prospects* 13, 2 (1983): 245.
47. Alec Fyfe, *The Worldwide Movement against Child Labour—Progress and Future Directions* (Geneva: ILO, 1997).
48. UNICEF, "Lesotho Launches Free and Compulsory Education," June 16, 2011. www.unicef.org/infobycountry/lesotho_58940.html (accessed November 10, 2012).
49. World Bank, "Progression to Secondary School, Male." http://data.worldbank.org/indicator/SE.SEC.PROG.MA.ZS (accessed February 23, 2013).
50. Kwame Akyeampong, "Revisiting Free Compulsory Universal Basic Education (FCUBE) in Ghana," *Comparative Education* 45, 2 (2009): 175–195.
51. Friedrich Huebler, "International Education Statistics: Official School Ages: Primary, Secondary, and Compulsory Education," January 27, 2007. http://huebler.blogspot.co.uk/2007/01/official-school-ages-primary-secondary.html (accessed November 10, 2012).
52. Human Development Unit South Asia Region, *Secondary Education in India: Universalising Opportunity* (Washington, DC: World Bank, 2009).
53. Richard Wilkinson and Kate Pickett, *The Spirit Level* (London: Penguin, 2010).
54. Santosh Mehrotra, "Education for All: Policy Lessons from High Achieving Countries," *International Review of Education* 44, 5–6 (1998): 461–484.
55. Constitution (Eighty-Sixth Amendment Act), 2002. http://indiacode.nic.in/coiweb/amend/amend86.htm (accessed November 10, 2012).
56. *Education for All. National Plan of Action. India* (New Delhi: Ministry of Human Resource Development, 2003).
57. The Right to Education Bill, November 14, 2005.
58. Krishna Kumar, "Quality of Education at the Beginning of the 21st Century: Lessons from India," background paper for EFA Global Monitoring Report, 2005 (Paris: UNESCO, 2004).
59. Ministry of Education, Science and Technology, "Overview." http://english.mest.go.kr/web/1692/site/contents/en/en_0203.jsp (accessed July 20, 2012).
60. Compare Carl J. Dahiman and Jean-Eric Aubert, *China and the Knowledge Economy. Seizing the 21st Century* (Washington, DC: World Bank Institute,

2001); and Andy Green, "Globalisation and the Changing Nature of the State in East Asia," *Globalisation, Societies and Education* 5, 1 (2007): 23–38.

61. Ministry of Education, Singapore, "Compulsory Education." www.moe.gov .sg/initiatives/compulsory-education/ (accessed July 5, 2010).

62. Ministry of Education, Singapore, *Report of the Committee on Compulsory Education in Singapore* (Singapore: MOE, 2000).

63. Josh Franken, "Analysis: Indonesia's 12-Year Compulsory Education Program," *Jakarta Post*, June 28, 2010. www.thejakartapost.com/news/2010/06/28/anal-ysis-indonesia%E2%80%99s-12year-compulsory-education-program.html (accessed November 10, 2011).

64. See Thomas Siedler, "Schooling and Citizenship in a Young Democracy: Evidence from Postwar Germany," *Scandinavian Journal of Economics* 112, 2 (2010): 315–338.

65. For example, Seymour M. Lipset, *Political Man* (London: Heinemann, 1976); Adam Przeworski, Michael E. Alvarez, Jose Antonio Cheibub, and Fernando Limongi, *Democracy and Development: Political Institutions and Well-Being in the World, 1950–1990* (Cambridge: Cambridge University Press, 1988); Philip Oreopoulos, "Estimating Average and Local Treatment Effects of Education When Compulsory Schooling Laws Really Matter," *American Economic Review* 96, 1 (2006): 152–175; Philip Oreopoulos, "Do Dropouts Drop Out Too Soon? Wealth, Health and Happiness from Compulsory Schooling," *Journal of Public Economics* 91 (2007): 2213–2229.

66. Wing-Wah Law, "Legislation and Educational Change: The Struggle for Social Justice and Quality in China's Compulsory Schooling," *Education and the Law* 19, 3 (2007): 177–199.

67. Chengzhi Wang and Mary Bergquist, "Basic Education Development in China: From Finance Reform to World Bank Projects," *International Journal of Educational Management* 17, 7 (2003): 303–311.

68. Zhao Litao and Lim Tin Seng, *China's New Social Policy* (New Jersey: London World Scientific, 2010), 4.

69. OECD, *Compulsory Schooling in a Changing World* (Paris: OECD, 1983).

70. Ibid.

71. Peter Meadmore, "'Free, Compulsory and Secular'? The Re-Invention of Australian Public Education," *Journal of Education Policy* 16, 2 (2001): 113–125.

72. Murtin and Viarengo, "Expansion and Convergence."

73. David Halpin and Barry Troyna, "The Politics of Education Policy Borrowing," *Comparative Education* 31, 3 (1995): 303–310.

74. Alison Wolf, "Education and Economic Performance: Simplistic Theories and Their Policy Consequences," *Oxford Review of Economic Policy* 20, 2 (2004): 315–333.

75. For example, Anthony Giddens, *Modernity and Self-Identity: Self and Society in the Late Modern Age* (Cambridge: Polity, 1991); Carol Reid and Helen Young, "The New Compulsory Schooling Age Policy in NSW, Australia: Ethnicity, Ability and Gender Considerations," *Journal of Education Policy* 27, 6 (2012): 795–814.

76. Joshua Angrist and Alan Krueger, "Does Compulsory Schooling Attendance Affect Schooling and Earnings?" *Quarterly Journal of Economics* 106, 4 (1991): 979–1014; Colm Harmon and Ian Walker, "Estimates of the Economic Return to Schooling for the United Kingdom," *American Economic Review* 85, 5 (1995): 1278–1286; Philip Oreopoulos, "Stay in School: New Lessons on the Benefits of Raising the Legal School-Leaving Age," in *Commentary* (Toronto: C.D. Howe Institute, 2005), 225; Philip Oreopoulos, "The Compelling Effects of Compulsory Schooling: Evidence from Canada," *Canadian Journal of Economics* 39, 1 (2006): 22–52; DfES, *Raising Expectations: Staying in Education and Training Post-16* (Norwich: Stationery Office, 2007).

77. Nicholas Rose and Pavla Miller, "Political Power beyond the State: Problematics of Government," *British Journal of Sociology* 43, 2 (1992): 173–205; Robin Simmons, "Raising the Age of Compulsory Education in England: A NEET Solution?" *British Journal of Educational Studies* 56, 4 (2008): 420–439.

78. See Colin Green and Maria Navarro Paniagua, "Does Raising the School Leaving Age Reduce Teacher Effort? Evidence from a Policy Experiment," *Economic Inquiry* 50, 4 (2012): 1018–1030.

79. Australian States and Territories, *Federalist Paper 2. The Future of Schooling* (Canberra: AST, 2007). See also Adelaide Declaration on National Goals for Schooling in the Twenty First Century, 1999. www.mceetya.edu.au /mceecdya/nationalgoals/natgoals.htm (accessed October 10, 2012).

80. Department of Education, Employment and Workplace Relations, "Compact with Young Australians Increasing Educational Attainment of Young People Aged 15–24." http://foi.deewr.gov.au/documents/compact-young-australians-questions-and-answers-1 (accessed November 10, 2012).

81. Carol Reid and Helen Young, "The New Compulsory Schooling Age Policy in NSW, Australia: Ethnicity, Ability and Gender Considerations," *Journal of Education Policy* 27, 6 (2012): 795–814.

82. NSW Government, *Raising the School Leaving Age. Consultation Paper* (Sydney: NSW Government, 2008).

83. David Hodgson, "Policy Rationalities and Policy Technologies: A Programme for Analysing the Raised School-Leaving Age in Western Australia," *Journal of Education Policy* 26, 1 (2011): 115–130.

84. Melodye Bush, "Compulsory School Age Requirements," State Notes, ECS (Education Commission of the States) June 2010. www.ecs.org/html/educationissues/StateNotes/2010-StateNotes.pdf (accessed July 10, 2010).

85. Barack Obama, "Remarks by the President in State of the Union Address," The White House, January 24, 2012. www.whitehouse.gov/the-press-office /2012/01/24/remarks-president-state-union-address (accessed November 24, 2012).

86. John M. Bridgeland, John J. Dilulio, and Ryan Streeter, *Raising the Compulsory School Attendance Age: The Case for Reform* (Washington, DC: Civic Enterprises, 2007); see also John M. Bridgeland, John J. Dilulio, and Karen Burke Morrison, *The Silent Epidemic. Perspectives of High School Dropouts* (Washington, DC: Civic Enterprises and the Bill and Melinda Gates Foundation, 2006).

87. National Association of Secondary School Principals, "Raising the Compulsory School Attendance Age," May 7, 2010. www.nassp.org/Content .aspx?topic=Raising_the_Compulsory_School_Attendance_Age_Proposed _ (accessed July 10, 2012).

88. Cindy Johnston, "The Cost of Dropping Out," July 24, 2011. www.npr. org/2011/07/24/138508517/series-overview-the-cost-of-dropping-out (accessed December 10, 2012); Sandra E. Black, Paul J. Devereaux, and Kjell Salvanes, "Staying in the Classroom and Out of the Maternity Ward? The Effect of Compulsory Schooling Laws on Teenage Births," *The Economic Journal* 118, 530 (2008): 1025–1054.

89. Ibid., 8–11. See also, Task Force to Study Raising the Compulsory Public School Attendance Age to 18, *Attending to Learn. The Implications of Raising the Compulsory Age for School Attendance* (Baltimore: Maryland State Department of Education, 2007).

90. For example, see Sheldon Richman and David Kopel, "End Compulsory Schooling," Issue Paper 1–96 (Golden, CO: Independence Institute, 1996).

91. Andrew Ujifusa, *"Obama Push on Mandatory Attendance Age Stalls in States,"* State EdWatch, *Education Week,* June 19, 2012. http://blogs.edweek. org/edweek/state_edwatch/2012/06/heavy_lifting_elsewhere_may_have _squashed_obamas_bully_pulpit%20_moment_on_attendance_age.html (accessed December 10, 2012).

92. Grover J. "Russ" Whitehurst and Sarah Whitfield, *Compulsory School Attendance. What Research Says and What It Means for State Policy* (Washington, DC: Brookings Institution, 2012).

93. Fyfe, *Worldwide Movement.*

3   Framework for ROSLA: Establishing Compulsion

1. Brian Simon, *Education and the Labour Movement, 1870–1920* (London: Lawrence and Wishart, 1965); D. Birch, *Our Victorian Education* (Oxford: Blackwell, 2008).

2. Harold Perkin, *The Rise of Professional Society*, 2nd ed. (London: Routledge, 2002).

3. See Paul Crook, *Darwin's Coat-Tails: Essays on Social Darwinism* (New York: Peter Lang Publishing, 2007).

4. See William Forster, "Elementary Education Bill," February 17, 1870. HC Deb February 17, 1870 vol. 199, col. 438–498, especially 459–460.

5. For an account of how the inspectors operated in relation to the Committee of Council: Richard Selleck, *James Kay-Shuttleworth: Journey of an Outsider* (Essex: Woburn Press, 1994), 142–313. For an account of how the administrative structure of the Education Department evolved between the 1830s to

the 1860s: A. S. Bishop, *The Rise of a Central Authority in English Education* (Cambridge: Cambridge University Press, 1971).

6. www.mylearning.org/victorian-school-and-work-in-preston/p-3215/

7. Jane Humphries, *Childhood and Child Labour in the British Industrial Revolution* (Cambridge: Cambridge University Press, 2010), 314–315.

8. W. B. Stephens, *Education, Literacy and Society, 1830–1870: The Geography of Diversity in Provincial England* (Manchester: Manchester University Press, 1987).

9. For example, Brian Simon, "Can Education Change Society?" in Gary McCulloch (ed.), *Routledge Falmer Reader in the History of Education* (London: Routledge, 2005).

10. See for example John Honey, *Tom Brown's Universe: The Development of the Public Schooling the 19th Century* (London: Millington Books, 1977); John Roach, *A History of Secondary Education in England, 1800–1870* (London: Longmans, 1986).

11. See for example John Roach, *Secondary Education in England 1870–1902: Public Activity and Private Enterprise* (London: Routledge, 1991); Hilary Steedman, "Defining Institutions: The Endowed Grammar Schools and the Systematisation of English Secondary Education," in Detlef Muller, Fritz Ringer, and Brian Simon (eds.), *The Rise of the Modern Educational System: Structural Change and Social Reproduction, 1870–1920* (Cambridge: Cambridge University Press, 1987), 111–134.

12. Gary McCulloch, "Education and the Middle Classes: The Case of the English Grammar Schools, 1868–1944," *History of Education* 35, 6 (2006): 689–704; Gary McCulloch, "Sensing the Realities of English Middle-Class Education: James Bryce and the Schools Inquiry Commission, 1865–1868," *History of Education* 40, 3 (2011): 599–613.

13. John Honey, "The Sinews of Society: The Public Schools as a 'System'," in Muller et al., *Rise of the Modern Educational System*, 151–162.

14. *Report of the Schools Inquiry Commission* (Taunton Report) (London: HMSO, 1868); David Allsobrook, *Schools for the Shires: The Reform of Middle-Class Education in Victorian England* (Manchester: Manchester University Press, 1986).

15. Humphries, *Childhood and Child Labour*, Chapter 9.

16. See Harold Silver, "Ideology and the Factory Child: Attitudes to Half-Time Education," in his *Education as History* (London: Methuen, 1983), 35–59.

17. See also for example Eric Hopkins, *Childhood Transformed: Working-Class Children in Nineteenth-Century England* (Manchester: Manchester University Press, 1994).

18. See also, Richard Johnson, "Really Useful Knowledge. Radical Education and Working Class Culture, 1790–1848," in Jon Clarke, Chas Critcher, and Richard Johnson (eds.), *Working Class Culture* (London: Hutchinson, 1972), 75–102.

19. *Report of the Commissioners Appointed to Inquire into the State of Popular Education in England* (Newcastle Report) (London: HMSO, 1861).

20. See W. H. G. Armytage, *Four Hundred Years of English Education* (Cambridge: Cambridge University Press, 1970), 144–145.

21. See Phil Gardner, *The Lost Elementary Schools of Victorian England* (London: Croom Helm, 1984).

22. Silver, *Education as History*, Chapter 4, Education, "Opinion and the 1870s" (London: Methuen, 1983), 85.

23. John Malcolm, Forbes Ludlow, and Lloyd Jones, *The Progress of the Working Class 1832–1867* (London: Strachan, 1867).

24. Prince Albert, "Inaugural Address," in Alfred Hill (ed.), *Essays Upon Educational Subjects Read at the Educational Conference of 1857* (London: Longman, Brown, Green, Longman and Roberts, 1857), 373.

25. On Mundella, see W. H. G. Armytage, *A.J. Mundella 1825–1897: The Liberal Background to the Labour Movement* (London: Ernest Benn, 1951).

26. See also Anne Rodrick, *Self-Help and Civic Culture: Citizenship in Victorian Birmingham* (Aldershot: Ashgate, 2004), Chapter 3.

27. Gillian Sutherland, *Policy-Making in English Elementary Education, 1870–1895* (Oxford: Oxford University Press, 1973), provides a full account of the period.

28. Asher Tropp, *The School Teachers* (London: William Heinemann, 1956), covers in considerable detail the early history of the NUT; Michael Barber, *Education and the Teacher Unions* (London: Cassell, London, 1992), offers a concise account of the first 40 years of the Union.

29. See Tony Taylor, "Conservative Politics, Compulsory Education, and Lord Sandon's Act, 1876: A Nineteenth-Century Case Study," *Paedagogica Historica* 25, 1 (1984): 265–279; John T. Smith, *Methodism and Education, 1849–1902: J.H. Rigg, Romanism, and Wesleyan Schools* (Oxford: Oxford University Press, 1998), Chapter 5.

30. *Report of the Royal Commission on the Elementary Education Acts* (Cross Report) (London: HMSO, 1888). See D. T. Roberts, "The Genesis of the Cross Commission," *Journal of Educational Administration and History* 17, 2 (1985): 30–38.

31. Susannah Wright, "Citizenship, Moral Education and the English Elementary School," in Laurence Brockliss and Nicola Sheldon (eds.), *Mass Education and the Limits of State Building, c. 1870–1930*, (New York: Palgrave Macmillan, 2012), 21–45.

32. See W. Gareth Evans, "The Welsh Intermediate and Technical Education Act, 1889: A Centenary Appreciation," *History of Education* 19, 3 (1990): 195–210; Bill Bailey, "Technical Education and Secondary Schooling, 1905–1945," in Penny Summerfield and Eric J. Evans (eds.), *Technical Education and the State since 1850: Historical and Contemporary Perspectives* (Manchester: Manchester University Press, 1990), 97–119.

33. Arthur Acland, *Studies in Secondary Education* (London: Perceval, 1892).

34. 1891 Elementary Education Act.

35. See Committee of Enquiry into the Education of Handicapped Children and Young People, *Special Educational Needs* (The Warnock Report) (London:

HMSO, 1978), 11; Ted Cole, *Apart or A Part? Integration and the Growth of British Special Education* (Milton Keynes: Open University Press, 1989).

36. Royal Commission on Secondary Education, *Report of the Commissioners* (Bryce Report) (London: HMSO, 1895).

37. Department of Science and Art, *Abstract of Returns Furnished to the Department of Science and Art: Showing the Manner in Which, and the Extent to Which, the Councils of Counties and County Boroughs in England and Wales, and the Town Councils and Police Burghs in Scotland, Are Devoting Funds to the Purposes of Science, Art, Technical and Manual Instruction* (London: HMSO, 1893).

38. *Report of a Conference on Secondary Education in England* convened by the vice-chancellor of the University of Oxford, Oxford, 1893.

39. Sir Henry Craik, *State Education: Its Scope and Responsibilities, a Speech Delivered at the Opening of Bruntsford School, Edinburgh, April 19th* (London: MacMillan, 1895).

40. See for example Gary McCulloch, *Failing the Ordinary Child? The Theory and Practice of Working-Class Secondary Education* (Buckingham: Open University Press, 1998), Chapter 2.

41. See Lionel Rose, *The Erosion of Childhood: Child Oppression in Britain, 1860–1918* (London: Routledge, 1991), 109–111.

42. Neil Daglish, *Education Policy-Making in England and Wales: The Crucible Years, 1895–1911* (London: Woburn, 1996).

43. *School Attendance of Children below the Age of Five* (London: HMSO, 1908); *Attendance, Compulsory or Otherwise, at Continuation Schools* (London: HMSO, 1909).

44. Education (Administrative Provisions) Act 1907.

45. James Scotland, "The Centenary of the Education (Scotland) Act of 1872," *British Journal of Educational Studies* 20, 2 (1972): 121–136.

46. H. M. Paterson, "Incubus and Ideology: The Development of Secondary Schooling in Scotland, 1900–1939," in W. Humes and H. M. Paterson (eds.), *Scottish Culture and Scottish Education, 1800–1980* (Edinburgh: John Donald Publishers, 1983), 197–215.

47. Warnock Report, 8–9.

48. Richard Stakes and Garry Hornby, *Change in Special Education* (London: Cassell: 1997).

49. T. Good, "Some Aspects of the Labour Problem," *Westminster Review* 167, 3 (1907): 288.

50. E. J. Urwick, "Introduction," in E. J. Urwick (ed.), *Studies of Boy Life in Our Cities* (London: J.M. Dent and Co, 1904), xii, vii–viii.

51. E. J. Urwick, "Conclusion," in Urwick, *Studies of Boy Life in Our Cities*, 255–318.

52. R. H. Tawney, "The Economics of Boy Labour," *The Economic Journal* (December 1909): 517–537.

53. C. P. Trevelyan, speech at opening of Brighouse Secondary School for Girls, September 26, 1910. Trevelyan papers, University of Newcastle CPT 39.

54. C. P. Trevelyan, speech to the North of England Education Conference, January 7, 1911. Trevelyan papers CPT 39. See also A. J. A. Morris, *C.P. Trevelyan 1870–1958: Portrait of a Radical* (London: Blackstaff Press, 1977).

55. 1911 School and Continuation Class Attendance Bill. See also C. Barber, "The Exemption System, 1833–1944," *Journal of Educational Administration and History* 12, 1 (1980): 10–17.

56. See also Geoffrey Sherington, *English Education, Social Change and War, 1911–20* (Manchester: Manchester University Press, 1981).

57. H. A. L. Fisher, speech to House of Commons, Parliamentary Debates, March 13, 1918, 5th Series, vol. 97, cols. 795–796, as cited in Perkin, *The Rise of Professional Society*, 541.

58. Arthur Marwick, *The Deluge: British Society and the First World War*, 2nd ed. (London: Palgrave Macmillan, 2006).

59. Report of the Board of Education 1917–18 (1919), Cd 8594, 1–4.

60. *Final Report of the Departmental Committee on Juvenile Labour in Relation to Employment after the War* (Lewis Report) (London: HMSO, 1917).

61. Ibid., 5.

62. Ibid., 7.

63. Ibid., 11–12.

64. H. A. L. Fisher, speech in House of Commons, Parliamentary Debates, March 13, 1918, 5th Series, vol. 97, cols. 795–796, as cited in Perkin, *The Rise of Professional Society*, 541. *Hansard*, August 10, 1917.

65. H. A. L. Fisher, *An Unfinished Autobiography* (London: Oxford University Press, 1940), 108.

66. Clive Griggs, *The Trades Union Congress and the Struggle for Education, 1868–1925* (London: Falmer, 1983), Chapter 2.

67. Ibid.

68. On the 1918 Education Act, see Denis W. Dean, "H.A.L. Fisher, Reconstruction and the Development of the 1918 Education Act," *British Journal of Educational Studies* 18, 3 (1970): 259–276; and Sherington, *English Education*, Chapter 5.

69. Sections 12–16 of the Act.

70. Section 20. See also Harry Hendrick, "'A Race of Intelligent Unskilled Labourers:' The Adolescent Worker and the Debate on Compulsory Part-Time Day Continuation Schools, 1900–1922," *History of Education* 9, 2 (1980): 152–173.

71. Section 21 of the Act.

72. 1921 Act, Part IV.

73. See "Capitalism and Education," *Athenaeum* 4627 (1918): 131–132.

74. "The Nation's Youth II Universal Secondary Education," *Athenaeum* 4616 (1917): 174.

4   ROSLA and the Emergence of Secondary Education

1. Brian Simon, *The Politics of Educational Reform 1920–1940* (London Lawrence and Wishart, 1974), 50–51.

2. Ibid., 52.
3. The government papers outlining all stages of the postwar economies can be found in the National Archives Ed 24 series.
4. R. H. Tawney, *Secondary Education for All—a Policy for Labour* (London: Labour Party, 1922).
5. See Gary McCulloch, "Educating the Public: Tawney, the *Manchester Guardian* and Educational Reform," in Richard Aldrich (ed.), *In History and in Education: Essays Presented to Peter Gordon* (London: Woburn, 1996), 116–137.
6. Useful accounts of Labour Party views during this period include Rodney Barker, *Education and Politics 1900–1951: A Study of the Labour Party* (Oxford: Clarendon Press, 1972); and Denis Lawton, *Education and the Labour Party:1900–2001 and beyond* (London: Routledge, 2005).
7. Tawney, *Secondary Education for All*, 12.
8. A. Morris, *C.P. Trevelyan, 1870–1958: Portrait of a Radical* (Belfast: Blackstaff Press, 1977).
9. Board of Education Consultative Committee, *The Education of the Adolescent* (Hadow Report) (London: HMSO, 1926).
10. Board of Education, *The Education of the Adolescent*, 145.
11. Ibid., paragraphs 161, 142.
12. Ibid., paragraphs 162/3, 143–144.
13. Ibid., paragraph 166.
14. Ibid., paragraphs 168, 148.
15. Reported in *The Schoolmaster and Woman Teacher's Chronicle*, October 27, 1927.
16. Ibid.
17. R. H. Tawney to C. P. Trevelyan, October 7, 1927. Trevelyan papers, University of Newcastle CPT 136.
18. Ibid.
19. R. H. Tawney to C. P. Trevelyan, October 10, 1927. Trevelyan papers, University of Newcastle CPT 136.
20. E. T. Good, "Too Much Schooling," *English Review* March (1926): 351, 353.
21. Ibid., 353.
22. The Labour Party, *We Can Conquer Unemployment* (London: Labour Party, 1929).
23. "The School-Leaving Age," editorial, *Manchester Guardian*, July 9, 1929.
24. David Rolf, "Education and Industry: The Malcolm Committee," *Oxford Review of Education* 7, 1 (1981): 95–106.
25. "The School-Leaving Age."
26. "The Educational Programme," leading article, *Manchester Guardian*, October 28, 1929.
27. Cabinet papers, National Archives July 18 CAB 24/205.
28. Ibid.
29. *Hansard*: House of Commons Debates, July 18, 1929, vol. 230, col. 611–615.
30. Board of Education Circular 1404.
31. Cabinet papers, National Archives July 18 CAB 24/205.

32. Ibid.
33. Eustace Percy, "The School Leaving Age," *Empire Review* October (1929): 269.
34. "Raising the School Leaving Age in the Country," *The Countryman* January (1930): 538
35. For example, see an earlier intervention by Isabel Cleghorn, "The Educational Ladder. The Presidential Address," *Practical Teacher* 31, 11 (1911): 744.
36. Bolton King, *Schools of To-Day. Present Problems in English Education* (London: J.M. Dent, 1929), 11, 15.
37. See Shena D. Simon, "Maintenance Allowances and the Raising of the School Leaving Age," *Contemporary Review* April (1930): 445–452.
38. Ibid.
39. Ibid.
40. *Education.* January 10 edition, 1930.
41. Marjorie Cruickshank, *Church and State in English Education* (London: MacMillan, 1963), 124–130. Also James Murphy, *Church, State and Schools in Britain 1800–1970* (London: Routledge and Kegan Paul, 1971), 104–107.
42. C. P. Trevelyan, letter of resignation to prime minister, February 19, 1931. Trevelyan papers, University of Newcastle CPT 142.
43. C. P. Trevelyan, speech Blenheim Street and Jubilee Road, Newcastle, March 12, 1931. Trevelyan papers CPT 176.
44. R. H. Tawney, "'Economy' in Education": 1. Present policy. Slump in capital expenditure. Arrested growth, *Manchester Guardian*, May 24, 1933; "'Economy' in Education": II. Admitted needs. Large classes and idle teachers. Juvenile unemployed, *Manchester Guardian*, May 25, 1933.
45. John Jewkes and Allan Winterbottom, *Juvenile Unemployment* (London: George Allen and Unwin, 1933).
46. Ibid., 15.
47. Ibid., 45.
48. Ibid., 75.
49. Ibid., 142.
50. Cabinet papers, National Archives CAB 24/256 marked SA 24696.
51. Cabinet meeting 8(35), February 6, 1935. Cabinet papers, National Archives CAB 24/256/3.
52. Oliver Stanley, Paper to Cabinet Education Policy Committee relating to "Compulsory Education Beyond 14." June 27, 1935. Cabinet papers, National Archives CAB/24/256E.
53. Ibid.
54. Cabinet papers, National Archives CAB 24/256.
55. Ibid., CAB 24/256, paragraph 6b.
56. Ibid., paragraph 12, p. 12.
57. Ibid., paragraph 12.
58. Ibid., paragraph 15.
59. Ibid.
60. Ibid.
61. *TES*, editorial, January 4, 1936.

62. For a detailed discussion of the opposition to exemptions, see Simon, *The Politics of Educational Reform*, 217–224.
63. Ibid.
64. *TES*, January 18, 1936.
65. "Questions in Parliament," *TES*, January 4, 1936.
66. *TES*, January 11, 1936.
67. *TES*, January 18, 1936, leading article.
68. 1936 Education Act, Section 2.2.
69. Henry Hope, *The Education Act 1936* (London: Eyre & Spottiswood, 1936).
70. Spens Report (1938).
71. Ibid., 353.
72. Ibid., Chapter 9, part 5, section 19, 380.
73. AEC and NUT, *The Extra Year* (London: University of London Press, 1938), 69.
74. Colonel Sir Thomas Polson, "School Leaving Age Folly," *Saturday Review* March 28 (1936): 399.
75. Kenneth Lindsay, *Social Progress and Educational Waste: Being a Study of the "Free-Place" and Scholarship System* (London: Routledge, 1926).
76. *Hansard*, HC Deb October 10, 1939, vol. 352 cc255–265.
77. F. H. Spencer, *Education for the People* (London: Routledge, 1941).
78. H. G. Stead, "Education of the Future II: Some Essential Reforms," *TES*, March 8, 1941.
79. Ed 136/312. Brief handwritten note records that a meeting took place in the office of Ernest Bevin, London on September 4, 1941.
80. National Archives Ed 136/312. File of correspondence between Ernest Bevin and Board officers.
81. Ibid.
82. Ibid.
83. Ibid.
84. Ibid., Corporals and Sergeants.
85. Ibid.
86. National Archives ED 136/312.
87. Ibid.
88. Board of Education, *Educational Reconstruction*, White Paper (London: HMSO, 1943), Section (2B), para. 22.
89. Ibid., Section (5A), paras. 63–76.
90. Richard Stakes and Garry Hornby, *Change in Special Education* (London: Cassell: 1997), 25–26.
91. Section 35. 1944 Education Act, 29.
92. Ernest Bevin, memorandum from the minister of Labour and national service. Cabinet papers, National Archives CAB 65/43/12 W.P. (44) 379.
93. Cabinet Paper, *Raising the School Leaving Age*, August 16, 1945. Cabinet papers, National Archives CAB 129/1/17.
94. Ibid.
95. CAB 129/140. This memorandum to cabinet was presented by Morrison to support Wilkinson's efforts. September 1, 1945.

96. Herbert Morrison, *Raising the School Leaving Age*. Memorandum September 1, 1945. Cabinet papers, National Archives CAB 129/1/40.
97. Ibid., 2.
98. Ibid., 6.
99. Wilkinson to Trevelyan, October 1, 1945. Trevelyan papers, University of Newcastle CPT 161.
100. B/T18/186. R. H. Tawney to A. P. Wadsworth, May 12, 1946.
101. Ibid.
102. Cabinet papers, National Archives CAB 129/13/37. Copy of King's Speech.
103. Cabinet papers, National Archives CAB. 129/16 (C.P. (47) 25), January 10, 1947.
104. Cabinet meeting, January 14, 1947. Cabinet papers, National Archives CAB 195/5.
105. Ibid.
106. Martin Chick, *Industrial Policy in Britain 1945–1951: Economic Planning, Nationalisation and Labour Governments* (Cambridge: Cambridge University Press, 2002). Cabinet papers, National Archives CAB 134/503.
107. Conservative Research Department, note, Education. Supply Day—Thursday, July 29, 1948 (Conservative Party archive, CRD 2/33/1).
108. Ibid.
109. Survey of public opinion on current politics, 1948. Abrams papers, Churchill College Cambridge ABMS 3/20.

5 FORWARD WITH ROSLA 1951–1964

1. CACE Ministry of Education, *15 to 18* (HMSO: London, 1959).
2. Meetings of Cabinet, November 28, 1951. Cabinet papers, National Archive CAB 195/10; December 16, 1952. Cabinet papers CAB 195/11; 29 November 1954. Cabinet papers, National Archives CAB 195/13.
3. Dennis Dean, "Conservative Governments, 1951–64, and Their Changing Perspectives on the 1944 Education Act," *History of Education* 24, 3 (1995): 247–266.
4. Cabinet minutes, November 29, 1954. Cabinet papers, National Archives CAB 128/27.
5. "Education Cuts," editorial, *Manchester Guardian*, December 12, 1951.
6. CACE, "The Age of Compulsory School Attendance," July 23, 1952. Ministry of Education papers, National Archives ED 146/24.
7. CACE, report, "The Age of Compulsory School Attendance," 1952, 5. Ministry of Education papers, National Archives ED 146/24.
8. Ibid., 5.
9. Ibid., 12.
10. Ibid., 13.
11. CACE, letter to minister of education, July 23, 1952. Ministry of Education papers, National Archives ED 146/24.

12. Ministry of Education, *Early Leaving* (Gurney-Dixon Report) (London: HMSO, 1954).
13. Essex County Council, "Length of School Life. Report of a Special Sub-Committee Adopted by the Education Committee," November 26, 1962. Essex County Record Office C/DO/10/1–2.
14. Ibid.
15. David Eccles, memorandum to cabinet, "Education Policy," Appendix B, "Economies in the Education vote," 2(b) Lowering the age of leaving, November 12, 1954. Cabinet papers, National Archives CAB (54) 343.
16. David Eccles, memo, "Secondary Education," September 18, 1956. Ministry of Education papers, National Archives ED 147/636.
17. See for further details Steve Cowan, Gary McCulloch, and Tom Woodin, "From HORSA Huts to ROSLA Blocks: The School Leaving Age and the School Building Programme in England, 1943–1972," *History of Education* 40, 3 (2012): 361–380.
18. D. M. Nenk, letter to F. F. Turnbull (Treasury), July 23, 1956. Ministry of Education papers, National Archives of Scotland, Edinburgh ED 48/1657.
19. Advisory committee on policy, "Education policy," May 6, 1957. Conservative Party Archive, Bodleian Library Oxford ACP 3/5 (57) 55.
20. Cabinet meeting, February 7, 1957. Cabinet papers, National Archives CAB 128/51.
21. Conservative Party education committee meeting February 25, 1957. Conservative Party papers, Bodleian Library Oxford CRD 2/33/4.
22. G. N. Flemming, draft paper for minister, "Long-Term Educational Programme: a Draft Paper for the Ministerial Committee on Higher Education," February 21, 1958. Ministry of Education papers, National Archives ED 136/945.
23. Conservative Party advisory committee on policy, memorandum, "Some Preliminary Ideas," April 18, 1958. Conservative Party archive, Bodleian Library Oxford ACP/3/5 (58) 61.
24. Conservative Party advisory committee on policy, "Summary of Comments on 'Some Preliminary Ideas'," n.d., c. April–May 1958. Conservative Party archive, ACP/3/5 (58) 63.
25. G. N. Flemming, note, Main action to be taken in 1960–1965, June 1, 1959. Ministry of Education papers ED 136/945.
26. Cabinet memorandum by the minister of education, "A Drive in Education," July 14, 1958. Cabinet papers, National Archives CAB 129/93.
27. Geoffrey Lloyd, letter to R. A. Butler, March 12, 1958. Ministry of Education papers, National Archives ED 136/945.
28. Ibid.
29. Cabinet memorandum, "A Drive in Education."
30. Ibid.
31. Ibid.
32. Ministry of Education, *Secondary Education for All: A New Drive* (HMSO: London, 1958).

33. Stephen Haseler, *The Gaitskellites: Revisionism in the British Labour Party, 1951–64* (Macmillan: London, 1969); Ilaria Favretto, "'Wilsonism' Reconsidered: Labour Party Revisionism, 1952–64," *Contemporary British History* 14, 4 (2000): 54–80.

34. Anthony Crosland, *The Future of Socialism* (Jonathan Cape: London, 1956), 276.

35. Margaret Cole, letter to Hugh Gaitskell, April 17, 1956. Stewart papers, Churchill College Cambridge STWR 9/2/10.

36. Michael Stewart and Margaret Cole, "Memorandum on Labour Party Policy for Education," May 1957. Stewart papers, Churchill College Cambridge STWT 9/2/12.

37. Michael Stewart, draft memo, "Memorandum on Labour Party Policy for Education," n.d., 1956–1957, Stewart papers, Churchill College Cambridge STWT 9/2/7.

38. Labour Party study group on education, 3rd meeting, item 3vi, July 16, 1957. Stewart papers, Churchill College Cambridge STWT 9/2/12.

39. Labour Party study group on education, 4th meeting, September 18, 1957, item 5 (a); 5th meeting, October 14, 1957, item 1; 6th meeting, October 29, 1957, item 1. Stewart papers, Churchill College Cambridge STWT 9/2/12.

40. Survey of educational attitudes, Report J.912, November 1957. Abrams papers, Churchill College Cambridge ABMS 3/64.

41. Labour Party study group on education, 10th meeting, December 10, 1957, item 3 (d). Stewart papers, Churchill College Cambridge STWT 9/2/12.

42. Labour party study group memo, "Some Political Implications of the Survey on Educational Attitudes," December 1957, RR, 257. Stewart papers, Churchill College Cambridge STWT 9/2/12.

43. Crowther Report, 143.

44. Ibid., 58.

45. Ibid., 60.

46. Gary Becker, *Human Capital* (New York: NBER, 1964); Mark Blaug, *Economics of Education 1* (Harmondsworth: Penguin, 1968).

47. Walt Whitman Rostow, *Stages of Economic Growth: A Non-Communist Manifesto* (Cambridge: Cambridge University Press, 1960).

48. Crowther Report, 34.

49. "Reactions to the Crowther Report," front-page leading article, *Education*, December 18 (1959): 1059–1060.

50. William Alexander, "Week by Week—15 to 18," *Education*, December 18 (1959): 1061–1062.

51. AEC, Memorandum of Evidence to the Central Advisory Council for Education (England) Extract from the Executive Committee Minutes, no. 248, November 30, 1961. AEC Archive, Leeds University MS618 A537.

52. For example, J. Jameson, letter to *The Guardian*, December 28, 1959; Harry Ree, letter to *The Guardian*, December 17, 1959.

53. Conservative Party education committee meeting, November 25, 1959. Conservative Party papers, Bodleian Library CRD 2/33/5.

54. Ibid.
55. Ibid.
56. Ibid.
57. Conservative Party education committee, meeting February 8, 1960. Conservative Party papers, Bodleian Library CRD 2/33/5.
58. Conservative Party education committee, meeting March 14. Conservative Party papers, Bodleian Library CRD 2/33/5.
59. Ibid.
60. Crowther working party, meetings January 19, February 17, February 25. Treasury papers, National Archives T 277/914.
61. Cabinet memorandum by the chancellor of the Exchequer, "The Crowther Report," March 15, 1960, Annex. Cabinet papers, National Archives CAB 129/101.
62. Cabinet memorandum by the secretary of state for the Home Department, "The Crowther Report," March 15, 1960. Cabinet papers, National Archives CAB 129/100.
63. Cabinet memorandum, "The Crowther Report," March 15, 1960. Cabinet papers, National Archives CAB 129/101.
64. Ibid.
65. Cabinet meeting, March 17, 1960. Cabinet papers, National Archives CAB 195/18.
66. No author, probably L. R. Fletcher, Raising the school-leaving age, draft n.d., c. August 1963. Ministry of Education papers, National Archives ED 147/516.
67. *Hansard*, "Education (Report of the Central Advisory Council), March 21, 1960 HC Deb vol. 620, col. 40–180.
68. "Smaller Classes Given First Priority: Decision on Higher School Leaving Age Deferred," report, *The Times*, March 22, 1960.
69. Ministry of Education, *The Youth Service in England and Wales* (Albemarle Report) (London: HMSO, 1960).
70. J. Smyth, report, "The Rising Tide: Youth in the 1960s," July 31, 1960. Conservative Party papers, Bodleian Library Oxford ACP 3/7 (60) 84.
71. Ibid.
72. Conservative and Unionist Teachers' Association, Recommendations with regard to the Crowther and Albemarle Reports, July 26, 1960. Conservative Party papers, Bodleian Library Oxford ACP 3/7 (60) 85.
73. L. R. Fletcher, Raising the school-leaving age, September 4, 1962. Ministry of Education papers, National Archives ED 147/516.
74. Association of Teachers in Colleges and Departments of Education, Submission to the Central Advisory Council for Education, London, January 1962. AEC Archives, Leeds University MS618 A537.
75. Fletcher, Raising the school-leaving age.
76. Mr Withrington, Comments. Ministry of Education papers, National Archives ED 147/516.
77. W. R. Elliot commenting on L. R. Fletcher's draft, December 20, 1962. Ministry of Education papers, National Archives ED 147/516.

78. Ibid.
79. M. E. Peston, Raising the school-leaving age. Ministry of Education papers, National Archives ED 147/516.
80. H. H. Donnelly, letter to T. R. Weaver, n.d. [1963]. Ministry of Education papers, National Archives ED 147/516.
81. Fletcher, Raising the school-leaving age.
82. T. R. Weaver, note to H. H. Donnelly, January 21, 1963. Ministry of Education papers, National Archives ED 147/516.
83. W. D. Pile, note to Toby Weaver, July 12, 1963. Ministry of Education papers, National Archives ED 147/516.
84. Reginald Maudling, *Memoirs* (London: Sidgwick and Jackson, 1978).
85. Ministry of Education, *Half Our Future* (Newsom Report) (London: HMSO, 1963).
86. Ibid., Chapter 1.
87. H. Andrew, note to H. F. Rossetti, August 22, 1963. Ministry of Education papers, National Archives ED 147/513.
88. L. R. Fletcher, revised draft, Raising the school-leaving age, October 1963. Ministry of Education papers, National Archives ED 147/516.
89. H. F. Rossetti, note to Herbert Andrew, October 22, 1963. Ministry of Education papers, National Archives ED 147/513.
90. Herbert Andrew, note, October 23, 1963. Ministry of Education papers, National Archives ED 147/513.
91. Lionel Robbins, *Higher Education* (Robbins Report) (London: HMSO, 1963).
92. Cabinet meeting, October 8, 1963. Cabinet papers, National Archives CAB 128/37.
93. Herbert Andrew, note to Mr Cockerill, November 1, 1963. Ministry of Education papers, National Archives ED 147/513.
94. Ibid.
95. C. S. Bennett, letter to D. E. Lloyd Jones (Ministry of Education), November 15, 1963. Ministry of Education papers, National Archives ED 147/513.
96. Prime minister's office, record of a meeting, December 4, 1963. Prime minister's papers, National Archives, PREM 11/4747.
97. Ibid.
98. Ibid.
99. "Raising the Leaving Age," leading article, *Education*, December 6, 1963.
100. Cabinet, memorandum by the lord president of the council and minister for science (Lord Hailsham), "The School Leaving Age," January 2, 1964. Cabinet papers, National Archives CAB 129/116.
101. Reginald Maudling, "The School Leaving Age," draft memorandum, n.d. [January 1964]. Cabinet papers, National Archives CAB.227/1349.
102. H. A. Harding, memo to J. A. Petch, "School Leaving Age," January 13, 1964. Treasury papers, National Archives T 2227/1349.
103. Burke Trend, memo to prime minister, "The School Leaving Age," January 13, 1964. Prime minister's office, National Archives PREM 11/4747.
104. Arthur Barton, "Wilkinson's Law," *The Guardian*, January 6, 1964.

105. Cabinet meeting, January 17, 1964. Cabinet papers, National Archives CAB 128/38.
106. Ibid.
107. Reginald Maudling and John Boyd-Carpenter, memorandum to cabinet, "Government Expenditure after 1968," January 21, 1964. Cabinet papers, National Archives CAB 129/116.
108. Burke Trend, memo to prime minister, "The School Leaving Age," January 22, 1964. Prime minister's office, National Archives PREM 11/4747.
109. Cabinet meeting, January 23, 1964, item 5. Cabinet papers, National Archives CAB 128/38.
110. Ibid., item 6.
111. "A Date at Last," leading article, The Times, January 28, 1964.

6 WAITING FOR ROSLA 1964–1968

1. CACE, Half Our Future (Newsom Report) (London: HMSO, 1963), xiii.
2. Ibid., xvii.
3. Ibid.
4. Ibid., 119.
5. Ibid., 117.
6. Ibid., 38.
7. See Gary McCulloch, "The Politics of the Secret Garden: Teachers and the School Curriculum in England and Wales," in Christopher Day, Alicia Fernandez, Trond E. Hauge, Jorunn Muller (eds.), The Life and Work of Teachers: International Perspectives in Changing Times (London, Routledge, 2000), 26–37.
8. Toby Weaver, note to secretary, February 20, 1961. Ministry of Education papers, National Archives ED 147/784.
9. Schools Council, Science for the Young School Leaver (London: HMSO, 1964), iii.
10. Ibid.
11. Schools Council internal memorandum, Preparations for raising the school-leaving age, December 1964. AEC Archive, Leeds University A31(c).
12. Ibid.
13. Ibid.
14. Schools Council, RSLA and 6th Form Exercises, Schools Council Archive, Institute of Education SC 351/355/03.
15. Co-ordinating Committee. Preparations for raising the school-leaving age. Relevance: the humanities. Memorandum by the Council's Staff CC paper no. 9, January 1965. AEC Archive, Leeds University MS618 A31 (c).
16. Schools Council, Raising the School Leaving Age: A Co-Operative Programme of Research and Development (London: HMSO, 1965), 1–2.
17. Ibid., 8.

18. Ibid., 9.
19. Ibid.
20. Ibid., 13.
21. Co-ordinating Committee, Sub-Committee on Preparations for Raising the School Leaving Age, May 25, 1966. Oral report on the meeting with the Review Committee of the Youth Service Development Council. See also Memo from National Association of Youth Service Offices, November 17, 1966. DES papers, National Archives ED 147/883.
22. Report by Working Party of the Yorkshire and Lincolnshire Federation of the Education Welfare Officers' National Association 1966/7. AEC Archive, Leeds University MS618 A675.
23. Slough Borough Council Education Committee. School Management Sub-Committee. Report on Youth Counselling Work at Westgate County Secondary School.
24. Schools Council, History and the Humanities. Sub-Committee on Preparations for the Raising of the School Leaving Age 1968 Papers. DES papers, National Archives ED 124/385.
25. Association of Teachers of Domestic Science, Memo on Preparations for the Raising of the School Leaving Age, September 28, 1967. DES papers, National Archives ED 147/884.
26. Schools Council, *Society and the Young School Leaver: A Humanities Programme in Preparation for the Raising of the School Leaving Age* (London: HMSO, 1967).
27. Lawrence Stenhouse, Letter to Joslyn (J. G. Owen), February 21, 1967. Schools Council Archive, Institute of Education SCC/318/440/019.
28. Schools Council, English Subject Committee, An Approach through English, September 28, 1967, Sub-Committee Raising of the School Leaving Age. DES papers, National Archives ED 147/884.
29. Anthony Crosland, School Leaving Age (industrial training) *Hansard,* July 10, 1967, HC Deb vol. 750, col. 28–29W.
30. Maurice Kogan, Memo to Mr Corder, May 9, 1967. DES papers National Archives ED 147/886.
31. E. F. L Brech, A Note on Basic Educational Development for Life and Living in an Industrial Society, 1967. DES papers, National Archives ED 147/884.
32. Roma Morton-Williams and Stewart Finch, *Young School Leavers: Report of a Survey Among Young People, Parents and Teachers* (London: HMSO, 1968).
33. Frank Barraclough, secretary, North Riding Education Committee, Northallerton to William Alexander, February 23, 1963. AEC Archive, Leeds University MS618 A594.
34. "An Extra Year at School," *The Guardian*, November 28, 1966, 8.
35. Schools Council, Organization of development work, Sub-Committee on Preparations for Raising the School Leaving Age, September 15, 1966. DES papers, National Archives ED 147/883.
36. Ibid.
37. "Regional Planning Proposed for Extra School Year," report, *The Guardian*, June 18, 1966.

38. "Crash Programme for Changing School-Leaving Age," report, *The Guardian*, November 28, 1966; "An Extra Year at School," leading article, *The Guardian*, November 28, 1966.

39. DES, Raising of the School Leaving Age Sub-Committee: Minutes and Papers 1968. DES papers, National Archives ED 147/885.

40. Schools Council, *The Educational Implications of Social and Economic Change. Report of a Conference Called by the Schools Council in Preparation for Raising the School Leaving Age* (London: HMSO, 1967).

41. Sub-Committee on Preparations for Raising the School Leaving Age, September 15, 1966, Invitational Conference on the Educational Implications of Social and Economic Change: An Outline Report. DES papers, National Archives ED 147/883.

42. DES, The Discussions—Relating to Nottingham Conference. DES papers, National Archives ED 147/884.

43. Ibid.

44. Schools Council, State of the Leaving Age Program, Sub-Committee on Preparations for Raising the School Leaving Age, September 28, 1967. DES papers, National Archives ED 147/884.

45. Ibid.

46. Schools Council, Teachers' Centers and Groups: An Informal Report on Progress. Sub-Committee on Preparations for Raising the School Leaving Age, November 16, 1967. DES papers, National Archives ED 147/884.

47. Meeting with directors of projects in the RSLA program. Sub-Committee on Preparations for Raising the School Leaving Age, December 14, 1967. DES papers, National Archives ED 147/884.

48. Ibid.

49. Ibid.

50. Letter from Stephen Wiseman to E. L. Britton, March 6, 1968. DES papers, National Archives ED 124/385.

51. D. O'Donovan to C. I. Mr Elliott, S. I. Mr Withrington, D. I. Mr Burrows, Proposed Working Party on Compensatory Education, September 19, 1966. DES papers, National Archives ED 147/886.

52. H. E. Egner, memorandum, The Problem of Courses for the Less Bright in the Sixth Form, December 20, 1966. Incorporated Association of Head Masters papers, University of Warwick Modern Records Centre MS. 58/3/5/13.

53. Handwritten note, Agenda for Subcommittee for Preparations for Raising the School-Leaving Age, September 28, 1967. DES papers, National Archives ED 147/884.

54. More Schools "Before Raised Leaving Age," *Daily Telegraph*, December 5, 1966, 13.

55. Newsom Report, 253.

56. Ibid., Chapter 25.

57. Ibid., 87.

58. Ibid., 87.

59. Ibid., 95, diagram 6.

60. F. Lincoln Ralphs to William Alexander, March 15, 1966. AEC Archive, Leeds University MS618 A1097 School Building Programme and Raising SLA.

61. Anthony Crosland, prime minister, Comprehensive Reorganisation and the Raising of the School Leaving Age, February 28, 1966. Prime minister's papers, National Archives PREM 13/3168.

62. *Building Bulletin* 32 (1967).

63. Memorandum by Architects and Building Branch, Raising the School Leaving Age. The Building Implications, October 1965, DES papers, National Archives ED 150/30.

64. Letter from J. A. Hudson to local education authorities, Accommodation for Raising the School Leaving Age to 16, November 9, 1965. DES papers, National Archives ED 150/30.

65. Memorandum by A & B Branch, Raising the School Leaving Age.

66. Ibid.

67. Ibid.

68. Ibid.

69. Ibid.

70. Ibid.

71. See papers in School Building Programme and Raising SLA Nov 65 to Oct 67, AEC Archive, Leeds University MS618 A1097.

72. George Taylor, "Can Schools Use the Extra Year?" *The Guardian*, January 5, 1966.

73. "A Fair Deal for Kids—How?" leading article, *The Guardian*, January 8, 1966.

74. Lady (Shena) Simon to Alastair Hetherington, January 10, 1966. *Manchester Guardian* papers, Manchester University, file C3/S62/108.

75. Lady Simon to Alastair Hetherington, January 13, 1966. *Manchester Guardian* papers, Manchester University C3/S62/110.

76. Ernest Armstrong, letter to the *Guardian,* December 6, 1966. Cutting in Raising of the School Leaving Age Sub-Committee: Internal Minutes and Discussions. DES papers, National Archives ED 147/886.

77. W. G. Jackson, City of Nottingham Education Committee to William Alexander, January 11, 1966. AEC Archive, Leeds University MS618 A1097.

78. "Concern Over New School Leaving Age," report, *The Guardian*, April 2, 1966; National Association of Schoolmasters, *Ready in Time?: Some Observations on the Raising of the School Leaving Age* (Hemel Hempstead: NAS, 1966).

79. NAS, *Ready in Time?* 26.

80. Edward Boyle, letter to Michael Shaw MP, July 22, 1966. Boyle papers, Leeds University MS 660/27610.

81. Michael Shaw, letter to Edward Boyle, July 23, 1966. Boyle papers, Leeds University MS 660/26293.

82. "Too Soon to Raise School-Leaving Age," *The Guardian*, March 30, 1967.

83. Scottish Education Department, "Raising of the School Leaving Age," Circular no. 562, June 24, 1964. Scottish Education Department, National Archives of Scotland, Edinburgh CO1/5/1611.

84. Ibid.

85. Ibid.

86. Dumfries County Council to Association of County Councils in Scotland, January 20, 1965. Scottish Education Department papers, National Archives of Scotland CO1/5/1611.

87. Scottish Education Department, "Building for Raising the School Leaving Age," memorandum, November 1965. SED papers, National Archives of Scotland CO1/5/1611.

88. Ibid.

89. Ibid.

90. Douglas McIntosh, director of education, Fife County Council, to Frank Inglis, secretary, Association of County Councils in Scotland, November 17, 1965. SED papers, National Archives of Scotland CO1/5/1611.

91. Douglas McIntosh to Frank Inglis, December 9, 1965. SED papers, National Archives of Scotland CO1/5/1611.

92. Caithness County Council to Frank Inglis, December 6, 1965. SED papers, National Archives of Scotland CO1/5/1611.

93. "Questions for Sir Edward," leading article, *Dundee Courier and Advertiser*, March 17, 1967.

94. Edward Boyle, letter to Michael Shaw, March 20, 1967. Boyle papers, Leeds University MS 660/26295.

95. "Raising School Age Act of Faith," report, *The Guardian*, January 21, 1966.

96. Ibid.

97. Ibid.

98. "Minister Forecasts Classroom Problem Solved by 1976," report, *The Guardian*, April 13, 1966.

99. "Mr Wilson's Priorities for Education," report, *The Guardian*, June 17, 1966.

100. Anthony Crosland, memorandum to cabinet, Comprehensive Reorganization and the Raising of the School-Leaving Age, February 25, 1966. Cabinet papers, National Archives CAB/129/124.

101. "Mr Crosland Optimistic on Money for Education," report, *The Guardian*, June 24, 1967.

102. James Callaghan, Cabinet memorandum, Public Expenditure: Civil Reviews: Education and Science, June 15, 1967, 10. Cabinet papers, National Archives CAB 129/130.

103. Ibid.

104. James Callaghan, Cabinet memorandum, Public Expenditure, June 21, 1967. Cabinet papers, National Archives CAB 129/131.

105. Anthony Crosland, Cabinet memorandum, Public Expenditure: Education, July 10, 1967. Cabinet papers, National Archives CAB 129/132.

106. Ibid.

107. Cabinet meeting, minutes, July 12, 1967. Cabinet papers, National Archives CAB 128/39.

108. Ibid.

109. Richard Crossman, *The Diaries of a Cabinet Minister*, vol. 2 (London: Hamish Hamilton, 1976), 408.

110. Ibid., diary for November 16, 1967, 575–576.

111. Cabinet meeting, minutes, November 16, 1967. Cabinet papers, National Archives CAB 128/42. See also Harold Wilson, *The Labour Government 1964–70: A Personal Record* (London: Penguin, 1974), 581.

112. Crossman, *Diaries of a Cabinet Minister*, diary for December 29, 1967, 624.

113. Roy Jenkins, Cabinet memorandum, Public Expenditure: Post-Devaluation Measures, January 3, 1968, annex B, Education, paragraph 18. Cabinet papers, National Archives CAB 129/135.

114. Ibid.

115. Ibid.

116. Ibid.

117. Ibid.

118. T. Benn, *Office without Power: Diaries 1968–72* (London: Hutchinson, 1972), diary for January 3, 1968, 2.

119. Ibid., 6.

120. Ibid.

121. Ibid.

122. Ibid.

123. Ibid., 7.

124. Crossman, *Diaries of a Cabinet Minister*, diary for January 5, 1968, 636.

125. Ibid., 637. Kenneth Morgan's biography of Callaghan notes that Callaghan as chancellor had rejected a proposal to defer the school-leaving age and insists that "an assault on working-class education aroused the strongest of personal feelings in him." See Kenneth O. Morgan, *Callaghan: A Life* (Oxford: Oxford University Press, 1987), 327.

126. Cabinet meeting, minutes, January 5, 1968. Cabinet papers, National Archives CAB 128/43.

127. "Where the Cuts Are Likely to Be Made," report, *The Guardian*, January 5, 1968.

128. "Did Minister Drop Hint on School Leaving Age?" report, *The Guardian*, January 6, 1968.

129. "Despondency," leading article, *Education*, January 12, 1968.

130. Tyrrell Burgess, "Up the School-Leaving Age," *The Guardian*, January 3, 1968.

131. "Masters' Plea to Mr Wilson," report, *The Guardian*, January 5, 1968; "NUT Again Demands a Leaving Age of 16," report, *The Guardian*, January 10, 1968. See also Clive Griggs, *The TUC and Education Reform, 1926–1970* (London, Woburn Press, 2002), 258–264.

132. Cabinet meeting, minutes, January 15, 1968. Cabinet papers, National Archives CAB 128/43.

133. Benn, *Office without Power*, 17.

134. Roy Jenkins, *A Life at the Centre* (London: Macmillan, 1991), 228.

135. Arthur Barton, "I'm Not Crying," *The Guardian*, January 29, 1968.

7 PREPARING FOR ROSLA 1968–1972

1. "Can We Do It?" *TES*, January 10, 1969.
2. "Compulsory School," editorial, *Daily Telegraph*, April 23, 1971.
3. Brian Simon, *Education and the Social Order, 1940–1990* (London: Lawrence and Wishart, 1991).
4. William Alexander to George Churchill, Northamptonshire County Council Education Committee, April 1, 1971. AEC Archive, Leeds University MS618 A1093.
5. Conservative Party Education Policy Group, "Conservative Education Policy for the Seventies," July 1968, Conservative Party Archive, Bodleian Library, Oxford ACP 3/16.
6. William Alexander letter to Wilma Harte, DES, April 17, 1969. AEC Archive, Leeds University MS618 A 731, Further Education 1967 to 1969.
7. Wilma Harte to William Alexander, December 15, 1969 and William Alexander to W. Harte, DES, May 22, 1969. Leeds University Special Collections MS 618 A 731 Further Education 1967 to 1969.
8. Frank Wood, Association of Principals of Technical Institutions, response to draft circular 8/71, July 5, 1971, DES papers, National Archives ED 207/121.
9. *National Institute Economic Review*, "The Economic Situation: Chapter 1, The Home Economy," 58 (November 1971) 13.
10. Miss J. M. Forsyth to Mr Widdup, Feasibility of RSLA in 1972, December 7, 1971. Treasury papers, National Archives T 227/3943.
11. Miss J. M. Forsyth, December 8, 1971, Note for record, Scottish Comments on the Feasibility of RSLA in 1972. Treasury papers, National Archives T 227/3943.
12. Mr Hunt to S. Goldman, December 8, 1971, School-leaving age. Treasury papers, National Archives T 227/3943.
13. Anthony Crosland to William Alexander, April 10, 1967. AEC Archive, Leeds University MS618 A782 Single School Leaving Date.
14. City of Manchester Education Committee, Raising the school-leaving age to 16. AEC Archive, Leeds University MS 618 A1093.
15. R. J. Gunter to Anthony Crosland, March 18, 1967. AEC Archives, Leeds University MS 618 A782 Single School Leaving Date.
16. *Hansard*, Single School Leaving Date, HC Deb June 12, 1969, vol. 784, col. 1653–1654. Margaret Thatcher followed suit: *Hansard*, School Leaving, December 2, 1970, HC Deb vol. 807, col. 416–417W.
17. ILEA, Single School Leaving Date, n.d., c. February 1971. AEC Archive, Leeds University MS618 A 782 Single School Leaving Date, April, 1967.
18. Herbert Andrew to secretary of state, December 17, 1968. DES papers, National Archives ED.
19. Herbert Andrew, minute to secretary of state. DES papers, National Archives ED 203/4. Redraft on deferment of RSLA program. See also H. O. Dovey

to Miss W. Harte, November 7, 1968. DES papers, National Archives ED 207/121.

20. Draft Circular, Raising the school-leaving age, January 15, 1968. DES papers, National Archives ED 203/4, Redraft on deferment of RSLA program.

21. H. O. Dovey to Mr Tanner, January 7, 1969. Raising the school-leaving age. DES papers, National Archives ED 147/886.

22. Sir Herbert Andrew, memo to secretary of state, January 1969, Redraft on deferment of ROSLA program. DES papers, National Archives ED 203/4.

23. P. S. Litton to Mr Hudson, November 19, 1968. Raising the school-leaving age. DES papers, National Archives ED 147/886, Raising of the School Leaving Age Sub-Committee: internal minutes and discussions.

24. Margaret Thatcher, "Speech at Royal Festival Hall, March 16, 1971," in Barry Turner (ed.), *Raising the School Leaving Age* (London: Encyclopaedia Britannica, 1971), 27–36.

25. No author, RSLA and the curriculum. DES papers, National Archives ED 233/7.

26. Minutes of Architectural Sub-Committee, January 4, 1971, Erection of RSLA type units. Lancashire County Record Office, EVF 95, Raising of school-leaving age.

27. Letter to Borough Education Officer, Keighley, November 22, 1967; RSLA special programs. Policy and Finance Sub-Committee, November 7, 1972. West Yorkshire Archive Service, WRD5/4/4/19, Raising of the school-leaving age, 1967–1973.

28. David Fletcher, "Classroom Ban Threatened Over Stay-On Pupils," *Daily Telegraph*, April 24, 1973, cutting in Lancashire County Record Office, EVF 95, Raising of school-leaving age.

29. Leaders Consultative Committee. Conservative Party Archives, Bodleian Library, Oxford LCC 1/2/15.

30. Alan Evans, NUT to Mr Richards, July 7, 1971. DES papers, National Archives ED 207/121, Raising the school-leaving age: policy and implementation; comments from educational organizations on draft circular.

31. C. L. Smith, Eastbourne Education Committee, Report of the chief education officer on the raising of the school-leaving age, October 4, 1971. East Sussex Record Office, R/C 70/39, Raising the school-leaving age to 16 years.

32. Nottingham County Council, minute, Raising the school-leaving age, c. 1974. DES papers, National Archives ED 233/7; City of Manchester Education Committee. The Raising of the School Leaving Age to 16; DES, Survey on RSLA, based on 50 returns from local authorities responding to circular 8/71. DES papers, National Archives ED 233/7; Chief Education Officer, Provision for ROSLA, Essex County Record Office, C/DE/5/10, Papers relating to raising the school-leaving age (ROSLA).

33. Mr Edward Taylor, School Leaving Age, *Hansard*, November 11, 1970, HC Deb vol. 806, col. 361.

34. Edward Short, School Leaving Age, *Hansard*, March 5, 1970, HC Deb vol. 797, col. 612.

35. Draft circular on ROSLA. AEC Archive, Leeds University MS 618 G14.
36. Edward Taylor, School Leaving Age, *Hansard,* January 13, 1971, HC Deb vol. 809 col. 60.
37. Mr Eadie and Mr Ross, School Leaving Age, *Hansard*, December 10, 1969, HC Deb vol. 793, col. 126W.
38. A. V. Slater, Borough of Haringey, Raising the school-leaving age to 16, December 22, 1971. AEC Archive, Leeds University MS618 A 1093, Raising of the school-leaving age to 16, April 1968–November 1973.
39. David Hopkinson, "The School Leaving Age," *Trends in Education*, October 1971. AEC Archives, Leeds University MS618 A849.
40. No author, "School Until 16 Will Help North," *Daily Express*, January 9, 1969. Lancashire County Record Office, EVF 95, Raising the school-leaving age.
41. "Minister Firm on School Leaving Age," report, *The Guardian*, March 17, 1971.
42. Lord Belstead, note to A. Hill, June 23, 1971. Conservative Party Archive, Bodleian Library Oxford, CCO 505/4/96.
43. James Scott, note to Miss Todd (Scottish Education Department), "School Leaving Age," December 2, 1970. Scottish Education Department papers, National Archives of Scotland ED 48/1917.
44. I. M. Robertson, note to Mr McClellan, December 31, 1970. SED papers, National Archives of Scotland ED 48/1917.
45. J. F. McClellan, note, January 29, 1971. SED papers, National Archives of Scotland ED 48/1917.
46. "Petition on School Age Is Rejected," report, *The Guardian*, June 29, 1971.
47. Note of meeting, minutes of meeting at Chequers with Edward Heath, January 12, 1972. Prime Minister's Office, National Archives PREM15/863.
48. Margaret Thatcher, School Leaving Age, *Hansard,* March 23, 1972, HC Deb vol. 833, col. 1839–1842.
49. DES, *Education: A Framework for Expansion* (London: HMSO, 1972).
50. "Mrs Thatcher: A Progressive Programme," leading article, *The Guardian*, December 7, 1972.
51. DES, Raising the School Leaving Age, Press release on RSLA, January 8, 1969. AEC Archive, Leeds University MS618 A699.
52. "Raising the Age" *Times* editorial, n.d. (ca. January 9, 1969), Lancashire County Record Office, EVF 95, Raising the school-leaving age.
53. Arthur Davidson, MP. Parliamentary Recess Diary. "School Leaving Age to Be Raised," *Accrington Observer*, January 18, 1969. Lancashire County Record Office, EVF 95, Raising of school-leaving age.
54. County Home Economics Advisor, The Home Economics Teacher's Role in the Future Development of the Pre-School Child. Essex County Record Office, C/DE/5/10. Papers relating to raising the school-leaving age (ROSLA). See also Lawrence Stenhouse, *Authority, Education and Emancipation* (London: Heinemann Educational, 1983).
55. Schools Council, *Society and the Young School Leaver* (London: HMSO, 1967).

56. City of Manchester Education Committee. The Raising of the School Leaving Age to 16.

57. Edward Short, quoted in *Lancashire Evening Post*, "Pupils 'Not Stretched Enough,'" January 10, 1972. Lancashire County Record Office, EVF 95, Raising of the school-leaving age.

58. "DP/LB," Paper on effects of raising the school-leaving age, April 20, 1967. East Sussex Record Office R/E/2/68/79, Raising the school-leaving age from 15 to 16.

59. Working Party of Secondary School Teachers, Raising the school-leaving age in Brighton's secondary schools, 1971. East Sussex Record Office, R/E/2/50/12.

60. Ibid.

61. Ibid.

62. Hertfordshire County Council, Local Bulletin no. 10, ROSLA, A report on preparations for ROSLA, September 1971. Essex County Record Office, C/DE/5/10, Papers relating to raising the school-leaving age (ROSLA).

63. HMI, a Survey of Fifth Forms in the Non-Selective Secondary Schools of Worcestershire, Autumn 1968 and Spring Term 1969. DES papers, National Archives ED 235/7.

64. Professor H. F. Halliwell, "Schools and Colleges," *Further Education Staff College Report of Study Conference* 3, 2 (1970): 2. AEC Archive, Leeds University MS618 716.

65. EYR Division Area Team, South Yorkshire: RSLA Enquiry. N.d., c. 1971. West Yorkshire Archive Service WRD 5/6/139 ROSLA.

66. Lancashire Education Committee Annual Report, 1970–1971 (Preston: LEC, 1971). Tameside Local Studies.

67. Lancashire Education Committee Annual Report, 1971–1972 (Preston: LEC, 1971): 19. Tameside Local Studies.

68. HMI, Survey of Courses for Fourth-Year Non-Examination Pupils in Selected Midland Secondary Schools, September 1968–March 1969. DES papers, National Archives ED 235/7.

69. EYR Division Area Team, South Yorkshire: RSLA Enquiry, West Yorkshire Archive Service, WRD 5/6/139 ROSLA.

70. Schools Council, Curriculum Development Work in Home Economics. a Report of a One Year Feasibility Study and Recommendations for a Development Stage, DES papers, National Archives ED 124/385 Schools Council: subcommittee on preparations for the raising of the school-leaving age, 1968 papers.

71. Lancashire Education Committee, Annual Report 1971–1972, 30. Tameside Local Studies

72. A Century of Change: Trends in United Kingdom statistics since 1900. www.parliament.uk/documents/commons/lib/research/rp99/rp99–111.pdf (accessed July 23, 2012).

73. HMI, a Survey of the Provision Made for the Raising of the School Leaving Age in 3 Secondary Schools in Salop, 1974. DES papers, National Archives ED 272/24.

74. Schools Council, History and the Humanities. DES papers, National Archives ED124/385, Schools Council: subcommittee on preparations for the raising of the school-leaving age, 1968 papers.

75. Working Party of Secondary School Teachers, Raising the school leaving age in Brighton's secondary schools, 18–19.

76. See papers on NAS, Essex County Record Office, C/DE/5/10, Papers relating to raising the school-leaving age (ROSLA).

77. EYR Division Area Team, South Yorkshire: RSLA Enquiry. West Yorkshire Archive Service, WRD5/6/139 ROSLA.

78. Ibid.

79. Slater, Raising the school-leaving age.

80. HMI, a Survey of the Provision Made for the Raising of the School Leaving Age in 3 Secondary Schools in Salop.

81. HMI, Survey of the Education of Young School Leavers in Huddersfield, October 14–24, 1968. DES papers, National Archives ED 235/5.

82. William Alexander to G. K. Greenwood, July 8, 1971. AEC Archive, Leeds University MS618 A1093, Raising of the school-leaving age to 16, April 1968–November 1973. A. C. Hetherington to N. W. Stuart, DES, September 10, 1971. AEC Archive, Leeds University MS618 A1093, Raising of the school-leaving age to 16, April 1968–November 1973.

83. Raising the school-leaving age: policy and implementation; comments from educational organizations on draft circular. DES papers, National Archives ED 207/121; also AEC Archives, Leeds University MS618 A1093, Raising of the school-leaving age to 16, April 1968–November 1973.

84. J. K. Brierley, Monitoring of the school-leaving age: a discussion paper, September 1, 1972. DES papers, National Archives ED 233/7.

85. Ibid.

86. EYR Division Area Team, South Yorkshire: RSLA Enquiry; also Curricular Developments Relating to ROSLA, Saturday, June 11. West Yorkshire Archive Service, WRD5/6/139 ROSLA.

87. Slater, Raising the school-leaving age.

88. C. H. Maude, Monitoring ROSLA (Huntingdon/Peterborough), November 20, 1972. DES papers, National Archives ED 233/7.

89. An outline of curriculum developments in Scotland. Appendix 7, n.d., c. 1971. National Archives LAB 19/876.

90. HMI, RSLA, Following based on 50 returns from local authorities responding to circular 8/71. DES papers, National Archives ED 233/7.

91. Ibid.

92. Brierley, Monitoring of the school-leaving age.

93. JLJ/LB, Raising the School Leaving Age, March 10, 1967. East Sussex Record Office, R/E/2/68/79, Raising the school-leaving age from 15 to 16.

94. Davigdor Girls School to Chief Education Officer, October 1971. East Sussex Record Office, R/E/5/5/56, Raising the school-leaving age: correspondence and reports, 1969–1973.

95. HMI, a Survey of Fifth Forms in the Non-Selective Secondary Schools of Worcestershire.

96. HMI, a Survey of Fourth and Fifth Year Work in Secondary Modern Schools of the Mid-Somerset Divisional Executive, September 1967–March 1968. DES papers, National Archives ED 235/3.

97. D. E. Morris, Knoll School for Boys to Chief Education Officer, October 8, 1971. East Sussex Record Office, R/E/5/5/56, Raising the school-leaving age: correspondence and reports, 1969–1973.

98. D. R. Stansbury, Report on progress toward a new objective for fifth-form pupils in preparation for the raising of the school-leaving age, September 14, 1971. Swindon Education Committee. Gloucestershire Record Office, 5152/2 12/27

99. Ibid.

100. J. Creedy, Southend on Sea: RSLA, October 19, 1972. DES papers, National Archives ED 233/7.

101. DES, Survey on RSLA, based on 50 returns.

102. F. J. Downs to J. K. Brierley, Monitoring RSLA: Suffolk, October 12, 1972; HMI, a Survey of the Provision of Full-Time Courses for Bristol Students (Age 16–18) in Schools and Colleges in the Bristol Area, October 1968–April 1969. DES papers, National Archives ED 235/7.

103. HMI, a Survey of Fifth Forms in the Non-Selective Secondary Schools of Worcestershire.

104. EYR Division Area Team, South Yorkshire: RSLA Enquiry.

105. Curricular Developments Relating to ROSLA conference, Saturday, June 11. West Yorkshire Archive Service, WRD5/6/139 ROSLA.

106. Brierley, Monitoring of the school-leaving age.

107. HMI, Preparation and Courses for Raising of the School Leaving Age, Prudhoe County Secondary School. N.d., c. 1972. DES papers, National Archives ED 272/23.

108. EYR Division Area Team, South Yorkshire: RSLA Enquiry. West Yorkshire Archive Service, WRD 5/6/139 ROSLA.

109. Creedy, Southend on Sea 1972.

110. Nottingham County Council, minute, Raising the leaving age 1974.

111. DES, Survey on RSLA: based on 50 returns; also C. H. Hopkins, Kingsholm Secondary School, Raising the school-leaving age, April 1972. Gloucestershire Record Office, 5154/2 12/27.

112. Director of education to permanent undersecretary of state, January 4, 1972. East Sussex Record Office, R/E/2/68/79, Raising the school-leaving age from 15 to 16.

113. R. Arnold to Mr J. K. Brierley, Monitoring RSLA, London Borough of Barking, October 29, 1972. DES papers, National Archives ED 233/7.

114. Ibid.

115. D. B. F. Billimore, Monitoring RSLA, Redbridge LB, October 20, 1972. DES papers, National Archives ED 233/7.

116. Schools Council, Planning of the secondary school curriculum, 1968. DES papers, National Archives ED 124/385 Schools Council: subcommittee on preparations for the raising of the school-leaving age, 1968 papers.

117. Stephen Wiseman to E. L. Britton, March 6, 1968. DES papers, National Archives ED 124/385 Schools Council: subcommittee on preparations of the school-leaving age, 1968 papers.

118. HMI, A Survey of Courses for Fourth-Year Non-Examination Pupils in Selected Midland Secondary Schools, 1968–1969. DES papers, National Archives ED 235/7.

119. Very Reverend Canon C. H. de Laubenque to N. Polmear, November 30, 1967. Centre for Kentish Studies C/ED9/2/41.

120. Handwritten note on ROSLA 1969. Chief education officer to permanent undersecretary of state, March 20, 1972. Centre for Kentish Studies C/ED9/241.

121. Raising the school-leaving age in Brighton's secondary schools. A report by a working party of secondary school teachers, 1971. East Sussex Record Office R/E/2/50/12.

122. HMI, A Survey of Readiness for Raising the School Leaving Age in Derby CB; Derbyshire; Lincoln CB; Lincolnshire (Lindsey); Nottingham CB; Nottinghamshire. October–November 1972. DES papers, National Archives ED 272/4.

123. HMI, a Survey of Fourth and Fifth Year Work in Secondary Modern Schools of the Mid-Somerset.

124. No author, "The Leaving Age," *Trends in Education*, October 1971, 2. AEC Archive, Leeds University MS618 A849.

125. Schools Council, Curriculum development for young school leavers. 1968. DES papers, National Archives ED 124/385 Schools Council: subcommittee on preparations for the raising of the school-leaving age, 1968 papers.

126. Brierley, Monitoring of the school-leaving age.

127. Schools Council, History and the Humanities, 1968. DES papers, National Archives ED124/385 Schools Council: subcommittee on preparations for the raising of the school-leaving age, 1968 papers.

128. CACE, *Half Our Future* (The Newsom Report) (London: HMSO, 1963), 166.

129. Morris, Knoll School for Boys to Chief Education Officer.

130. HMI, a Survey of the Provision Made for the Raising of the School Leaving Age in 3 Secondary Schools in Salop.

131. HMI, A Survey of Fifth Year Work in Secondary Modern Schools in Yeovil, Somerset, Spring/Summer 1967. DES papers, National Archives ED 235/3.

132. Edmund Noblett, quoted in Robert Satchwell, "Teachers Groups All Back Extra Year," *Lancashire Evening Post*, May 1, 1973. Lancashire County Record Office, EVF 95, Raising of school-leaving age.

133. Central Youth Employment Executive CYEE Memorandum no. 40. "Wider Employment Opportunities for Girls," December 4, 1968; also CYEE Memorandum no. 48, "Raising the School Leaving Age," January 25, 1971. West Yorkshire Archive Service C603/2/7 ROSLA.

134. HMI, A Survey of the Education of Young School Leavers in Huddersfield, October 1968. DES papers, National Archives ED 235/5.

135. *The Problems of Coloured School Leavers*. Report from the Select Committee on Race Relations and Immigration (London: HMSO, 1969).

136. "Teachers' Lives Shortened," report, *The Guardian*, April 16, 1971.

137. DES Press Notice, April 3, 1968. AEC Archive, Leeds University MS618 A 699, Building Programmes, March 1968–November 1969; Schools Council, North West Regional Curriculum Development Project. DES papers, National Archives ED 124/383 Schools Council: subcommittee on preparations for the raising of the school-leaving age. See also Ronald Cave, *All Their Futures* (Harmondsworth: Penguin, 1968).

138. A. E. Mason, *Third Pilot Course for Experienced Teachers: The Education of the Socially Handicapped* (London: Goldsmiths College, 1966), 3.

139. Richard Stakes and Garry Hornby, *Change in Special Education* (London: Cassell, 1997), 70–71.

140. Eastbourne Education Committee. Report of the chief education officer.

141. Sir Edward Boyle, 1973: opening address to BACIE (British Association for Commercial and Industrial Training), April 25, 1968. Lord Boyle Archive, Leeds University MS660 47893.

142. S. G. Sharp, "Raising the School Leaving Age—Implications for the 16–19 Age Group," Coombe Lodge, *Further Education Staff College Report of Study Conference* 3, 2 (1970): 15–19. AEC Archive, Leeds University MS618 716.

8   Achieving ROSLA

1. See School Leaving Age, *Hansard*, March 23, 1972, HC Deb vol. 833, col. 1821–1846.

2. Mrs R. H. S. Johnson (Scottish Education Department) to B. M. Radley, February 20 1973. Incorporated Association of Head Masters papers, Modern Records Centre 58B/3/32. Section 9 of the Education Act of 1962 had provided that pupils in their final year of compulsory schooling in England and Wales who reached the upper age level between the end of January and the start of September were deemed to attain the upper limit of compulsory school age at the end of the summer term. This remained the situation when the school-leaving age was increased to 16. Under section 33 of the Education (Scotland) Act of 1962, local authorities were able to set up to three different leaving dates.

3. DES Report 1974. DES papers, National Archives ED 272/24.

4. J. A. Widdows, Ryburn Secondary School to Mr Carpenter, Divisional Educational Offices, Todmorden, October 27, 1972. West Yorkshire Archive Service WRD 5/4/4/19 Raising of the school-leaving age.

5. Note headed Sir Alec Clegg, October 1, 1972, Raising of the School Leaving Age. Major Building Programme 1972/3. West Yorkshire Archive Service WRD 5/4/4/19 Raising of the school-leaving age.

6. H. O. Dovey, DES to LEA, Canterbury, April 1, 1969; also H. O. Dovey, DES to LEA, Canterbury, January 5, 1967. Centre for Kentish Studies, C/ED9/2/41.

7. Chief education officer to Reverend Canon L. G. Appleton, January 15, 1969. Centre for Kentish Studies C/ED9/2/41.

8. Chief education officer to permanent undersecretary of state, Circular 8/71 Raising of the School Leaving Age to 16, December 8, 1971. Centre for Kentish Studies C/ED9/2/41.

9. M. F. Atkins, Monitoring RSLA: Great Yarmouth, November 14, 1972. DES papers, National Archives ED 233/7.

10. J. Creedy, ROSLA: Southend on Sea, October 19, 1972. DES papers. National Archives ED 233/7.

11. B. C. Peatey to Mr Jordan, The higher leaving age and school leaving dates, January 17, 1975. DES papers, National Archives ED 233/7.

12. Ernest Armstrong, *Hansard*, July 8, 1974, col. 1000.

13. Alasdair Aston, "The Humanities Curriculum Project," in Lawrence Stenhouse (ed.), *Curriculum Research and Development in Action* (Heinemann: London, 1980), 139–148; M. D. Shipman, *Inside a Curriculum Project* (Longman: London, 1974).

14. Paul Medlicott, "The Rosla Children," *New Society,* May 17, 1973, 357.

15. Roger White and David Brockington. *In and Out of School. The ROSLA Community Education Project* (London: Routledge and Kegan Paul, 1978).

16. Tom Woodin, "Building Culture from the Bottom-Up: The Educational Origins of the FWWCP," *History of Education* 39, 4 (2005): 345–363.

17. D. G. Lambert, Assessing the First Year of the Raising of the School Leaving Age, November 1974. DES papers, National Archives ED 233/7.

18. HMI, Survey of Readiness for Raising the School Leaving Age in Derby CB; Derbyshire; Lincoln CB; Lincolnshire (Lindsey); Nottingham CB; Nottinghamshire. November 1972. DES papers, National Archives ED 272/4.

19. HMI, Raising the School Leaving Age—a Note on Twelve Schools in Bristol and Gloucestershire Report, 1974. DES papers, National Archives ED 272/8.

20. Ibid.

21. HMI, a Survey of the Provision Made for the Raising of the School Leaving Age in 3 Secondary Schools in Salop, 1974. DES papers, National Archives ED 272/24.

22. HMI, Provision for rsla in Some Small Secondary Schools in Plymouth, November 1973 and February 1974. DES papers, National Archives ED 272/14.

23. Ibid.

24. Ibid.

25. HMI, Raising the School Leaving Age—A Note on Twelve Schools in Bristol.

26. Ibid.

27. DES, Meeting on first year of ROSLA, December 12, 1974. DES papers, National Archives ED 233/7.
28. HMI, a Survey of the Provision Made for the Raising of the School Leaving Age in 3 Secondary Schools in Salop.
29. HMI, Survey of Readiness for Raising the School Leaving Age in Derby.
30. HMI, Preparation and Courses for Raising of the School Leaving Age, Prudhoe County Secondary School. DES papers, National Archives ED 272/23; Lambert, Assessing the First Year.
31. Ibid.
32. HMI, Provision for RSLA in Some Small Secondary Schools in Plymouth.
33. HMI, Survey of Readiness for Raising the School Leaving Age in Derby.
34. HMI, a Survey of the Provision Made for the Raising of the School Leaving Age in 3 Secondary Schools in Salop.
35. HMI, Raising the School Leaving Age—a Note on Twelve Schools in Bristol.
36. Lambert, Assessing the First Year.
37. HMI, A Survey of Link Courses between a Selected Sample of Schools and Technical Colleges in the Counties of Dorset and Hampshire. September 1968–December 1969. DES papers, National Archives ED 235/7.
38. HMI, The Implementation of RSLA in Four 11–16 Schools in Wolverhampton. 1974. DES papers, National Archives ED 235/29/11; HMI, a Survey of the Provision of Full-Time Courses for Bristol Students (Age 16–18) in Schools and Colleges in the Bristol Area. October 1968–April 1969. DES papers, National Archives ED 235/7.
39. Lambert, Assessing the First Year.
40. HMI, Survey of the Education Provided for the 15–18 Year Olds in the Borough of Reigate and Redhill, 1970. DES papers, National Archives ED 235/8; HMI, A Survey of the Educational Provision for the 15–18 Age Group in the Borough of Blackpool. Autumn 1968–Spring term 1969. DES papers, National Archives ED 235/7.
41. Medlicott, "Rosla children."
42. HMI, A Survey of Fifth Year Work in Secondary Modern Schools in Yeovil, Somerset, Sprint/Summer 1967. DES papers, National Archives ED 235/3.
43. HMI, a Survey of the Provision Made for the Raising of the School Leaving Age in 3 Secondary Schools in Salop.
44. HMI, A Survey of Fifth Year Work in Secondary Modern Schools in Yeovil.
45. DES, The Raising of the School Leaving Age: Some Effects on Curriculum and Organisation, 1978. DES papers, National Archives ED 233/7.
46. Ibid.
47. Lambert, Assessing the First Year. Appendix B Raising the School Leaving Age.
48. HMI, a Survey of Fourth and Fifth Year Work in Secondary Modern Schools of the Mid-Somerset Divisional Executive, September 1967 and March 1968. DES papers, National Archives ED 235/3.

49. HMI, J. A. Davies, Effects of the New School Leaving Date in 12 Secondary Schools in NE Essex, June 1976. DES papers, National Archives ED 233/7.
50. C. H. Maude, Monitoring ROSLA (Huntingdon/Peterborough) 20 Nov 1972. DES papers, National Archives ED 233/7.
51. The Raising of the School Leaving Age: Some Effects on Curriculum and Organisation, 1978. DES papers, National Archives ED 233/7.
52. HMI, *The Raising of the School Leaving Age in Scotland* (Edinburgh: Scottish Education Department, 1976).
53. HMI, A Survey of Courses for Fourth-Year Non-Examination Pupils in Selected Midland Secondary Schools, September 1968–March 1969. DES papers, National Archives ED 235/7.
54. HMI, A Survey of Fifth Year Work in Secondary Modern Schools in Yeovil.
55. HMI, Provision for rsla in Some Small Secondary Schools in Plymouth.
56. HMI, Survey of Readiness for Raising the School Leaving Age in Derby.
57. HMI, Provision for RSLA in Some Small Secondary Schools in Plymouth.
58. For example, Susan Hart, Annabelle Dixon, Mary Jane Drummond, and Donald McIntyre, *Learning without Limits* (Maidenhead: Open University Press, 2004).
59. DES, The Raising of the School Leaving Age: Some Effects on Curriculum and Organisation; David Gareth Lewis, *Assessment in Education* (London: University of London Press, 1974).
60. HMI, a Survey of Fourth and Fifth Year Work in Secondary Modern Schools of the Mid-Somerset Divisional Executive.
61. DES, The Raising of the School Leaving Age: Some Effects on Curriculum and Organisation.
62. Lambert, Assessing the First Year.
63. NAS (National Association of Schoolmasters) *Ready in Time?* (Hemel Hempstead: NAS, 1966). NAS, *Provision for the Raising of the School Leaving Age* (Hemel Hempstead: NAS, 1973).
64. Schools Council, Raising of the School Leaving Age Sub-Committee: minutes and papers 1968, DES papers, National Archives ED 147/885.
65. DES, The Raising of the School Leaving Age: Some Effects on Curriculum and Organisation.
66. M. F. Atkins, Monitoring RSLA, Norfolk, November 14, 1972. DES papers, National Archives ED 233/7.
67. J. K. Brierley, Monitoring of the School Leaving Age: a discussion paper, September 1, 1972. DES papers, National Archives ED 233/7.
68. Schools Council, A raising the school leaving age project: how teachers plan their courses and pupils perceive their educational objectives, University of Birmingham, 1969. AEC Archive, Leeds University MS 660 A682.a.
69. Lambert, Assessing the First Year. John Nisbet, "The Schools Council, United Kingdom," April 1971, in Centre for Educational Research and Innovation (CERI), *Case Studies of Educational Innovation: 1. At the Centre Level* (OECD: Paris, 1973), 69; Maurice Plaskow (ed.), *Life and Death of the Schools Council* (Barcombe: Falmer Press, 1985).
70. DES, The Raising of the School Leaving Age: Some Effects on Curriculum and Organisation.

71. DES, RSLA, Following based on 50 returns from local authorities responding to circular 8/71. DES papers, National Archives ED 233/7.
72. See John E. B Hill, MP, School Leaving Age, *Hansard*, March 23, 1972, HC Deb vol. 833, col. 1826.
73. HMI, a Survey of the Provision Made for the Raising of the School Leaving Age in 3 Secondary Schools in Salop.
74. Lambert, Assessing the First Year
75. D. Price, County Careers Officer, Durham County Council to Mrs Leitch, Raising the school-leaving age. National Archives LAB 19/876.
76. Sir William Reid, Rise in school-leaving age 1973, Bridging the gap, October 24, 1972. Treasury papers, National Archives T 227/3943.
77. Letter sent to industrial training boards.
78. Adam Hunter, School Leaving Age (Exemption Certificates), *Hansard*, December 12, 1973. HC Deb vol. 866, cc391–393.
79. HMI, Provision for rsla in Some Small Secondary Schools in Plymouth.
80. James Prior to Robert Carr MP, n.d., c. October/November 1973; Mr Widdup to Mr Baldwin (Treasury) December 10, 1973. Treasury papers, National Archives T 227/3943.
81. H. F. Rossetti, I.L.O. to L. G. Morgan, CYEE, June 8, 1971. National Archives LAB 19/876.
82. Letter sent to industrial training boards, November 10, 1969, Raising of the school-leaving age in 1972. National Archives LAB 19/876.
83. Engineering Industry Training Board. A report to the board by a working party on the raising of the school-leaving age to 16 years in September 1972. August 1970. National Archives LAB 19/876.
84. Letter sent to industrial training boards, National Archives LAB 19/876.
85. An outline of curriculum developments in Scotland. Appendix 7. National Archives LAB 19/876.
86. DES, The Raising of the School Leaving Age: Some Effects on Curriculum and Organisation.
87. Lambert, Assessing the First Year.
88. DES, Trends in Education. DES papers, National Archives ED 233/7.
89. City architect to chief education officer, January 22, 1973. Gloucestershire Record Office, 5154/2 12/27.
90. HMI, Raising the School Leaving Age—A Note on Twelve Schools in Bristol and Gloucestershire.
91. K. G. Sherriff, SW Regional Office June 4, 1973 to MR Hanson CYEE. National Archives LAB 19/876.
92. Northern Regional office, Central Youth Employment Executive to Mr M. R. Hanson, June 15, 1973. National Archives LAB 18/976.
93. Education and Training Bulletin, "Industrial Training Boards and the New School Leaving Age," (February 1972), 6. National Archives LAB 19/876.
94. Letter sent to industrial training boards, National Archives LAB 19/876.
95. Information Unit of IMITED, Raising the school-leaving age. The recruitment implications for commerce, industry, and the public services, November 1971. National Archives, LAB 19/876.

96. David Jones, "Competition for the School Leavers," *The Times,* January 14, 1972.
97. For example, E. R. F. Pluck, Hawker Siddeley Power Transformers Limited to CYEE, July 7, 1971. National Archives LAB 19/876.
98. Alan S. Willmott, *CSE and GCE Grading Standards: The 1973 Comparability Study Report* (Basingstoke: Macmillan, 1977); and *Daily Mail,* July 3, 1976, reported in Alex Smith, "The Review," in Maurice Plaskow (ed.), *Life and Death of the Schools Council* (Barcombe: Falmer Press, 1985), 111–112.
99. Lambert, Assessing the First Year
100. Norman St John-Stevas, Secondary Schools, *Hansard,* October 24, 1973, HC Deb vol, 861, col. 519–20W.
101. Mr Edward Taylor, School Leaving Age, *Hansard,* November 11, 1970, HC Deb vol. 806, col. 361–362.
102. Edward Taylor, MP, School Leaving Age (Exemption Certificates), *Hansard,* December 12, 1973, HC Deb vol. 866, col. 391–393.
103. Miss Shields, Headmistress, Knoll C. Secondary School for Girls, to Mr O'Sullivan, Hove Committee for Education, December 3, 1973. East Sussex Record Office, R/E/5/5/56, Raising the school-leaving age: correspondence and reports, 1969–1973.
104. Clement Freud, Amendment of School Leaving Age Bill, *Hansard,* July 2, 1974, HC Deb vol. 876, col. 220–230. Amendment of School Leaving Age, *Hansard,* December 17, 1974, HC Deb vol. 883, col. 1358–1368.
105. "Leaving Age 'Led to Crime,'" *The Guardian,* January 4, 1975.
106. Nigel Lawson, School Leaving Age, *Hansard,* July 8, 1974, HC Deb vol. 876, cc955–1024.
107. Lambert, Assessing the First Year; Appendix B, Raising the School Leaving Age.
108. Lambert, Assessing the First Year.
109. William Alexander to H. Jordan, DES, February 6, 1974. AEC Archive, Leeds University MS618 E72 School Leaving Dates.
110. Education in Approved Schools, November 30, 1971. National Archives, BN 29/2034, The effect on approved schools of raising the school-leaving age to 16 years, 1967–1972.
111. Lambert, Assessing the First Year.
112. Gordon Campbell to James Prior, Lord President, December 19, 1973. Treasury papers, National Archives T 227/3943.
113. Margaret Thatcher, School Leaving Regulations, *Hansard,* January 29, 1974, HC Deb vol. 868, cc235–236.
114. Mrs D. M. White to Mr Jordan, January 15, 1975. DES papers, National Archives ED233/7.
115. C. K. R. Pearce (headmaster, Leek High School, Staffordshire) to M. R. St J. Pitts-Tucker (secretary, Headmasters' Association), March 13, 1973; C. K. R. Pearce, memorandum, The post-exam period for those not eligible to leave. Incorporated Association of Head Masters papers, Modern Records Centre 58B/3/38.
116. G. S. V. Petter (DES) to V. J. Wrigley (head, Longdean School, Hemel Hempstead, Hertfordshire), March 5, 1973; Mrs R. H. S. Johnson (SED) to

B. M. Radley (CYEE), February 20, 1973. IAHM papers, Modern Records Office 58B/3/32.

117. R. J. Cook (general secretary, NAHT) to Margaret Thatcher, January 16, 1973. IAHM papers, Modern Records Office 58B/3/32.

118. Thatcher to Cook, February 8, 1973. IAHM papers, Modern Records Office 58B/3/32.

119. R. J. Cook to R. St J. Pitts-Tucker, March 21, 1973. IAHM papers, Modern Records Office 58B/3/32.

120. Thatcher to Cook, December 6, 1973. IAHM papers, Modern Records Office 58B/3/32.

121. N. Jordan to Mr Hudson, January 16, 1975. DES papers, National Archives ED 233/7.

122. Mrs DM White to Mr Jordan, Assessment of RSLA, January 15, 1975. DES papers, National Archives ED 233/7.

123. *Hansard*, House of Lords, January 15, 1976.

124. HMI J. A. Davies, Effects of the new school leaving date.

125. The Raising of the School Leaving Age: Some Effects on Curriculum and Organisation.

126. "M.L.M." to Mr Millwood, Report on Education no. 83. DES papers, National Archives ED 233/7.

127. Paper headed Mr Millwood. DES papers, National Archives ED 233/7.

128. The Raising of the School Leaving Age: Some Effects on Curriculum and Organisation.

129. The Youth Opportunities Scheme operated under the Manpower Services Commission and acted as a bridge from school into work for 16- to 18-year-olds.

130. HMI, Raising the School Leaving Age—A Note on Twelve Schools in Bristol and Gloucestershire.

131. J. A. Hudson to Mr Evans, January 23, 1975. DES papers, National Archives ED 233/7.

132. Lambert, Assessing the First Year; Appendix B, Raising the School Leaving Age.

133. Lambert, Assessment of the First Year.

134. Ernest Armstrong, School Leaving Age, *Hansard*, July 8, 1974, HC Deb vol. 876, col. 1000.

135. James Callaghan, speech at Ruskin College Oxford, October 18, 1976. www.educationengland.org.uk/documents/speeches/1976ruskin.html (accessed November 24, 2012).

9 Raising the Participation Age: Policy Learning from the Past?

1. Robert Beloe, *Secondary School Examinations Other Than the G.C.E: A Report by a Committee Appointed by the Secondary School Examinations Council.* The Beloe Report (London: HMSO, 1960).

2. See also Christopher Knight, *The Making of Tory Education Policy in Post-War Britain, 1950–1986* (London: Falmer, 1986); and Denis Lawton, *The Tory Mind on Education, 1979–1994* (London: Falmer, 1994).

3. *The Guardian*, report, "Leaving Age 'Led to Crime'," January 4, 1975.

4. Dan Finn, *Training without Jobs: New Deals and Broken Promises, from Raising the School Leaving Age to the Youth Training Scheme* (London: Macmillan, 1987).

5. Caroline Benn, *Challenging the MSC on Jobs, Training and Education* (Milton Keynes: Open University Press, 1986); Geoffrey Walford and Henry Miller, *City Technology College* (Milton Keynes: Open University Press, 1991); Patrick Ainley, *Vocational Education and Training* (London: Cassell, 1991).

6. On the TVEI, see also for example Denis Gleeson (ed.), *TVEI and Secondary Education* (Milton Keynes: Open University Press, 1987).

7. Andrew Gamble, *The Free Economy and the Strong State* (London: Macmillan, 1989).

8. Andy Green, *Education, Equality and Social Cohesion: A Comparative Analysis* (London:Palgrave Macmillan, 2006); Centre for Research and Innovation (CERI) *Think Scenarios, Rethink Education* (Paris: OECD, 2006).

9. Sandy Leitch, *Prosperity for All in the Global Economy: World Class Skills: The Final Report* (Leitch Review of Skills) (London: Stationery Office, 2006).

10. DfES, *Raising Expectations: Staying in Education and Training Post-16* (Norwich: Stationery Office, 2007).

11. DCSF, *Raising Expectations: Staying in Education and Training Post-16. From Policy to Legislation* Nottingham: DCSF, 2007); DCSF, *Impact Assessment of the Education and Skills Bill* (London: DCSF, 2007).

12. DfES, *14–19 Education and Skills White Paper* (Norwich: Stationery Office, 2005a); DfES, *Youth Matters: Next Steps. Something to Do, Somewhere to Go, Someone to Talk to* (Nottingham: Stationery Office, 2005b); DfES, *Further Education: Raising Skills, Improving Life Chances* (Norwich: Stationery Office, 2006).

13. Meg Maguire and Stephen Ball, "Researching Politics and the Politics of Research: Recent Qualitative Studies in the UK," *International Journal of Qualitative Studies in Education* 7, 3 (1994): 269–285.

14. John Furlong, "BERA at 30. Have We Come of Age?" *British Educational Research Journal* 30, 3 (2004): 343–358; Geoff Whitty, "Education(al) Research and Education Policy Making: Is Conflict Inevitable?" *British Educational Research Journal* 32, 2 (2006): 159–176.

15. Jeremy Higham and David Yeomans, "Policy Memory and Policy Amnesia in 14–19 Education: Learning from the Past?" in David Raffe and Ken Spours (eds.), *Policy Making and Policy Learning in 14–19 Education* (London: Institute of Education, 2007), 33–60; Gary McCulloch, *The Struggle for the History of Education* (London: Routledge, 2011).

16. Peter A. Hall, "Policy Paradigms, Social Learning and the State: The Case of Economic Policy Making in Britain," *Comparative Politics* 25, 3 (1993): 275–296.

17. DfES, *Raising Expectations*, 3.
18. Ibid., 9.
19. Francisco O. Ramirez and John Boli, "The Political Construction of Mass Schooling: European Origins and Worldwide Institutionalisation," *Sociology of Education* 60, 1 (1987): 2–17.
20. Ed Balls, "Raising the Participation Age: Opportunity for All Young People," Fabian Society Lecture, Institute of Education, London, November 5, 2007; also DCSF, *Raising Expectations*.
21. Ibid.
22. Raffe and Spours, *Policy Making*.
23. James Kewin, Mark Tucker, Sarah Neat, and Mark Corney, *Lessons from History: Increasing the Number of 16 and 17 Year Olds in Education and Training* (Reading: CfBT, 2009), 9.
24. Jeremy Higham and David Yeomans, "Curriculum Choice, Flexibility and Differentiation in 14–19 Education: The Way Forward or Flawed Prospectus?" *London Review of Education* 5, 3 (2007b): 281–297; also "Thirty Years of 14–19 Education and Training in England: Reflections on Policy, Curriculum and Organisation," *London Review of Education* 9, 2 (2007c): 217–230.
25. Harold Silver, *Education, Change and the Policy Process* (Barcombe: Falmer Press, 1990); David Tyack and Larry Cuban, *Tinkering towards Utopia: A Century of Public School Reform* (Cambridge: Harvard University Press, 1995).
26. Richard Henry Tawney, "Keep the Workers' Children in Their Place," in *The Radical Tradition* (Harmondsworth: Penguin, 1966), 49.
27. CACE (Central Advisory Council for Education [England]) *Early Leaving* (London: HMSO, 1954).
28. CACE, *15 to 18* (Crowther Report) (London: HMSO, 1959).
29. Theodore Schultz, *The Economic Value of Education* (New York: Columbia University Press, 1963); Gary S. Becker, *Human Capital* (New York: NBER, 1964); Mark Blaug, *Economics of Education 1* (Harmondsworth: Penguin, 1968).
30. Sir Edward Boyle, 1973: Opening Address, BACIE (British Association for Commercial and Industrial Training), April 25, 1968. Boyle Archive, Leeds University MS 660 47893.
31. Gary McCulloch, Steven Cowan, and Tom Woodin, "The British Conservative Government and the Raising of the School Leaving Age, 1959–1964," *Journal of Education Policy* 27, 4 (2012): 509–527.
32. CACE, *15 to 18*, 147–148.
33. W. D. Pile, Note to Toby Weaver, July 12, 1963. Ministry of Education Papers, National Archives, ED 147/516.
34. First Secretary of State, Possible Deferment of the SLA. Reductions in Expenditure on Education, memorandum, draft version December 5, 1967. Cabinet Papers, National Archives CAB 152/4.
35. J. L. Rampton, Possible Deferment of the SLA. Letter to P. R. Odgers, December 1, 1967. Cabinet Papers, National Archives, CAB 152/4.

36. DIUS, *World Class Skills: Implementing the Leitch Review of Skills in England* (Norwich: Stationery Office, 2007), 3.
37. Leitch Review
38. DCSF, *Impact Assessment.*
39. Alison Wolf, *Diminished Returns: How Raising the Leaving Age to 18 Will Harm Young People and the Economy* (London: Policy Exchange, 2007).
40. DfE, "Development of New Academic Diplomas Stops," June 7, 2010. www.education.gov.uk/childrenandyoungpeople/strategy/laupdates/a0071145/development-of-new-academic-diplomas-stops (accessed July 10, 2010).
41. House of Commons Education Committee, *Participation by 16–19 Year-Olds in Education and Training,* fourth report of session 2010–2012, 1 (London: HMSO, 2011).
42. DfE, Statistical First Release, Participation in Education, Training and Employment By 16–18 Year Olds in England, February 21, 2013. http://media.education.gov.uk/assets/files/pdf/m/sfr12–2012.pdf (accessed February 25, 2013).
43. Angela Harrison, "Young Jobless 'NEETS' Reach Record Level," BBC News online, www.bbc.co.uk/news/education-15870240? (accessed December 1, 2011).
44. DfE, Statistical First Release.
45. Michael Gove, "Education for Young People." Written Ministerial Statements. *Hansard* July 22, 2012, col. 33WS.
46. DfE, *The Importance of Teaching. The Schools White Paper* (Norwich: Stationery Office, 2010), 50; Liberal Democrats, *Our Manifesto* (London: Chris Fox, 2010), 36.
47. Education and Skills Act 2008, paragraph 173, subsection 10, 115.
48. DCSF, *Raising Expectations,* 1, 8.
49. Ibid., 5–6.
50. For a view downplaying the school-leaving age in favor of an adult and vocational education, see Sir Richard Livingstone, *The Future in Education* (Cambridge: Cambridge University Press, 1941).
51. CACE, *15 to 18,* 143.
52. AEC 1960–63, Report of the Sub-Committee on County College Provision (n. d.). AEC Archive, Leeds University MS618 A32(a), Day Release 1960–63.
53. Tom Woodin, "Working Class Education and Social Change in Nineteenth and Twentieth Century Britain," *History of Education* 36, 4–5 (2007): 483–496.
54. Richard Pring, Geoffrey Hayward, Ann Hodgson, Jill Johnson, Ewart Keep, Alis Oancea, Gareth Reese, Ken Spours, and Stephanie Wilde, *Education for All. The Future of Education and Training for 14–19 Year Olds* (London: Routledge, 2009); Jeremy Higham and David Yeomans, "Working Together? Partnership Approaches to 14–19 Education in England," *British Educational Research Journal* 36, 3 (2010): 379–400.
55. DfE, *Review of Vocational Education* (The Wolf Report) (London: DfE, 2011).

56. For recent context see DfE, The Importance of Teaching: Schools White Paper (Norwich: Stationery Office, 2010).

57. DfES and DIUS, Raising Expectations: Enabling the System to Deliver (Norwich: Stationery Office, 2008).

58. National Audit Office, Raising the Participation Age: An Assessment of the Cost-Benefit Analysis (London: National Audit Office, 2011).

59. ISOS, Evaluation of the Phase 2 Raising the Participation Age Trials—Final Report. Research Report DFE-RR135 (London: DfE, 2011), 6.

60. DfE, "The Role of Schools and Local Authorities in Careers Guidance." www.education.gov.uk/childrenandyoungpeople/youngpeople/a0064052/the-role -of-schools-and-local-authorities-in-careers-guidance (accessed February 22, 2013).

61. Letter from John Hayes, Minister of State for Further Education, Skills and Lifelong Learning, March 28, 2012. http://media.education.gov.uk/assets/files/pdf/l/jh%20letter%20re%20enrolling%2014–16%20year%20olds%20 in%20colleges%2028march.pdf (accessed November 7, 2012).

62. NUT, Stephen Twigg's speech to Labour Party conference—press release. October 4, 2012. www.teachers.org.uk/node/16703 (accessed December 12, 2012).

63. Tom Woodin, "Co-operative Schools: Building Communities for the 21st Century," Forum 54, 2 (2012): 327–340. Tom Woodin (ed.), Co-operation, Learning and Co-operative Values (London: Routledge, forthcoming 2014).

64. Ron Brooks, Contemporary Debates in Education. An Historical Perspective (London: Longman, 1991).

65. For example, CYEE (Central Youth Employment Agency), "Raising of the School Leaving Age," memorandum No. 48, January 25, 1971. West Yorkshire Archive Service C603/ 2/7 ROSLA.

66. Ann Hodgson and Ken Spours, Education and Training 14–19: Curriculum, Qualifications and Organization (London: Sage, 2008).

67. Graeme Paton, "New Diplomas 'Have Been Fatally Undermined,'" Daily Telegraph, August 24, 2010. www.telegraph.co.uk/education /educationnews/7962111/New-diplomas-have-been-fatally-undermined. html (accessed September 1, 2010).

68. Richard Wilkinson and Kate Pickett, The Spirit Level. Why Equality Is Better for Everyone (London: Penguin, 2009).

69. Boyle, 1973: Opening Address.

70. Hansard, "Education (Report of the Central Advisory Council), March 21, 1960, HC Deb vol. 620, col. 40–180.

71. Schools Council, "A Raising the School Leaving Age Project: How Teachers Plan Their Courses and Pupils Perceive Their Educational Objectives," November 1969. AEC Archive, Leeds University MS 618 A682.a.

72. ISOS Partnership, Raising the Participation Age (RPA) Trials: Phase 1 Evaluation. Research Report DfE RR02 (London: DfE, 2010).

73. ISOS, Evaluation of the Phase 2 Raising the Participation Age Trials—Final Report. Research Report DFE-RR135 (London: DfE, 2011), 6.

10 CONCLUSION

1. Brian Simon, "Can Education Change Society?" in Brian Simon (ed.), *Does Education Matter?* (London: Lawrence and Wishart, 1985), 13–31.
2. Shirley Brice Heath, *Ways with Words: Language, Life and Work in Communities and Classrooms* (Cambridge: Cambridge University Press, 1983); Concha Delgado-Gaitan, "The Value of Conformity: Learning to Stay in School," *Anthropology and Education Quarterly* 19, 4 (1988): 354–381.
3. NSW Government, "Raising the School Leaving Age. Consultation Paper" 2008 (Sydney: NSW Government, 2008), 14.
4. Ann Hodgson and Ken Spours, "An Analytical Framework for Policy Engagement: The Contested Case of 14–19 Reform in England," *Journal of Education Policy* 21, 6 (2006): 679–696.
5. Keith Middlemas, *Politics in Industrial Society: The Experience of the British System since 1911* (London: Andre Deutsch, 1979).
6. Bruce Curtis, *Building the Educational State: Canada West 1836–1871* (Falmer: Lewes, 1988).
7. Stephen J. Ball, "Policy Sociology and Critical Social Research: A Personal Review of Recent Education Policy and Policy Research," *British Educational Research Journal* 23, 3 (2006): 257–274.
8. Peter Preston, "Two More Futile Years," Guardian online, January 15, 2007. www.guardian.co.uk/commentisfree/2007/jan/15/comment.politics2 (accessed February 24, 2007).
9. Alison Wolf, Professor of Economics, King's College, London, *Does Education Matter? Myths about Education and Economic Growth* (London: Penguin 2002).
10. BBC, "Cut School Leaving Age to 14, Says Sir Chris Woodhead," October 3, 2011. www.bbc.co.uk/news/education-15146240; BBC, "Lord Digby Jones: 'Connect Getting a Skill With Earning Money,'" July 29, 2011, www.bbc.co.uk/news/education-14338977.

Bibliography

Archival Sources and Collections

Bodleian Library, Oxford:
    Conservative Party

Centre for Kentish Studies

Churchill College Cambridge:
    Michael Stewart

Essex County Record Office

East Sussex Record Office

Gloucestershire Record Office

Institute of Education, London:
    Schools Council for Curriculum and Examinations
    R. H. Tawney

John Rylands University Library, Manchester:
    Manchester Guardian

Lancashire County Record Office

Leeds University Special Collections:
    Association of Education Committees
    Edward Boyle

London Metropolitan Archives

Manchester Archives and Local Studies:
    Ernest Simon
    Shena Simon

Modern Records Office, University of Warwick:
    Confederation of British Industry
    National Union of Teachers

National Archives, Kew, London:
    Board of Education
    Cabinet

Department of Education and Science
Ministry of Labour
Treasury

National Archives of Scotland:
Scottish Office

Newcastle University Library:
C. P. Trevelyan

Tameside Local Studies

West Yorkshire Archive Service

Newspapers and Journals

Education
Guardian
Times
Times Educational Supplement

Published Government Reports

Beloe, R. (1960), *Secondary School Examinations Other Than the G.C.E: A Report by a Committee Appointed by the Secondary School Examinations Council. The Beloe Report*, London: HMSO.
Board of Education (1908), *School Attendance of Children below the Age of Five*, London: HMSO.
———. (1909), *Attendance, Compulsory or Otherwise, at Continuation Schools*, London: HMSO.
Board of Education Consultative Committee (1926) (The Hadow Report), *The Education of the Adolescent*, London: HMSO.
———. (1938) (Spens Report), *Report of The Consultative Committee on Secondary Education with special reference to Grammar Schools and Technical High Schools*, London: HMSO.
CACE Ministry of Education (1952), "The Age of Compulsory School Attendance," London: HMSO.
———. (1959) (Crowther Report), *15–18: A Report of the Central Advisory Council for Education* (England), London: HMSO.
———. (1963) (Newsom Report), *Half Our Future*, London: HMSO.
Committee on Higher Education (1963) (Robbins Report), *Higher Education Report of the Committee appointed by the Prime Minister*, London: HMSO.
Department of Science and Art (1893), Abstract of returns furnished to the Department of Science and Art: showing the manner in which, and the

extent to which, the councils of counties and county boroughs in England and Wales, and the town councils and police burghs in Scotland, are devoting funds to the purposes of science, art, technical, and manual instruction, London: HMSO.

DCSF (2007), *Raising Expectations: Staying in Education and Training Post-16. From Policy to Legislation*, Nottingham: DCSF.

———. (2007), *Impact Assessment of the Education and Skills Bill*, London: DCSF.

DfE (2010a), *The Importance of Teaching. The Schools White Paper*, Norwich: Stationery Office.

———. (2010b), "Development of New Academic Diplomas Stops," June 7, available at www.education.gov.uk/childrenandyoungpeople/strategy/laupdates /a0071145/development-of-new-academic-diplomas-stops (accessed July 10, 2010).

———. (2010c), Statistical First Release. SFR 18/2010, London: DfE.

DfE website, "16- to 18-Year-Olds Not in Education, Employment or Training (NEET)," available at www.education.gov.uk/a0064101/16-to-18-year-olds -not-in-education-employment-or-training-neet (accessed November 2012).

DfE (2011), *Review of Vocational Education. The Wolf Report*, London: DfE.

DfES (2005a), *14–19 Education and Skills White Paper*, Norwich: Stationery Office.

———. (2005b), *Youth Matters: Next Steps. Something to Do, Somewhere to Go, Someone to Talk to*, Nottingham: Stationery Office.

———. (2006), *Further Education: Raising Skills, Improving Life Chances*, Norwich: Stationery Office.

———. (2007), *Raising Expectations: Staying in Education and Training Post-16*, Norwich: Stationery Office.

DfES and DIUS (2008), *Raising Expectations: Enabling the System to Deliver*, Norwich: Stationery Office.

DIUS (2007), *World Class Skills: Implementing the Leitch Review of Skills in England*, Norwich: Stationery Office.

Education (Administrative Provisions) Act 1907.

Final Report of the Departmental Committee on Juvenile Labour in Relation to Employment after the War (1917) (Lewis Report), London: HMSO.

ISOS Partnership (2010), *Raising the Participation Age (RPA) Trials: Phase 1 Evaluation*. Research report DfE RR02, London: DfE.

ISOS (2011), *Evaluation of the Phase 2 Raising the Participation Age Trials—Final Report*. Research Report DFE-RR135, London: DfE.

Ministry of Education (1954) (Gurney-Dixon Report), *Early Leaving*, London: HMSO.

———. (1958), *Secondary Education for All: a New Drive*, London: HMSO.

———. (1960) (Albermarle Report), *The Youth Service in England and Wales*, London: HMSO.

Report of the Commissioners Appointed to Inquire into the State of Popular Education in England (1861) (Newcastle Report), London: HMSO.

Report of the Royal Commission on the Elementary Education Acts (1888) (Cross Report), London: HMSO.

Royal Commission on Secondary Education (1895) (Bryce Report), *Report of the Commissioners*, London: HMSO.

Schools Council (1964), *Science for the Young School Leaver*, London: HMSO.

———. (1965), *Raising the School Leaving Age: A Co-operative Programme of Research and Development*, London: HMSO.

———. (1967a), *The Educational Implications of Social and Economic Change. Report of a Conference Called by the Schools Council in Preparation for Raising the School Leaving Age*, London: HMSO.

———. (1967b), *Society and the Young School Leaver: A Humanities Programme in Preparation for the Raising of the School leaving Age*, London: HMSO.

———. (1968), *Young School Leavers: Report of a Survey Among Young People, Parents and Teachers*, London: HMSO.

———. (1969), *a Raising the School Leaving Age Project: How Teachers Plan Their Courses and Pupils Perceive Their Educational Objectives*, Birmingham: University of Birmingham.

Schools Inquiry Commission (1868) (Taunton Report), *Report of the Commissioners*, London: HMSO.

Australia

Australian States and Territories (2007), *Federalist Paper 2. The Future of Schooling*, Canberra: AST.

Department of Education, Employment and Workplace Relations, Australia, "Compact with Young Australians Increasing Educational Attainment of Young People Aged 15–24," available from http://foi.deewr.gov.au/documents/compact-young-australians-questions-and-answers-1 (accessed November 10, 2012).

New South Wales Government (2008), *Raising the School Leaving Age. Consultation Paper* Sydney, NSW Government 14.

Singapore

Ministry of Education, Singapore, "Compulsory Education," available from www.moe.gov.sg/initiatives/compulsory-education/ (accessed July 5, 2010).

India

Department of Elementary Education and Literacy (2003), *Education for All. National Plan of Action*. India. New Delhi: Ministry of Human Resource Development.

Constitution (Eighty-Sixth Amendment Act) (2002), available from http://indiacode.nic.in/coiweb/amend/amend86.htm (accessed November 10, 2012).

The Right to Education Bill (2005), India, November 14, 2005.

South Korea

Ministry of Education, Science and Technology, "Overview," available from
   http://english.mest.go.kr/web/1692/site/contents/en/en_0203.jsp   (accessed
   July 20, 2012).

Other Sources and Publications

Abeje, H. (1983), "How to Provide Universal Schooling," *Prospects* 13, 2,
   pp. 245–249.
Acland, A. (1892), *Studies in Secondary Education*, London: Perceval.
Adelaide Declaration on National Goals for Schooling in the Twenty First Century
   (1999), available from www.mceetya.edu.au/mceecdya/nationalgoals/natgoals.
   htm (accessed October 10, 2012).
AEC/NUT (1938), *The Extra Year: A Report of the Joint Committee of Investigation
   Representing the Association of Education Committees and the National Union of
   Teachers*, London: University of London.
Ainley, P. (1991), *Vocational Education and Training*, London: Cassell.
Akyeampong, K. (2009), "Revisiting Free Compulsory Universal Basic Education
   (FCUBE) in Ghana," *Comparative Education* 45, 2, pp. 175–195.
Alexander, W. (1959), "Week by Week—15 to 18," *Education*, December 18,
   pp. 1061–1062.
Allsobrook, D. (1986), Schools for the Shires: The Reform of Middle-Class
   Education in Victorian England, Manchester: Manchester University Press.
Angrist, J. and Krueger, A. (1991), "Does Compulsory Schooling Attendance Affect
   Schooling and Earnings?" *Quarterly Journal of Economics*, 106, pp. 979–1014.
Armytage, W. H. G. (1951), A.J. Mundella 1825–1897: The Liberal Background
   to the Labour Movement, London: Benn.
———. (1970), *Four Hundred Years of English Education*, Cambridge: Cambridge
   University Press, pp. 144–145.
Aston, A. (1980), "The Humanities Curriculum Project," in Lawrence Stenhouse
   (ed.), *Curriculum Research and Development in Action*, London: Heinemann,
   pp. 139–148.
Auerback, S. (2012), "'The Law Has No Feeling for Poor Folks Like Us!': Everyday
   Responses to Legal Compulsion in England's Working Class Communities,"
   Journal of Social History 45, 3, pp. 686–708.
Bailey, B. (1990), "Technical Education and Secondary Schooling, 1905–1945," in
   Penny Summerfield and Eric J. Evans (eds.), *Technical Education and the State
   since 1850: Historical and Contemporary Perspectives*, Manchester: Manchester
   University Press, pp. 97–119.

Bailyn, B. (1960), *Education in the Forming of American Society*, New York: Random House.

Ball, S. J. (2006), "Policy Sociology and Critical Social Research: A Personal Review of Recent Education Policy and Policy Research," *British Educational Research Journal* 23, 3, pp. 257–274.

Balls, Ed (2007), "Raising the Participation Age: Opportunity For All Young People," Fabian Society Lecture, Institute of Education, London, November 5; also DCSF, 2007.

Barber, M. (1992), *Education and the Teacher Unions*, London: Cassell.

Barker, C. (1980), "The Exemption System, 1833–1944," *Journal of Educational Administration and History*, 12, 1, pp. 10–17.

Barker, R. (1972), *Education and Politics 1900–1951: A Study of the Labour Party*, Oxford: Clarendon Press.

Barton, A. (1964) "Wilkinson's Law," *The Guardian*, January 6.

Becker, G. (1964), *Human Capital*, New York: NBER.

Benn, C. (1986), *Challenging the MSC on Jobs, Training and Education*, Milton Keynes: Open University Press.

Benn, T. (1988), *Office without Power: Diaries 1968–72*, London: Hutchinson.

Birch, D. (2008), *Our Victorian Education*. Oxford: Blackwell.

Bishop, A. S. (1971), *The Rise of a Central Authority in English Education*, Cambridge: Cambridge University Press.

Black, S. E., Devereaux, P. J. and Salvanes, K. (2008), "Staying in the Classroom and out of the Maternity Ward? The Effect of Compulsory Schooling Laws on Teenage Births," *The Economic Journal* 118, 530, pp. 1025–1054.

Blaug, M. (1968), *Economics of Education 1*, Harmondsworth: Penguin.

Boyle, E. (1973), "Opening Address," BACIE (British Association for Commercial and Industrial Training), April 25, 1968, Leeds University Special Collections, Lord Boyle Archive, MS660 47893.

Brice Heath, S. (1983), Ways with Words: Language, Life and Work in Communities and Classrooms, Cambridge: Cambridge University Press.

Bridgeland, J. M., Dilulio, J. J., and Burke Morrison, K. (2006), *The Silent Epidemic. Perspectives of High School Dropouts*, Washington, DC: Civic Enterprises and the Bill and Melinda Gates Foundation.

Bridgeland, J. M., Dilulio, J. J., and Streeter, R. (2007) *Raising the Compulsory School Attendance Age: the Case for Reform*, Washington, DC: Civic Enterprises.

Brooks, R. (1991), Contemporary Debates in Education. An Historical Perspective, London: Longman.

Bush, M. (June 2010), "Compulsory School Age Requirements," State Notes, ECS (Education Commission of the States), available at www.ecs.org/html /educationissues/StateNotes/2010-StateNotes.pdf (accessed July 10, 2010).

Centre for Research and Innovation (CERI) (2006), *Think Scenarios, Rethink Education,* Paris: OECD.

Chick, M. (2002), *Industrial Policy in Britain 1945–1951: Economic Planning, Nationalisation and Labour Governments*, Cambridge: Cambridge University Press.

Cipolla, C. M. (1969), *Literacy and Development in the West*, Harmondsworth: Penguin.

Cleghorn, I. (1911), "The Educational Ladder. The Presidential Address," *Practical Teacher* 31, 11, pp. 744–748.

Cooke, D. H. and Pruet, E. G. (1939), "Constitutional and Statutory Development of Compulsory School Attendance in Alabama," *Peabody Journal of Education*, 16, 5, pp. 330–334.

Corrigan, P. and Sayer, D. (1982), *The Great Arch: English State Formation as Cultural Revolution*, Oxford: Blackwell.

Cowan, S., McCulloch, G., and Woodin, T., (2012), "From HORSA Huts to ROSLA Blocks: The School Leaving Age and the School Building Programme in England, 1943–1972," *History of Education*, 40, 3, pp. 361–380.

Craik, H., Sir (1895), State Education: Its Scope and Responsibilities, a Speech Delivered at the Opening of Bruntsford School, Edinburgh, April 19, London: MacMillan.

Crook, D. (2005), "Compulsory Education in the United Kingdom. Historical, Comparative and Contemporary Perspectives," *Journal of Educational Planning and Administration*, 3, pp. 397–414.

Crook, P. (2007), *Darwin's Coat-Tails: Essays on Social Darwinism*, New York: Peter Lang Publishing.

Crosland, A. (1956), *The Future of Socialism,* London: Jonathan Cape.

Crossman, R. (1975, 1976, 1977), *The Diaries of a Cabinet Minister,* 3 Vols., London: Hamish Hamilton.

Cruickshank, M. (1963), *Church and State in English Education*, London: MacMillan.

Cubberley, E. P. (1909), *Changing Conceptions of Education*, Boston: Houghton Mifflin.

Cunningham, H. (1998), "Review Essay: Histories of Childhood," *The American Historical Review*, 103, 4, pp. 1195–1208.

Curtis, B. (1988), *Building the Educational State: Canada West 1836–1871*, Lewes: Falmer Press.

Daglish, N. (1996), *Education Policy-Making in England and Wales: The Crucible Years, 1895–1911*, London: Woburn.

Davey, I. (1987), "Capitalism, Patriarchy and the Origins of Mass Schooling," *History of Education Review* 16, 2, pp. 1–12.

Davin, A. (1996), *Growing Up Poor: Home, School and Street 1870–1914*, London: Rivers Oram.

Dean, D. (1995), "Conservative Governments, 1951–64, and Their Changing Perspectives on the 1944 Education Act," *History of Education*, 24, 3, pp. 247–266.

Delgado-Gaitan, C. (1988), "The Value of Conformity: Learning to Stay in School," *Anthropology and Education Quarterly* 19, 4, 354–381.

Dahiman, C. J., and Aubert, J. (2001), *China and the Knowledge Economy. Seizing the 21st Century,* Washington, DC: World Bank Institute.

Duane, M. (1995), *The Terrace: An Educational Experiment in a State School,* London: Freedom Press.

Durkheim, E. (1938/1977), *The Evolution of Educational Thought: Lectures on the Formation and Development of Secondary Education in France*. London: Routledge and Kegan Paul.

Everhart, R. B. (1977), "From Universalism to Usurpation: An Essay on the Antecedents to Compulsory School Attendance Legislation," *Review of Educational Research* 47, 3, pp. 499–530.

Ewing, J. L. (1972), National Commission on Education, *Compulsory Education in New Zealand*, Paris: UNESCO.

Favretto, H. (2000), "'Wilsonism' Reconsidered: Labour Party Revisionism, 1952–64," *Contemporary British History*, 14, 4, pp. 54–80.

Finn, D. (1987), *Training without Jobs: New Deals and Broken Promises, from Raising the School Leaving Age to the Youth Training Scheme*, London: Macmillan.

Fisher, H. A. L. (1940), *An Unfinished Autobiography*, Oxford: Oxford University Press.

Franken, J. (2010), "Analysis: Indonesia's 12-Year Compulsory Education Program," *Jakarta Post*, June 28, 2010, available at www.thejakartapost.com /news/2010/06/28/analysis-indonesia%E2%80%99s-12year-compulsory -education-program.html.

Furet, F. and Ozouf, J. (1982), *Reading and Writing: Literacy in France from Calvin to Jules Ferry*, Cambridge: Cambridge University Press.

Furlong, J. (2004), "BERA at 30. Have We Come of Age?" *British Educational Research Journal* 30, 3, pp. 343–358.

Fyfe, A. (1997), *The Worldwide Movement against Child Labour—Progress and Future Directions*, Geneva: ILO.

Gamble, A. (1989), *The Free Economy and the Strong State*, London: Macmillan.

Gardner, P. (1983), *The Lost Elementary Schools of Victorian England*, London: Croom Helm.

Gareth Evans, W. (1990), "The Welsh Intermediate and Technical Education Act, 1889: A Centenary Appreciation," *History of Education*, 19, 3, pp. 195–210.

Giddens, A. (1991), *Modernity and Self-identity: Self and Society in the Late Modern Age*, Cambridge: Polity.

Gleeson, D. (ed.), (1987), *TVEI and Secondary Education*, Milton Keynes: Open University Press.

Good, E. T. (1926), "Too Much Schooling," *English Review* March.

Green, A. (1990), *Education and State Formation: The Rise of Education and Training Systems in England, France and the USA*, London: Macmillan.

———. (2006), *Education, Equality and Social Cohesion: A Comparative Analysis*, London: Palgrave Macmillan.

———. (2007), "Globalisation and the Changing Nature of the State in East Asia," *Globalisation, Societies and Education*, 5, 1, pp. 23–38.

Green C. and Paniagua, M. N. (2012), "Does Raising the School Leaving Age Reduce Teacher Effort? Evidence from a Policy Experiment," *Economic Inquiry* 50, 4, pp. 1018–1030.

Griggs, C. (1988), *The Trades Union Congress and the Struggle for Education, 1868–1925*, Lewes: Falmer Press.

Griggs, C. (2002) *The TUC and Education Reform, 1926–1970*, London: Woburn Press.

Grover, J., Whitehurst, R., and Whitfield, S. (2012), *Compulsory School Attendance. What Research Says, What It Means for State Policy*, Washington, DC: Brookings Institution.

Hall, C. (2002), *Civilising Subjects: Metropole and Colony in the English Imagination, 1830–1867*, Cambridge: Polity.

Hall, P. A. (1993), "Policy Paradigms, Social Learning and the State: The Case of Economic Policy Making in Britain," *Comparative Politics*, 25, 3, pp. 275–296.

Halliwell, H. F. (1970), "Schools and Colleges," *Further Education Staff College Report of Study Conference* 3, 2. Leeds University College Publications.

Halpin, D. and Troyna, B. (1995), "The Politics of Education Policy Borrowing," *Comparative Education* 31, 3, pp. 303–310.

Harmon, C. and Walker, I. (1995), "Estimates of the Economic Return to Schooling for the United Kingdom," *American Economic Review* 85, pp. 1278–1286.

Harrison, A. "Young Jobless 'NEETS' Reach Record Level," BBC News online, available at www.bbc.co.uk/news/education-15870240? (accessed December 1, 2011).

Hart, S., Dixon, A., Drummond, M. J., and Donald McIntyre, D. (2004), *Learning without Limits*, Maidenhead: Open University Press.

Haseler, D. (1969), *The Gaitskellites: Revisionism in the British Labour Party, 1951–64*, London: Macmillan.

Hendrick, H. (1980), "'a Race of Intelligent Unskilled Labourers': The Adolescent Worker and the Debate on Compulsory Part-Time Day Continuation Schools, 1900–1922," *History of Education*, 9, 2, pp. 152–173.

Higham, J. and Yeomans, D. (2007a), "Policy Memory and Policy Amnesia in 14–19 Education: Learning from the Past?" in David Raffe and Ken Spours (eds.), *Policy Making and Policy Learning in 14–19 Education*, London: Institute of Education, pp. 20, 33–60.

———. (2007b), "Curriculum Choice, Flexibility and Differentiation in 14–19 Education: The Way Forward or Flawed Prospectus?" *London Review of Education* 5, 3, pp. 281–297.

———. (2007c), "Thirty Years of 14–19 Education and Training in England: Reflections on Policy, Curriculum and Organisation," *London Review of Education*, 9, 2, pp. 17–230.

———. (2010), "Working Together? Partnership Approaches to 14–19 Education in England," *British Educational Research Journal* 36, 3, pp. 379–400.

Hodgson, A. and Spours, K. (2006), "An Analytical Framework for Policy Engagement: The Contested Case of 14–19 Reform in England," *Journal of Education Policy* 21, 6, pp. 679–696.

———. (2008), *Education and Training 14–19: Curriculum, Qualifications and Organization*, London: Sage.

Hodgson, D. (2011), "Policy Rationalities and Policy Technologies: A Programme for Analysing the Raised School-Leaving Age in Western Australia," *Journal of Education Policy* 26, 1, pp. 115–130.

Honey, J. (1977), *Tom Brown's Universe: The Development of the Public Schoolin the 19th Century*, London: Millington Books.

———. (1987), "The Sinews of Society: The Public Schools as a 'System,'" in D. Muller, F. Ringer, and B. Simon (eds.), *The Rise of the Modern Educational System: Structural Change and Social Reproduction, 1870–1920*, Cambridge: Cambridge University Press, pp. 151–162.

Hope, H. (1936), *The Education Act 1936*. London: Eyre & Spottiswood.

Hopkins, E. (1994), *Childhood Transformed: Working-Class Children in Nineteenth-Century England*, Manchester: Manchester University Press.

Hopkinson, D. (ed.) (1971), "The School Leaving Age," *Trends in Education* (October), DES, pp. 17–22. AEC Archive, Leeds University MS618 A849.

House of Commons Library (1999), Research Paper 99/111, A Century of Change: Trends in UK Statistics since 1900, available at www.parliament .uk/documents/commons/lib/research/rp99/rp99–111.pdf (accessed August 23, 2012).

Huebler, F. (2007), "International Education Statistics: Official School Ages: Primary, Secondary, and Compulsory Education," January 27, available from http://huebler.blogspot.co.uk/2007/01/official-school-ages-primary-second-ary.html (accessed November 10, 2012).

Human Development Unit South Asia Region (2009), *Secondary Education in India: Universalising Opportunity*, Washington, DC: World Bank.

Humes, W. and Paterson, H. M. (eds.) (1983), *Scottish Culture and Scottish Education*, Edinburgh: John Donald, Chapter 3.

Humphries, J. (2010), *Childhood and Child Labour in the British Industrial Revolution*, Cambridge: Cambridge University Press.

Illich, I. (1973), *Deschooling Society*, Harmondsworth: Penguin.

ILO (1951), *Child Labour in Relation to Compulsory Education*, Paris: UNESCO.

INTERNATIONAL BUREAU OF EDUCATION (1979), "Compulsory Education and the Raising of the School Leaving Age (1934)," in *International Conference on Education. Recommendations 1934–1977*, Paris: UNESCO.

Jenkins, R. (1991), *A Life at the Centre*, London: Macmillan.

Jewkes, J. and Winterbottom, A. (1933), *Juvenile Unemployment*, London: George Allen and Unwin.

Johnson, R. (1970), "Educational Policy and Social Control in Early Victorian England," *Past and Present*, 49, pp. 96–119.

———. (1972), "Really Useful Knowledge. Radical Education and Working Class Culture, 1790–1848," in Jon Clarke, Chas Critcher, and Richard Johnson (eds.), *Working Class Culture*, London: Hutchinson, pp. 75–102.

Johnston, C. (2011), "The Cost of Dropping Out," July 24, available at www.npr .org/2011/07/24/138508517/series-overview-the-cost-of-dropping-out (accessed December 10, 2012).

Kandel, I. L. (1951), *Raising the School Leaving Age*. Paris: UNESCO.

Katz, M. (1968), *The Irony of Early School Reform*, Cambridge: Harvard University Press.

———. (1977), "Compulsion and the Discourse on Compulsory School Attendance," *Educational Theory* 27, 3, pp. 179–185.

Katznelson, I., Gille, K., and Weir, M. (1982), "Public Schooling and Working Class Formation: The Case of the United States," *American Journal of Education* 90, 2, pp. 111–143.

Kett, J. F. (1973), "Juveniles and Progressive Children," *History of Education Quarterly* 13, pp. 191–194.

Kewin, J., Tucker, M., Neat, S., and Corney, M. (2009), *Lessons from History: Increasing the Number of 16 and 17 Year Olds in Education and Training.* Reading: CfBT.

King, B. (1929), *Schools of To-Day. Present Problems in English Education,* London: J.M. Dent.

Knight, C. (1986), *The Making of Tory Education Policy in Post-War Britain, 1950–1986,* London: Falmer Press.

Kozol, J. (1978), "A New Look at the Literacy Campaign in Cuba," *Harvard Educational Review* 48, pp. 341–377.

Kumar, K. (2004), "Quality of Education at the Beginning of the 21st Century: Lessons from India," background paper for EFA Global Monitoring Report. 2005. Paris: UNESCO.

Labour Party (1929), *We Can Conquer Unemployment,* London: Labour Party.

Lancashire Education Committee Annual Report (1971–72), Preston, I EC, Ashton Under Lyne Local Studies.

Landes, W. M. and Solomon, L. C. (1972), "Compulsory Schooling Legislation: An Economic Analysis of Law and Social Change in the Nineteenth Century," *Journal of Economic History* 32, 1, p. 78.

Law, W. (2007), "Legislation and Educational Change: The Struggle for Social Justice and Quality in China's Compulsory Schooling," *Education and the Law,* 19, 3, pp. 177–199.

Lawton, D. (1994), *The Tory Mind on Education, 1979–1994,* London: Falmer Press.

———. (2005), *Education and the Labour Party: 1900–2001 and beyond,* London: Routledge.

Leitch, S. (2006), Prosperity for All in the Global Economy: World Class Skills: The Final Report (Leitch Review of Skills), London: Stationery Office.

Lester Smith, W. O. (1951), *Compulsory Education in England,* Paris: UNESCO.

Lewis, D. G. (1974), *Assessment in Education,* London: University of London Press.

Liberal Democrats (2010), *Our Manifesto,* London: Chris Fox.

Lindsay, K. (1926), *Social Progress and Educational Waste: Being a Study of the "Free-Place" and Scholarship System,* London: Routledge.

Lipset, S. M. (1976), *Political Man,* London: Heinemann.

Lodge, P. and Blackstone, T. (1982), *Educational Policy and Educational Inequality,* Oxford: Martin Robertson.

Lowe, R. (2007), *The Death of Progressive Education. How Teachers Lost Control of the Classroom.* London: Routledge.

Lowndes, G. A. N. (1937/1969), *The Silent Social Revolution. An Account of the Expansion of Public Education in England and Wales 1895–1965,* Oxford: Oxford University Press.

McCulloch, G. (1996), "Educating the Public: Tawney, the *Manchester Guardian* and Educational Reform," in R. Aldrich (ed.), *In History and in Education: Essays Presented to Peter Gordon*, London: Woburn, pp. 116–137.

———. (1998), *Failing the Ordinary Child? The Theory and Practice of Working-Class Secondary Education*, Buckingham: Open University Press.

———. (2000), "The Politics of the Secret Garden: Teachers and the School Curriculum in England and Wales," in C. Day, A. Fernandez, T. E. Hauge, and J. Muller (eds.), *The Life and Work of Teachers: International Perspectives in Changing Times*, London: Routledge, pp. 26–37.

———. (2001), "Sensing the Realities of English Middle-Class Education: James Bryce and the Schools Inquiry Commission, 1865–1868," *History of Education*, 40, 3, pp. 599–613.

———. (2006), "Education and the Middle Classes: The Case of the English Grammar Schools, 1868–1944," *History of Education*, 35, 6, pp. 689–704.

———. (2011), *The Struggle for the History of Education*, London: Routledge.

McCulloch, G., Cowan, S., and Woodin, T. (2012), "The British Conservative Government and the Raising of the School Leaving Age, 1959–1964," *Journal of Education Policy*, 27, 4, pp. 509–527.

McNair, J. (1981), "Education in Spain, 1970–1980: The Years of Compulsory Schooling," *Comparative Education*, 17, 1, pp. 47–57.

Maguire, M. and Ball, S. J. (1994), "Researching Politics and the Politics of Research: Recent Qualitative Studies in the UK," *International Journal of Qualitative Studies in Education* 7, 3, pp. 269–285.

Majault, J. (1956), "The Transition from the Primary to the Secondary School and Its Influence on the School Curriculum," Summary report of International Advisory Committee on the School Curriculum, Paris: UNESCO, available at http://unesdoc.unesco.org/images/0014/001459/145906eb.pdf (accessed July 10, 2010).

Malcolm, J., Ludlow, F., and Lloyd Jones, L. (1867), *The Progress of the Working Class 1832–1867*, London: Strachan.

Marwick, A. (2006), *The Deluge: British Society and the First World War*, 2nd edition, London: Palgrave Macmillan.

Maryland State Department of Education (2007), Task Force to Study Raising the Compulsory Public School Attendance Age to 18, *Attending to Learn: The Implications of Raising the Compulsory Age for School Attendance*, Baltimore.

Matthews, M. (1982), *Education in the Soviet Union*, London: George Allen and Unwin.

Maudling, R. (1978), *Memoirs*, London: Sidgwick and Jackson.

Maynes, M. (1985), *Schooling in Western Europe. A Social History*, Albany, New York: SUNY.

Meadmore, P. (2001), "'Free, Compulsory and Secular'? The Re-Invention of Australian Public Education," *Journal of Education Policy*, 16, 2, pp. 113–125.

Medlicott, P. (1973), "The Rosla Children," *New Society* May 17, p. 357.

Mehrotra, S. (1998), "Education for All: Policy Lessons from High Achieving Countries," *International Review of Education* 44, 5–6, pp. 461–484.

Meghir, C. and Palme, M. (2005), "Education Reform, Ability, and Family Background," *American Economic Review* 95, 1, pp. 414–424.

Middlemas, K. (1979), *Politics in Industrial Society: The Experience of the British System since 1911*, London: Andre Deutsch.

Miller, P. (1989), "Historiography of Compulsory Schooling: What Is the Problem," *History of Education* 18, 2, pp. 123–144.

Moore, R. (1987), "Education and the Ideology of Production," *British Journal of Sociology of Education* 8, 2, pp. 227–242.

———. (1994), "Vocationalism and Educational Change," *Curriculum Journal* 5, 3, pp. 281–293.

Morgan, K. O. (1987), *Callaghan: A Life*, Oxford: Oxford University Press.

Morris, A. J. A. (1977), *C.P. Trevelyan 1870–1958: Portrait of a Radical*, Belfast: Blackstaff Press.

Murphy, J. (1971), *Church, State and Schools in Britain 1800–1970*, London: Routledge and Kegan Paul.

Murtin, F. and Viarengo, M. (2011), "The Expansion and Convergence of Compulsory Schooling in Western Europe, 1950–2000," *Economica* 78, pp. 501–522.

Musgrove, F. (1964), *Youth and the Social Order*, London: Routledge and Kegan Paul.

NAS (National Association of Schoolmasters) (1966), *Ready in Time?* Hemel Hempstead: NAS.

———. (1973), *Provision for the Raising of the School Leaving Age*, Hemel Hempstead: NAS.

National Association of Secondary School Principals (2010), "Raising the Compulsory School Attendance Age," May 7, available at www.nassp.org /Content.aspx?topic=Raising_the_Compulsory_School_Attendance_Age _Proposed_ (accessed July 10, 2012).

National Audit Office (2011), *Raising the Participation Age: An Assessment of the Cost-Benefit Analysis*, London: National Audit Office.

Norris, Nigel (2007), "Raising the School Leaving Age," *Cambridge Journal of Education*, 37, 4, pp. 471–472.

Obama, B. (2012), "Remarks by the President in State of the Union Address," The White House, January 24, available at www.whitehouse.gov/the-press -office/2012/01/24/remarks-president-state-union-address (accessed November 24, 2012).

OECD (1983), *Compulsory Education in a Changing World*, Paris: OECD.

O'Keefe, D. (1975), "Some Economic Aspects of Raising the School Leaving Age in England and Wales in 1947," *Economic History Review*, 28, 3, pp. 500–516.

———. (1977), "Towards a Socio-Economy of the Curriculum," *Journal of Curriculum Studies*, 9, 2, pp. 101–109.

Oreopoulos, P. (2006), "Estimating Average and Local Treatment Effects of Education when Compulsory Schooling Laws Really Matter," *American Economic Review*, 96, 1, pp. 152–175.

Oreopoulos, P. (2007), "Do Dropouts Drop Out Too Soon? Wealth, Health and Happiness from Compulsory Schooling," *Journal of Public Economics*, 91, pp. 2213–2229.

Paton, P. (2010), "New Diplomas 'Have Been Fatally Undermined'," *Daily Telegraph*, August 24, 2010, available online at www.telegraph.co.uk/education/educationnews/7962111/New

Percy, E. (1929), "The School Leaving Age," *Empire Review* October, pp. 265–270.

Perkin, H. (2002), *The Rise of Professional Society: England Since 1880*, London: Routledge.

Pischke, J. S. and von Wachter, T. (2008), "Zero Returns to Compulsory Schooling in Germany: Evidence and Interpretation," *Review of Economics and Statistics* 90, pp. 592–598.

Pring, R. (2012), *The Life and Death of Secondary Education for All*. London: Routledge.

Pring, R., Hayward, G., Hodgson, A., Johnson, J., Keep, E., Oancea, A., Rees, G., Spours, K. and Wilde, S. (2009), *Education for All. The Future of Education and Training for14–19 Year Olds*, London: Routledge.

Przeworski, A. M., Alvarez, M., Cheibub, J. A., and Limongi, F. (1988), *Democracy and Development: Political Institutions and Well-Being in the World, 1950–1990*, Cambridge: Cambridge University Press.

Raffe, D. and Spours, K. (2007), *Policy Making and Policy Learning in 14–19 Education*. London: Bedford Way Papers, Institute of Education.

"Raising the School Leaving Age in the Country," *The Countryman* January (1930), pp. 536–540.

Ramirez, F. and Boli, J. (1987), "The Political Construction of Mass Schooling: European Origins and Worldwide Institutionalization," *Sociology of Education*, 60, 1, pp. 2–17.

Reid, C. and Young, H. (2012), "The New Compulsory Schooling Age Policy in NSW, Australia: Ethnicity, Ability and Gender Considerations," *Journal of Education Policy* 27, 6, pp. 795–814.

Report of a Conference on Secondary Education in England convened by the Vice-Chancellor of the University of Oxford, Oxford, 1893.

Richardson, J. (1980), "Variation in Enactment of Compulsory School Attendance Laws: An Empirical Inquiry," *Sociology of Education* 53, 3, pp. 153–163.

Richardson, J. G. (1994), "Common, Delinquent and Special: On the Formalization of Common Schooling in the American States," *American Educational Research Journal* 31, 4, pp. 695–723.

Richman, S. and Kopel, D. (1996), "End Compulsory Schooling," Issue Paper 1–96, Golden, Colorado: Independence Institute.

Roach, J. (1986), *A History of Secondary Education in England, 1800–1870*, London: Longmans.

———. (1991), *Secondary Education in England 1870–1902: Public Activity and Private Enterprise*, London: Routledge.

Roberts, D. T. (1985), "The Genesis of the Cross Commission," *Journal of Educational Administration and History*, 17, 2, pp. 30–38.

Rodrick, A. (2004), *Self-Help and Civic Culture: Citizenship in Victorian Birmingham*, Ashgate: Aldershot, Chapter 3.

Rolf, D. (1981), "Education and Industry: The Malcolm Committee," *Oxford Review of Education*, 7, 1, pp. 95–106.

Rose, L. (1991), *The Erosion of Childhood: Child Oppression in Britain, 1860–1918*, London: Routledge, pp. 109–111.

Rose, N. and Miller, P. (1992), "Political Power beyond the State: Problematics of Government," *British Journal of Sociology* 43, 2, pp. 173–205.

Rostow, W. W. (1960), *Stages of Economic Growth: A Non-Communist Manifesto*, Cambridge: Cambridge University Press.

Savage, Jon (2007), *Teenager. The Creation of Youth 1875–1945*, London: Chatto and Windus, 2007.

Schultz, T. (1963), *The Economic Value of Education*, New York: Columbia University Press.

Scotland, J. (1972), "The Centenary Of the Education (Scotland) Act of 1872," *British Journal of Educational Studies*, 20, 2, pp. 121–136.

Seaborne, M. (1970), "The Historical Background," in J. W. Tibble (ed.), *The Extra Year. The Raising of the School Leaving Age*, London: Routledge, pp. 9–19.

Selleck, R. (1994), *James Kay-Shuttleworth: Journey of an Outsider*, Essex: Woburn Press.

Sherington, G. (1881); *English Education, Social Change and War 1911–20*, Manchester: Manchester University Press, Chapter 3.

Shipman, M. D. (1974), *Inside a Curriculum Project*, Longman: London.

Shturman, D. (1988), *The Soviet Secondary School*, London: Routledge.

Siedler, T. (2010), "Schooling and Citizenship in a Young Democracy: Evidence from Postwar Germany," *Scandinavian Journal of Economics* 112, 2, pp. 315–338.

Silver, H. (1983), "Education, Opinion and the 1870s," in *Education as History: Interpreting Nineteenth- and Twentieth-Century Education*, London: Methuen.

———. (1990), *Education, Change and the Policy Process*, Barcombe: Falmer Press.

Simmons, R. (2008), "Raising the Age of Compulsory Education in England: A NEET Solution?" *British Journal of Educational Studies*, 56, 4, pp. 420–439.

Simon, B. (1974), *The Two Nations and the Educational Structure 1780–1870*, London: Lawrence and Wishart.

———(1974) *The Politics of Educational Reform 1920–1940*, London: Lawrence and Wishart,

———. (1991), *Education and the Social Order 1940–90*, London: Lawrence and Wishart.

———. (2005), "Can Education Change Society?" in Gary McCulloch (ed.), *The Routledge Falmer Reader in the History of Education*, London: Routledge.

Simon, S. D. (1930), "Maintenance Allowances and the Raising of the School Leaving Age," *Contemporary Review* April, pp. 445–452.

Smith, A. (1985), "The Review," in Maurice Plaskow (ed.), *Life and Death of the Schools Council*, Barcombe: Falmer Press, pp. 111–112.

Smith, J. T. (1998), *Methodism and Education, 1849–1902: J.H. Rigg, Romanism, and Wesleyan Schools*, Oxford: Oxford University Press.

Spencer, F. H. (1941), *Education for the People*, London: Routledge.

Stead, H. G. (1941), "Education of the Future ii: Some Essential Reforms," *TES*, March 8.

Stakes, R. and Hornby, G., *Change in Special Education*, London: Cassell.

Steedman, H. (1987), "Defining Institutions: The Endowed Grammar Schools and the Systematisation of English Secondary Education," in D. Muller, F. Ringer, and B. Simon (eds.), *The Rise of the Modern Educational System: Structural Change and Social Reproduction, 1870–1920*, Cambridge: Cambridge University Press, pp. 111–134.

Stenhouse, L. (1983), *Authority, Education and Emancipation*, London: Heinemann Educational.

Stephens, W. B. (1987), *Education, Literacy and Society, 1830–1870: The Geography of Diversity in Provincial England*, Manchester: Manchester University Press.

Sutherland, G. (1973), *Policy-Making in English Elementary Education, 1870–1895*, Oxford: Oxford University Press.

Taylor, T. (1984), "Conservative Politics, Compulsory Education, and Lord Sandon's Act, 1876: A Nineteenth-Century Case Study," *Paedagogica Historica*, 25, 1, pp. 265–279.

Tawney, R. H. (1909), "The Economics of Boy Labour," *The Economic Journal* December, pp. 517–537.

———. (1918/1964), "Keep the Workers' Children in Their Place," in R. H. Tawney (ed.), *The Radical Tradition*, London: Penguin, pp. 49–54.

———. (1922), *Secondary Education for All*, London: The Labour Party.

———. (1933), "'Economy' in Education": 1. Present policy. Slump in capital expenditure. Arrested growth. May 24, 1933. "'Economy' in Education": II. Admitted needs. Large classes and idle teachers. Juvenile unemployed, *Manchester Guardian*, May 25.

———. (1936), *The School Age and Exemptions*, London: Workers' Educational Association.

Thatcher, M. (1971), "Speech at Royal Festival Hall, March 16, 1971," in Barry Turner (ed.), *Raising the School Leaving Age*, London: Encyclopaedia Britannica, pp. 27–36.

Tibble, J. W. (ed.) (1970), *The Extra Year. The Raising of the School Leaving Age*, London: Routledge.

Tosh, J. "In Defence of Applied History: The History and Policy Website," available at www.historyandpolicy.org/papers/policy-paper-37.html (accessed June 3, 2011).

Tropp, A. (1956), *The School Teachers*, London: William Heinemann.

Tyack, D. B. (1976), "Ways of Seeing: An Essay on the History of Compulsory Schooling," *Harvard Educational Review* 46, 3, pp. 355–389.

Tyack, D. and Cuban, L. (1995), *Tinkering towards Utopia: A Century of Public School Reform*, Cambridge: Harvard University Press.

Ujifusa, A. (2012), "*Obama Push on Mandatory Attendance Age Stalls in States,*" State EdWatch, *Education Week,* June 19, available fromhttp://blogs.edweek. org/edweek/state_edwatch/2012/06/heavy_lifting_elsewhere_may_have _squashed_obamas_bully_pulpit%20_moment_on_attendance_age.html (accessed December 10, 2012).

UNESCO (1951a), "Extension of Free and Compulsory Education," Second Regional Conference of National Commissions, WS 091/64, available from http://unesdoc.unesco.org/images/0015/001554/155412eb.pdf (accessed May 21, 2010).

———. (1951b), "Extension of Free and Compulsory Education," Second Regional Conference of National Commissions, WS 091/64, available from http://unesdoc.unesco.org/images/0015/001554/155412eb.pdf (accessed May 21, 2010).

———. (2011), "Lesotho Launches Free and Compulsory Education," available from www.unicef.org/infobycountry/lesotho_58940.html (accessed November 10, 2012).

Urwick, E. J. (ed.) (1904), *Studies of Boy Life in our Cities*, London: J. M. Dent and co, pp. xii, vii–viii.

van Horn Melton, J. (1988), *Absolutism and the Eighteenth Century Origins of Compulsory Education in Prussia and Austria*, Cambridge: Cambridge University Press.

Vernon, B. (1982), *Ellen Wilkinson 1891–1947*, London: Croom Helm.

Walford, G. and Miller, H. (1991), *City Technology College*, Milton Keynes: Open University Press.

Wang, C. and Bergquist, M. (2003), "Basic Education Development in China: From Finance Reform to World Bank Projects," *International Journal of Educational Management* 17, 7, pp. 303–311.

White, R. and Brockington, D. (1978), *In and Out of School: The ROSLA Community Education Project*, London: Routledge and Kegan Paul.

Whitty, G. (2006), "Education(al) Research and Education Policy Making: Is Conflict Inevitable?" *British Educational Research Journal* 32, 2, pp. 159–176.

Wilkinson, R. and Pickett, K. (2009), *The Spirit Level Why Equality Is Better for Everyone*, London: Penguin.

Williams, R. (1961), *The Long Revolution*, London: Chatto and Windus.

———. (1989), "Culture Is Ordinary," in Robin Gable (ed.), *Resources of Hope: Culture, Democracy, Socialism*, London: Verso.

Williams, S., Ivin, P., and Morse, C. (2001), *The Children of London: Attendance and Welfare at School, 1870–1990*, London: Institute of Education.

Willmott, A. S. (1977), *CSE and GCE Grading Standards: The 1973 Comparability Study Report*, Basingstoke: Macmillan.

Wilson, H. (1974), *The Labour Government 1964–70: A Personal Record*, London: Penguin.

Woltz, C. K.(1955), "Compulsory Attendance at School," *Law and Contemporary Problems* 20, 1/6, pp. 3–22, School of Law, Duke University.

World Bank (2013), "Progression to Secondary School, Male," available from http://data.worldbank.org/indicator/SE.SEC.PROG.MA.ZS (accessed Februrary 23, 2013).

Wright, S. (2012), "Citizenship, Moral Education and the English Elementary School," in L. Brockliss and N. Sheldon (eds.), *Mass Education and the*

Limits of State Building, c. 1870–1930, New York: Palgrave Macmillan, pp. 21–45.

Wright, T. (1872), "Mis-Education," *Fraser's Magazine* 6, 35, pp. 641–650.

Wolf, A. (2002), *Does Education Matter? Myths about Education and Economic Growth*, London: Penguin.

———. (2004), "Education and Economic Performance: Simplistic Theories and Their Policy Consequences," *Oxford Review of Economic Policy* 20, 2, pp. 315–333.

———. (2007), *Diminished Returns: How Raising the Leaving Age to 18 Will Harm Young People and the Economy*, London: Policy Exchange.

Woodin, T. (2005), "Building Culture from the Bottom-Up: The Educational Origins of the FWWCP," *History of Education* 39, 4, pp. 345–363.

———. (2007), "Working Class Education and Social Change in Nineteenth and Twentieth Century Britain," *History of Education* 36, 4/5, pp. 483–496.

———. (2012), "Co-operative Schools: Building Communities for the 21st Century," *Forum* 54, 2, pp. 327–340.

Woodin, T. (forthcoming 2014) ed. *Co-operation, Learning and Co-operative Values*, London: Routledge.

Woodin, T., McCulloch, Gary, and Cowan, Steven (2013), "Raising the Participation Age: Policy Learning from the Past?" *British Educational Research Journal* 39, 4, pp. 635–653.

Zajda, J. (1982), *Education in the USSR*, Oxford: Pergamon.

Zhao, L. and Lim, T. (2010), *China's New Social Policy*, New Jersey: London World Scientific.

Index

Printed and bound in the United States of America